Essays in Biography

1680–1726

RATISBON IN 1666

(*British Museum*)

Essays in Biography
1680–1726

BY

BONAMY DOBRÉE

Essay Index Reprint Series

BOOKS FOR LIBRARIES PRESS, INC.
FREEPORT, NEW YORK

First published 1925
Reprinted 1967

''Tis opportune to look back upon old times, and contemplate our forefathers. Great examples grow thin, and to be fetched from the passed world. Simplicity flies away, and iniquity comes at long strides upon us. We have enough to do to make up ourselves from present and passed times, and the whole stage of things scarce serveth for our instruction.' — *Urn Burial* (Epistle Dedicatory).

PREFACE

" QUAND donc ", Flaubert once wrote, " Quand donc consentira-t-on à faire de l'histoire comme on fait du roman, c'est-à-dire sans amour et sans haine pour les personnages en jeu, au point de vuc d'une blague supérieure, exactement comme le bon Dieu voit les choses d'en haut ? " The answer must be, never, certainly so far as the biographical corner of history is concerned : for during many months the historian—if he can be called by so grave a title—must live at close quarters with his original, and such intimacy must bring with it more than a little measure of love or hate.

Yet there is a natural antidote to this evil. When all is said and done we are ready to accept the shortcomings of our friends, and love them, perhaps, not only in spite of, but by reason of their failings. Such an admission may be shocking to those who seek for perfect integrity, or to those strange persons who admire it ; but it is only by contact of mind with mind, and of heart with heart, that we can know our fellows. We are not so constituted that we can " exactement comme le bon Dieu voir les choses d'en haut ". The danger is greater where intimacy has brought dislike, and here again, perhaps the recognition of our own dubious nature may piece out the imperfection of our intellectual judgement ; thus we need not grieve at our failure to reach the dizzy height of an historical Flaubert.

A worse danger is that of distortion for the purposes of art, of sacrificing the humdrum likeness for the sake of contrast. And to avoid this I have tried in a limited degree to see and describe the events in the lives of my subjects from their own point of view. It goes without saying that to write as it were autobiographically, though it presents temptations, would be to give but half, or less, of the picture, and the method has its evident restrictions. But I have the more been able to use it, as my object in writing these studies has been not so much to show what effect these men had upon the thought and movement of their times, as to indicate what results the ideas and factions of their age had upon their lives. And if I have in any way succeeded in doing this, I shall hold myself excused from the fault of ‘ wandering too much in the light ’, to use Bolingbroke’s favourite phrase, of too much indulging my ‘ wantonness of curiosity ’, of being anecdotal where, on another scheme, I should have been analytical, or a moralist. And if it be asked where, in default of this last, the essential qualification of an historian, the lesson or the philosophy of my studies may be sought, I can only reply that to extend the circle of our acquaintance may be enriching as well as entertaining ; and concluding the paragraph from Sir Thomas Browne quoted on the title-leaf, argue that “ A complete piece of virtue must be made from the Centos of all ages, as all the beauties of Greece could make but one handsome Venus ”.

In pursuance of my object of bringing out the disharmony of the individual with society, which in any civilized community must always to some degree exist, I have deliberately chosen men who did not altogether belong to their age. Etherege, to be sure, is the true child of his time, but only when the place is London or Paris ; in Ratisbon he was quite incongruous. Vanbrugh, I think, should have been born fifty years later, in a less factious age, when men's qualities were more taken for granted, and art and letters farther removed from the gritty political arena. And Addison would surely more properly have found his place among those eminent (as distinguished from great) Victorians, to whom the appearance of consistency was too important to hazard in simple dealing, and who, although ambitious, contrived to play for safety.

B. D.

CONTENTS

LIST OF ILLUSTRATIONS

HIS EXCELLENCY
SIR GEORGE ETHEREGE

" The names of Buckingham and Rochester, of Etheridge, Killigrew and Sedley, still maintain a bad pre-eminence in the annals of English vice."—BISHOP WILBERFORCE.

" Plato, we have little doubt, was a much better man than Sir George Etherege."—MACAULAY.

To

A. J. C. Brown

I

TOWARDS the end of the year 1685 a 'fair, slender, genteel Englishman' of over fifty summers made his way from the Hague into Bavaria. He wore 'the pantaloon very well mounted, the tassels new and pretty, and the best cut coat ever seen'. His suit was by Barroy, the garniture by Le Gras, the shoes Piccat, and the periwig Chédreux, while his gloves, 'well-fringed, large and graceful', were scented with orangerie. In Holland he had now and again been met staking at the gaming tables; or, it was maliciously reported, haunting 'pitiful and mean houses'; he had, moreover, been caught 'making love, for which he was sufficiently laughed at'. When playgoing he had invariably taken a box or a seat in the pit, where, gaily flexible amid the good Dutch stiffness approved by William of Orange, the indomitable old beau held himself 'with his head standing for the most part on one side, and his looks more languishing than a lady's when she lolls at stretch in her coach'.

Any Englishman entering into conversation with this dazzling person as he pursued his journey, would have found him to be the intimate of Sedley and Buckhurst, and of the late Earl of Rochester, men who were the arbiters at once of vice and of poetry, who knew not only how to rhyme, but how to enjoy all the freedom of that happy age. He would have found him ready of wit, with a boisterous laugh, in manner easy and elegant, and might have judged him an idler voyaging in search of pleasure. Here he would have been wrong, for the traveller was bent on affairs of state, being no less a person than Sir George Etherege, on his way to Ratisbon to take up the position of envoy from his Majesty King James II, to become, as we should say to-day, ambassador to Austria.

To us it seems a puzzling appointment: there is no obvious reason why Etherege should have been selected for it. To be the author of three famous comedies was, or at any rate had been, the way to Court favour, but not to a responsible post. A trifle of diplomatic experience did, indeed, lie behind him; for some fifteen years earlier he had been sent as secretary to Constantinople; but in view of the popular couplet:

> Ovid to Pontus sent for too much wit,
> Eth'rege to Turkey for the want of it,

the recommendation hardly seems sufficient. Nor would a man

> For gaming, writing, speaking, keeping,
> His Excellence for all but sleeping,

as Dryden laughingly wrote to him, be likely to clothe himself in virtue and uphold the dignity of English manners. For it was not as though this last rhyme referred to salad days, it being notorious that not so very long ago Etherege had been involved, together with Rochester, in an affray near Epsom which had cost one of their party his life. This episode had meant for Etherege a short retirement into hiding. And again, a man who was to write to Dryden that "nature no more intended me for a politician than she did you for a courtier", and to Godolphin that he was "too lazy and too careless to be ambitious", would not seem best fitted for the management of weighty affairs, or the handling of diplomatic perplexities.

It is possible that he had been given this post as an easy way of getting rid of him. Times were changing, and there was no room for old sparks. Little escapades that were very well twenty years back would decidedly not do now. For although James, in spite of the protests of his wife, was still inclined to distribute duchies to ladies who had been kind, the atmosphere of the Court was hardening. The ' land of cuckoldry ' was becoming a stage for Jesuitical intrigues, and the forces of Catholicism were massing to their final doom. But if Etherege was to be side-tracked, there were a dozen ways of doing it other than giving him a diplomatic berth. However, we may be sure that polite society was not much astonished at the event. Etherege was a gentleman, and could thus turn his hand naturally to anything. The finest fruits of literature were thrown off by young dandies in their idle hours, or so the young dandies pretended ; and if literature was none the worse for being approached in this, to use the modern term, amateurish spirit, affairs of state were not likely to suffer by being tackled with the same carelessness. There was nothing so difficult in being an envoy.

To us, looking back, it would seem that Etherege, himself so much the ' idle sport of a witty fancy ', felt prophetically that the England of the next few years was not for such as he, and that he was fleeing, not without sadness, from the wrath to come. But to the polite world the appointment seemed just the thing for Etherege. He had latterly been wasting his time in roystering, when he should have been amusing the world with his plays. Now, however, he would be removed from the evil influence of his friends, and at the same time have leisure to write in sober earnest. " Finish what you here began, But scribble faster if you can ", Dryden urged him. Yet this view, reasonable as it was, did not altogether fall in with Etherege's notions. " I will endeavour not to be wanting in my duty ", he wrote of his labours in statecraft, and the habit began 'to beget in him', he told the Earl of Sunderland, " such a relish of business that I should be more vain of making a good dispatch, than of writing a witty letter ". But his relish for business stood him in no good stead; it was for nothing that he sat down twice a week to concoct laborious accounts of the proceedings of the Diet; it was in vain he amassed piles of paper concerning 'Austrian moneths', that is to say the revenue from taxation, or made brilliant *aperçus* of what the Empire designed to the Turk. Nobody wanted mere tedious reports; it was not to write stuff such as that for which he had been sent to Ratisbon. Therefore the Earl of Middleton, one of the Secretaries of State, wrote him a hint: " I hope in a little time we may hear something of your diversions, as well as of your business, which would be much pleasanter and perhaps as instructive. . . . The last time Sir Fopling appeared with the usual applause, and the King was pleased to tell me, that he expected you should put on your socks. . . . This you are to consider as an instruction." It is, however, hard to have your virtue flouted, especially if you " dare affirm Cato left not the world with more firmness of soul than I did England ". Thus Etherege did not put on his socks, and the exhaustive dispatches went on.

2

Yet, on the face of it, there was something to be said for the notion of sending Etherege to Bavaria to write more plays. Life pursued a tranquil course in the little, dignified old Gothic town on the banks of the Danube, its quietude hardly disturbed by the sittings of the Diet. For centuries the placid burghers had at intervals seen walking in the narrow, gable-capped streets, important personages gathered there to discuss affairs of state or disentangle knotty ecclesiastical problems. The Diet, representing the Electors, sat there sleepily, all the more gladly since the Turkish threat to Vienna, and the foreign envoys barely ruffled the calm of old German provincial aristocratic life. There if at all, a man cram-full of lively experience and endowed with a talent for writing, might produce mellow work. But in the case of Etherege it was an error in psychology to send him there.

For apart from the fact that Etherege took his duties seriously, it was of no use to send him to a place like Ratisbon and expect him to ' scribble faster ', or indeed to scribble at all. Although he was a lazy man, proud of the ' noble laziness of the mind ' he vaunted as belonging solely to himself, it was not the leisure brooding over his new abode that he needed to make him blossom into plays. It was the stimulus of gay society, for ' poetry ' to him was inseparable from silks and perfumes, gallantry and graceful sarabandes. He was acutely aware of it himself. Thus he wrote to his friend Poley, " I must confess I am a fop in my heart. I have been so used to affectation that without the help of the air of the court what is natural cannot touch me." And again, to another friend, " I wear flannel, sir, wherefore pray talk to me no more of poetry ", as though that settled the question. Besides, he was now an important public personage, no longer an idle dandy. Writing comedies was not, maybe, a very serious matter, but if done at all, it ought to be done well. Perhaps it is too much to say he had respect for his craft, but at any rate he owed it to himself not to try in unpropitious surroundings. So he told Dryden, " Though I have not been able formerly to forbear playing the fool in verse and prose, I have judgement enough to know how much I ventured, and am rather amazed at my own good fortune, than vain upon a little success, and did I not know mine own error, the commendations you give me would be enough to persuade me of it". Dryden had said, "I will never enter the lists in prose with the undoubted best author of it which our nation has produced". It is well to rest on one's laurels when there are no more to be gained: and if one is notoriously lazy, one may as well make the most of that reputation, especially in a place where it would be harder than ever to do any work.

Etherege at once saw that the atmosphere was not right. "This was a fine place to correct the laziness of my nature", he once commented, as though slightly huffed. There was no gaiety, no conversation with Sedley, who could speak more wit at supper than most of the plays then written could boast. There were no romps with Buckhurst; no gay parties in the Mulberry Garden with Mrs. Barry or Mrs. Wright; no musical evenings with the Bettertons; none of the brilliant talk of the coffee-house, and no Piazza or New Exchange in which to ogle the ladies, or barter amenities with a vizard. So far from such a mode of living were the people in this outlandish Ratisbon, that they wasted the night in sleep. Etherege complained of this to Sunderland: "Is it not enough to breed an ill habit of body in a man who was used to sit up till morning to be forced for want of knowing what to do with himself to go to bed in the evening; one who has been used to see his friends with all freedom never to approach anybody but with ceremony instead of rattling about the streets to seek variety of company; to sit at home and entertain himself with solitude and silence. . . . If I do well after this, you must allow me to be a philosopher."

"Never to approach anybody but with ceremony. . .", that was what killed life in *ce misérable endroit*, as he termed it. Indoors and out, punctilio baffled converse at every point. You might never look in unexpectedly on a friend, or hope for a delightful impromptu festival at your own house. It was deadly. "On ne rend jamais des visites qu'à une heure *assignée*, et si vous manquez un peu de votre temps vous courez risque de morfondre un pauvre ministre qui se tient en sentinelle pour vous recevoir à la portière de votre carrosse." The gentlemen of the Diet, of whom the society of the place almost wholly consisted, were always clothed in their dignity, so much so that they did not even doff it in the most cloistered intimacies of the home; or so Etherege believed. Even the ladies were spoiled by this punctilio, so that you could not approach them. If nothing else could, this might well spur a man into rhyming—*facit indignatio versum*—and, in fact, Etherege burst forth to Middleton:

> The plague of ceremony infects
> Even in love the softer sex,
> Who an essential will neglect
> Rather than lose the least respect.

Yet the ladies were hardly worth a rhyme. There were only two handsome ones in the whole town (probably the daughters of the Countess of Zinzendorf), "and their unconscionable price was marriage", which made any advance by Sir George out of the question, for there was a Lady Etherege, far away in London. And apart from these two handsome ones, the rest of the ladies were terrible creatures:

> Whose brawny limbs and martial face
> Proclaim them of the Gothic race,

who only appeared the more ridiculous by bedizening themselves with jewels, ugly old-fashioned gee-gaws that had come to them with their quarterings, and were indeed, worn for that reason. " Every stone as well as she Can boast an ancient pedigree ", his Lordship was told. Moreover they had no restraint in wearing them :

> Such ropes of pearls her hands encumber
> She scarce can deal the cards at ombre.
> So many rings each finger freight
> They tremble at the mighty weight.

It was labour wasted to tie your cravat at such dreadful apparitions. But you had to meet them if you wanted to play ombre, and ombre was the only fun to be had. Unless you considered the sittings of the Diet fun, as Etherege tried to do ; but these again were pompous and heavy, for the gentlemen who composed it were always wrangling over questions of ceremony. They were, however, leisurely folk. " The Diet sleeps still, and when they will awake I know not " ; or on another occasion ; " The Diet is at present in devotion, and will not be at leisure until after the holydays to mind worldly matters ". Moreover they worked irritatingly by fits and starts. " Generally once a week or a fortnight here uses to blow a trade wind, which makes us see the Diet under sail, though she suddenly casts anchor again ; but now we have had a dead calm ever since the instructions of the Electors are come to their deputies against the Count de Windischgrätz's pretensions." But diversion was not denied them, so long as it was enjoyed within the forms. " On Tuesday last the ninth instant (in matters of consequence a man cannot be too exact) the three colleges met in the *Neben Stube* (the room where the general conferences are always held), and after a grave debate which took up some time, by reason of unhappy difficulties, which I shall acquaint you with anon, a conclusion was unanimously made that they should go and see a farce that afternoon, to which they were invited by a deputy from a company of strollers, who are lately come from Nuremberg to divert us here. . . . This is all has been done in the Diet since my last, and it is but reasonable they should breathe awhile." It must have relieved the anxieties of Lord Middleton to hear that these worthy gentlemen had resolved their 'unhappy difficultics' to unanimity, especially as they concerned a matter of precedence. Still, Etherege must have found it hard work to make a good dispatch or write a witty letter. Luckily they were sometimes much the same thing.

Nor was there anything to be done out of doors ; there was no Whitehall down which to ruffle it, and no sport. For this place, added to its other inconveniences, had an odious climate, and you could not go out without finding yourself knee-deep in snow. However, there are possibilities in snow, and the envoy found he might now and again count on a trifle of sledge-driving. He told the French ambassador in London, " Le divertissement le plus galant du pays cet hiver c'est le traîneau où l'on se met en croupe de quelque belle Allemande en manière que vous pouvez ni la voir ni lui parler à cause d'un diable de tintamarre des sonnets dont les harnais sont tous garnis. Le droit néanmoins du traîneau est quelque chose de considérable ; vous pouvez prétendre un baiser dans tous les carrefours de la belle que vous menez, et la faveur n'est pas méprisable puisque le baiser ne se donne pas en cérémonie comme chez nous." Yet if there were only two 'belles Allemandes' worth saluting, the deprivation cannot have been very great. He ended up, however, with a little inverted plea for pity : " Je ne veux pas plus dire sur cet chapitre de peur de vous dégoûter des plaisirs de Londres." How he must have sighed for those pleasures of London, where punctilio was not, and young women still maintained the custom "which cannot be too much honoured" lauded by Erasmus in the famous passage, "They kiss you when you come, they kiss you when you go, and when you return they kiss you again". And it was not only the young priest who remembered with regret that their lips were 'fragrant and soft'.

But when a bird of paradise is suddenly introduced into a rookery, what do the rooks think of their new companion? The bird of paradise from very shame will not reveal what they say, and the rooks only caw to each other. But luckily there is among feathered creatures the secretary bird, and he was not absent from Ratisbon.

3

At about the end of February or the beginning of March 1686 another Englishman made his way across Holland into the Empire. This time it was a humbler sort of man, not addicted to pleasures, unless we count keeping one's ears well open as such. And those ears had poured into them strange things about Sir George, distressing things for one who was about to become the envoy's confidential man. For not only had His Excellency behaved, while in the Low Countries, in a shockingly frivolous manner, but he had uttered indiscreet things. He had even made derogatory remarks about Mr. Skelton, the Envoy at the Hague. Moreover, he had spread rumours ascribing success to the Monmouth rebellion, and it was hinted that he had openly jested about the shipful of arms for Monmouth that Skelton, through bungling, had allowed to slip away. Mr. H. H., such were the worthy man's initials, could not believe his well-opened ears. This sober, upright, and cautious scribe would tell his employer all the scandalous things that were being rumoured about him : he ought to know ; and once he knew, everything would, of course, be put right.

But when on his arrival at Ratisbon Mr. H. H. was so civil as to tell the envoy of the slurs being cast in Holland upon his good name, Sir George rounded upon him, and asked him how he was concerned. He even put the pithy question as to whether his secretary 'had been sent him as his governor?' The secretary decided that they should hear about this at home. If Sir George was going to 'follow his own course' in that manner, it would not be the secretary's fault if he was forced to use his pen in getting things altered, for such a state of affairs was a disgrace to the country. Naturally it was not very nice to play the spy upon your employer, but it would be in the national cause. Besides, in writing thus, he would be acting in some sort under instructions. "You see, Sir," he reminded the Honoured Sir to whom he addressed his epistles, "I cannot forbear to write to you, for fear of neglecting my promise which you may call duty." You may call it duty, and you may also call it by a harsher name. Still, the phrase is in its way an apology ; and besides, truth cannot prevail, if there is no one to bear her witness. So that if Mr. H. H. did not prove a good friend to Etherege, he has proved an admirable one to history ; which is no mean thing, especially when history is pleased to be so entertaining.

So he used his pen, which could be caustic on occasion, and his labours are preserved in a Letter-book, now housed in the British Museum. And as though he foresaw posterity would know him by this work, he determined it should be well done. If it was to begin in style, it must have a suitable heading, thus :

> They are a people pampered up in ease
> That no King can govern nor no God can please.

But what people? Mr. H. H. was surely too good a patriot to mean this as the common criticism of his own countrymen, and the misquotation from *Absalom and Achitophel* does not seem quite relevant to the context. Is it possible that the lines were meant to designate Etherege himself under the faint disguise of the plural? It would not be contrary to the secretary's humour to adorn his work with a hidden thrust at—well, the man who would not be governed by his secretary.

It would be a good book. Everything, of course, would not go in, only such things as served most clearly to portray his master. Some letters need only be in précis, and might be headed, "Expressions in a letter to . . ." where only the cream was to be saved for inclusion. Comment would be unnecessary, though now and again a short parenthesis might be slipped in ; even a word here and there might help to point a moral. And perhaps one might underline grammatical errors when His Excellency chose to write in French. For instance, a little stroke under a *devant* that should have been *avant* would show that such mistakes were at least not due to the secretary's ignorance, or to his carelessness in copying. Indeed, he would be very careful. Letters that were not revelatory of the envoy's habits would be omitted, thus making the collection more concise. Those two screeds to the Duke of Buckingham, for instance, were so unimpeachable in sentiment that any gentleman might have written them. Therefore there was no need to preserve them. There would, perforce, be the official dispatches, but that could not be helped ; they might even act as a foil to richer material.

Certainly somebody at home should know all about Sir George Etherege. To the letters he wrote would be added the private letters he received, those at least that could be got hold of. Then there would be a list of Sir George's books, ranging from Plato through Boccaccio to Molière, with not a devotional one among them, unless one should so rank a History of the Council of Trent. Finally there would come Mr. H. H.'s " acct of Sr G's life and manner of living, writ in several letters from Ratisbon ". When all was over the various papers would be bound together to make a neat, informative volume.

As to more active work, he would keep those excellent ears of his open, and his eyes as well. It was a pity that after the secretary's original advance Sir George " did all his endeavours to keep things from my hearing ", lest his exploits ' should be told him again ' ; for owing to this unfortunate reticence Mr. H. H. had sadly to admit that " I believe there has passed a great many things which I have not heard ". No doubt. But Mr. H. H. had one great advantage over his master—he could speak German, a language the envoy obstinately refused to learn ; and he soon found out what people thought of his master.

4

The Germans did not like the envoy, nor trouble to understand him ; indeed the divergence was too fundamental. He seemed to think life was a matter to be taken in your stride. ' Easy Etherege ' might be a term of commendation in London, at least in certain circles, but not in their Bavaria. In London, of course, circles intersected curiously, and there was little to be said for the propriety of that habit which prevailed there, of kissing when you come and when you go. But then, if your nobility, with the example of your late monarch, consort with stage players devoid of quarterings or even of coats of arms, nothing better can be expected. Etherege, however, must learn that he could not do those things here. The worst of it was, he seemed to have no sense of the fitness of things. He actually had the impertinence to try to 'salute' the Countess of Schalemberg! How right of her to reprimand him, saying in the hearing of all, "Monsieur, je vous prie, ne faites pas tant de familiarité avec moi, parce que je suis la Comtesse de Schalemberg et non pas une comédienne". Decidedly he must be taught that kissing was not part of the ceremony at Ratisbon.

Indeed, his conversation and manner were altogether too free for that company. He was not even punctual in his visits, and neglected to pay some altogether, evidently thinking they were of small account. He put aside this first duty to fritter away his time with the French ambassador, of all people. He did not seem to be aware that to pay attentions to the French was to insult the Empire. Did he not know that once "one of the Diet having lent money to another was offered to be paid back in French money, which the person refused to accept of, calling it the money of corruption". As a matter of fact he did know, but he still insisted upon paying court to Monsieur de Crécy. He used to go to his house every night of the week. Such behaviour was so marked that one of the Austrians said, "On voudrait savoir si c'est par l'ordre du roi qu'il donne tant d'ombrage à tous les ministres de l'Empire".

Yet Etherege himself could see no way out of it. "If I have visited the Count de Crécy more than the Emperor's ministers, it is because I was admitted without ceremony, which is the plague of this place, there being scarce another house where I could enjoy my freedom, and find any diversion." Ceremony apart, to be allowed in at all was no small thing. For after a first visit the other ministers were, strangely, not receiving when the British envoy made his next appearance ; or if they were, they did not return the second visit. The Elector of Bavaria's representative absolutely refused to admit him at the first, " so that ", Mr. Secretary observed to his Honoured Sir, " it is now near seven months since he received the last [visit] from anyone whatsoever ". Why this treatment ? The secretary guessed, but Sir George shrugged his shoulders, and since " His Majesty did not send me here to live in solitude ", went over the way to the de Crécy's, where the delightful Countess found him very charming—for a while. Apart from this, his only moment of happiness was when Mr. FitzJames, the son of the king and of his acquaintance Miss Churchill, paid him a fleeting visit on his way to the wars, where he was to qualify himself for the title of Duke of Berwick.

Thus Sir George became more than ever 'of the French faction '. At the same time it was unwise not to have shown a livelier enthusiasm at the taking of Buda in the autumn of 1686. He was even reported to have said that he neither believed the news nor hoped it to be true. He had evidently acquired Turkish sympathies in the old Constantinople days. But his saying flew abroad, it was noised about the streets, the Jesuit students got hold of it, and they put it into a comedy they happened to be acting a few days later, " where every minister but himself was invited. However he went thither, and heard his very words repeated on the stage, *neg credo neg spero*." It was supposed that nothing could be more humiliating to an envoy than to have his words lampooned in a stage play. Yet if we may hazard a guess, Etherege probably only laughed, as any decent writer of comedy would. Besides, had he not sent his ' compliment ' to the Imperial Commission ?

The Imperial Commission, however, took no notice of the compliment, and when they celebrated the feat of arms, inviting all the ministers and many cavaliers to a ride and a dinner, left out the English envoy, as " thought unworthy to partake in the public rejoicings ", as he complained later. But he would *not* be left out : he tacked himself on to the procession to assert his country's dignity. And since " Sir George would be of the number, they contrived it so that he was the nineteenth and last of all the gang, which the meanest minister but himself would have been ashamed of ". But this was " nothing to what followed, which seems to have been done by complot on purpose to affront him. One person being left to keep Sir George in discourse, the rest of the company sat down at table, and reserved only a place for one. Sir George approaching and thinking to sit down, the other without ceremony prepossessed the place, leaving Sir George a noun substantive. To expose him the more, the Anhalt minister, whom he had formerly abused, asked him faintly to sit down, but without any further care of him, they fell to it, all strutting and stretching to keep him out ; when otherwise they could have made place enough for half a dozen more. Sir George seeing himself thus abandoned, immediately sent for his coach, and told them upbraidingly that he could find a supper at home."

5

Perhaps it was largely the fault of the president of the Diet, who was an insufferable person : not the most docilely German minister could like the Count de

Windischgrätz. " Nobody can imagine the pride and malice of that man, who esteems himself the emperor of this place, and can not suffer anyone who will not neglect all besides to cringe to him." He was altogether too overbearing, and at last even the electoral colleges kicked against the pricks, and that more than once. It was hardly to be wondered at, for " he is hot and imperious, and uses those of the Diet who have some dependence on him as scurvily as he does his domestics ". Nor was he a good official, for though he ' understood his master's interests ', he would " sacrifice anything to his pride and ambition ; and indeed all his passions are so violent, that he does him little service for want of conduct. . . . These qualities (some of his countrymen say) got him this employment. The ministers at Vienna for their own quiet favouring him in this honourable occasion of his absence."

He was a little older than Etherege, tormented too with the gout and gravel, which added to his natural ill-humour. Moreover he was jealous, a crime no man of Etherege's generation could stomach. At home, Chesterfield had almost been ousted from society for this same crying sin, and this man was even worse than Chesterfield. He was " of a temper so jealous that he tormented his wife before her time, when he was her lover ; if he observed her speaking to any man in the drawing-room, he would get her into a corner and pinch her black and blue ".

Besides, he was a bore. He would buttonhole Etherege and tell him twenty times over how he had been received at the French court, " with as much heat as an old lady tells some pleasant passage of her youth which warms her ". And he recounted it all in horribly mutilated French, roaring loudly, since he was ' vehement even in trifles '. But he could be handled, for " if you flatter him the lion becomes a lamb, and . . . will (like the Lord Chamberlain in *Hamlet*) cry, oh, very like a weasel ".

But on no account would Sir George flatter de Windischgrätz. This dignitary, therefore, showed his displeasure, and though the envoy paid him " a hundred visits, never so much as sent a man to make him a compliment ". Etherege stoutly refused to ' play the fool to please him '. It was obviously " not becoming in a person His Majesty employs " to dance to any tune the Count might like to pipe. Thus they were not on the most cordial terms ; but his omitting to cringe was, Etherege averred, the only ' pique ' the Count had to him. Perhaps not the only one ; for when the bird of paradise found he could nowise get on in the rookery, he took measures to amuse himself, measures that had been well tried and not found wanting in the best days of Charles II's reign.

The secretary told of them in several scornful pages, in which too there is zest ; for is there not a rare pleasure in telling the truth by way of ' what you may call duty ' ? And what did Sir George not do ? He gathered friends about him with whom to gamble and be ' free ', chief among them a Frenchman, a Count Purpurat, a companionable person. The secretary bluntly called him a sharper, and went on to say that when not playing or quarrelling, the ' trade ' of this convivial band " was to drink till two or three o'clock in the morning, and (if they were able) to go and walk about the streets with clubs in their hands to guard themselves and their music . . . and sometimes they returned all covered with blows and bruises, the true recompense of such knight-errantry ". The secretary evidently had no memory of the palmy days of the early Restoration period, or he would not have been so greatly impressed. Still, Sir George need not have gone about the streets with a certain Le Febure, with nothing on but his shirt. It is true that previously he had, with two sisters, danced in a manner that may be found in certain editions of Pepys, but of which it will suffice to say here that the performance was African. To recount, then, another escapade, on one, or perhaps several nights, he visited " all the ale-houses of the town accompanied with his servants, his *valets de chambre*, his host-master, and his dancing and fighting-master, all with their coats turned inside outwards ".

All things considered, the secretary thought he could very well understand why Sir George's visits were not returned, why the Elector of Bavaria's envoy would not receive one at all, and why Etherege was left out of the public rejoicings. But Etherege himself hardly seemed to notice anything was amiss ; that little affair of being refused a supper did not deserve mention. Mr. H. H. was somewhat astonished at this bland attitude, and thought it worth while to make a précis of a letter " to Mr. Wynne, telling him that he had his visits constantly returned (though nothing can have less truth in it) " the secretary slips in. . . . " That grave fops abound here ; that nature who is the best poet, and in all her works shows the inclination she has for a comedy, would be thought degenerated into a farce to give a true description of them. That the fowls at the Bishop of Passau's feast for the taking of Buda, were brought from his bishopric to save charges ; and that they stunk . . ." and so on. Truly the English envoy was giving scant heed to what others might be thinking of him.

He was probably more concerned at the behaviour of the ladies, who did not receive him with that rapture to which he had been accustomed. The Countess de

Schalemberg, we remember, reproved him in front of all, while the Countess de Windischgrätz took sterner measures: for being partial to her sleep, she did not approve of the 'knights errant' who enlivened the dark hours. She was 'most angry', and "by her jealous husband's instigation, she threatened them publicly, and laid an ambuscade of stout fellows to watch for them, whose clutches they escaped narrowly one night, and so saved drubbing". However, she was of no great account, for though not unhandsome, she was more affected than that most *maniérée* of English ladies, Mrs. Middleton: and besides, she had married that wretch von Windischgrätz solely because the Empress ordered her to do so. The case of the Countess de Crécy was more serious: matters had gone well between them to begin with, but of late something had seemed to tarnish their relationship. Etherege had been so far ready to die for her, that he was actually ill. The secretary analysed the disease as one due to gratified rather than thwarted love, but "even before it was known what distemper Sir George was sick of, the Countess of Crécy was pleased to tell one of her women: "J'entends que Monsieur d'Etherege est malade pour l'amour de moi. S'il l'est, qu'il meurt."

But what, after all, did even the Countess of Crécy matter? A few verses in French would meet the case, a few trifles in this vein:

> Son humeur, à l'amour rebelle,
> Exile tous les doux désirs,
> Et la tendresse est criminelle
> Qui veut lui parler en soupirs.

For there came to Ratisbon a lady so handsome "that it may be said she has robbed the whole country, for the rest of the women look as if nature had spared from them what she has bestowed on this"; a lady "as fière as she is fair which may be allowed to a beauty that has no rival" : in short, something which if not quite a bird of paradise, was at least not a rook.

This time it was not Apollo, as a well-known rhyme had it, but another god that had " gentle George in his eye" : or perhaps one should say a goddess.

6

She managed it beautifully, with all the skill of a Greek tragedian whose victim moves innocently towards his doom. When, unsuspecting, Etherege had written that the Diet had made conclusion that they would go and see a farce, he had had no idea that he was spelling out the letters of his own fate. He had, of course, gone too, for it was unthinkable that he should miss a play. And there he had seen a comedian as handsome as the Fair Maid of the West he and Middleton had seen together at Newmarket in the good old days. Our envoy was enchanted ; he grew lyrical, and this time it was not indignation that caused him to burst into rhyme, once again in French, though he doubted if his command of the language permitted him to do justice to his subject. " Mr. Vice-chamberlain is so able a Frenchman that I fear his criticisms, but pray tell him I am not the only man, who have engaged myself in a love business, without considering whether I was able to go through with it." Moreover, " It is well known that when play or women are in the case I am no sleeper". At any rate it would enliven the town a little.

It did : but we will leave Mr. H. H. to tell the tale.

" Amongst a company of strollers lately come hither from Nuremberg (under the name of comedians) there happened to be one woman, who seemed to have something of grace in her face, though none in her manners. She had not been here many days, before His Excellence

Sir George Etherege intending to forestall the rest of the ministers in paying the honour due to her character (of an errant whore) was civilly pleased to send his steward to make her a compliment, and to desire audience (which is the only kind he has hitherto had). It was not to be doubted but so forward a zeal was accepted, especially in such a place as this, where people stand so much upon the punctillo's of honour, that none certainly but himself would have done it. Having seen her credentials, and finding her *plein pouvoir* conformable to his own, though not according to the style of the Empire, he gently proposed that without cavil or contestation, they should presently proceed to name a place *ad designandos limites* (as France and the Empire had done some days before). The Whalefish (a paltry little alehouse) where she lodged was pitched upon for one, and his Excellence's house for another. They lost no time in their negotiation: for either he sent his coach to fetch her, or went himself to her lodgings, where he would make his coach wait on him for whole nights and most part of the day, for fear (as it were) that the town should not come to the knowledge of the scandal.

" She was so bare in clothes as His Excellence was of money and credit at that time, which made him pawn his watch to buy her a new suit. The Jew who had it was afraid of his bargain, and therefore showed it in so many places, till at last the whole town came to ring of it. But he was so far from being concerned at what anyone said, that sometimes after the play was ended, he has put her into his coach before all the company, notwithstanding all the giggling and hishing of the Austrian ladies and of the ministers' wives and daughters: himself humbly walking home on foot."

They might do these things every day in London, but they were assuredly not in the style of the Empire, and there was a terrible outcry in the Bavarian rookery. The Baron de Sensheim especially was furious, and decided to take active measures. So when "on Monday 15th November, about three o'clock, his Excellence Sir George Etherege sent his coach for the comedian to come and dine with him in private according to his custom, several young fellows hearing of this entertainment (though it was no news to them) resolved to show some feats for the honour of their country. . . . About seven o'clock several parties of them appeared in sight and posted themselves in several places about the house and garden according to their orders; by eight o'clock they had formed the siege; and within less than half an hour after they began to make their regular approaches, advancing within five or six yards of the very door. They continued to carry on their works in silence, till nine, then they loudly proclaimed an open war, and threatened if this Helena was not delivered into their hands, they would presently let Paris see the dire effects of his obstinacy. In expectation of an answer, they lost no time in whetting their swords on the stone walls, and pavements; in fixing their firearms, etc: A little before ten his Excellence began to parley with them out at the window, and desired they would grant him an hour's time to consider of their proposition. Having obtained it with some difficulty, he resolved to make the best use he could of it, to prepare for his defence. This shows Mahomet was no true lover who brought out his fair Irene, and sacrificed her with his own hands to the rage of the multitude; and in spite of all his soldiers Titus Vespasian had never banished Berenice out of Rome if he had had but half the courage of this truly heroic and valiant knight."

The secretary's sense of fun, we see, was as ponderous as the Baron de Sensheim's plan of battle; but we can forgive the display of erudition which brings him too within the comic zone.

"Much about eleven, his Excellence with a detachment of his three footmen, two French laquays, his fencing- dancing- and host-masters . . . sallied out upon seven or eight persons, who were left to keep the trenches, and being seconded by his French Vice-Bassa, who commanded the reserve (the cook, coachman, and kitchen wench) would have totally routed them, but that his second thoughts proved better than his first. However, some blows happened, for a lute-player having clapped his Excellence two or three times on the back (pretending likely to take him prisoner) was answered with a slap on the face ; and the dancing-master, more accustomed to a capriole than the use of the sabre, gave another of the enemies a slight cut in the neck, for which the Vice-Bassa knocked him down for fear of farther mischief."

The secretary did not " think fit to concern himself at all with their broils ".

The makers of the sortie then retired, and the attackers, taking this for a sign of victory, made a brave noise ; and since they used " language so opprobrious and scurrilous as none but those who have been at Billingsgate ever heard the like ", Sir George determined to escort the lady home.

Thus his party once more sallied forth into the street, " two footmen marching before with pistols ready cocked in one hand and flambeaux in the other ; the damsel with a man and a musquetoon followed after in the coach, which was guarded on each side by two persons, and behind by three more all well-furnished with swords and pistols. Baron de Sensheim and his company pursued them closely, but fearing by their appearance they might make too great an opposition, they were forced to content themselves with hooting and hollowing, except only one action that happened on this manner: the fencing-master perceiving that some of the enemy were like to fall in upon them in the flank, by the favour of a *défilé* where they annoyed them with stones, betook himself to pursue them with all his might "—it is more than the secretary would have done—" till by running he happened to stumble over a turnstile which was like to cost him his neck. . . . And so they continued on, some crying one thing and some another ; but all with one voice agreed in this ; that *great was the Diana of the English envoy*."

There was a tremendous to do about it all. " It is not known which was the greater—the show, and the music that went along with it, or the noise it made in the town next morning." Something obviously had to be done ; but one could not very well arrest the English envoy. It was a most delicate and unheard of situation. Clearly the lady must be bundled out of the town, or, since that might provoke reprisals, at least be warned privately to go. The necessary steps were taken, and she ' trooped immediately away ' for Nuremberg. Besides this capital measure, a footman was cashiered, and the lute-player put in prison for two or three days. All was over ; and when it was heard that Sir George had promised ' to live more regular for the future ', Ratisbon sighed its relief.

But not so Nuremberg. This town was averse to receiving back the viper it had unknowingly nourished so long, and could not abide the notion of vice walking unabashed about its streets. But it was difficult to know what to do, for one could not send the lady forth to spread pestilence to the confines of the Empire. Happily one of the councillors remembered the town had a prison. So in prison she was put, where, Mr. H. H. suggested, " Sir George's fine clothes are like to maintain her for some years on bread and water ".

But soon an alarming rumour reached the ears of the councillors of Nuremberg ; it was repeated ; it grew to a certainty. The British envoy was coming to release the lady. What would he do, or not do? And what were they to do? He would cause unholy riot in the streets after dark ; he might even walk about with nothing on but his shirt ! One does not know what was said to the unlucky councillor who had suggested the prison. In any case the only thing now to do was to release the lady. She was turned loose, therefore, and went the sixty miles back to Ratisbon, or rather to one of its suburbs. Thus once again Nuremberg had peace, but once again it was the turn of Ratisbon to tremble. The situation was more delicate than ever, and the councillors of Ratisbon took the precaution of doubling the guards at the city gates.

But they need not have been afraid: for though Etherege would sometimes " declare his intention of coaching the lady triumphantly into the town in spite of all the magistrates so as to vindicate his own honour and authority ", he did nothing of the sort. " It is true some few visits were made her, but they were looked upon to be merely out of formality, and for fashion's sake." For after all, the affair had gone on long enough. " It is not, Celia, in our power To say how long our love will last ", but with the author of those lines you might be sure it would not last very long. If he was the Dorimant of his own play, as he was reported to have admitted, he will have thought that " when love grows diseased, the best thing we can do is to put it to a violent death ", since no reasonable man would " endure the tortures of a consumptive passion ". Besides, he had promised to live more regular.

The lady, however, was a little more reluctant to disengage. She had ambitions, not having heard there was a Lady Etherege. So she disguised herself as a soldier, and slipped through the double guard. But her high spirit was unrewarded, for she found that " after all Sir George is run out of all his money, and therefore trading is like to be broke ". It probably was, for after a reference in a letter of the 1st January, nothing more is heard of her.

The whole affair caused shocking scandal, and the only person who did not seem to think the envoy had behaved abominably was the envoy himself. He had not even tried to conceal anything. Indeed a year or so later he wrote airily to Middleton, " not to affect to be le Chevalier à bonnes fortunes, the best adventure I have had here has been with a comedian no less handsome and no less kind in Dutchland, than Mrs. Johnson was in England ", as though it had all been a matter for congratulation. In the England Etherege knew, it certainly would have been.

Obviously, the only real offender in the whole story was the Baron de Sensheim, and Etherege let him know it in a letter written the day after the great affray.

" J'étais surpris d'apprendre que ce joli gentilhomme travesti en Italien hier au soir était le Baron de Sensheim. Je ne savais pas que les honnêtes gens se mêlaient avec des laquais ramassés pour faire le fanfaron et les batteurs de pavés. Si vous avez quelque chose à me dire faites-le moi savoir comme vous le devez, et ne vous amusez plus à venir insulter mes domestiques ni ma maison. Soyez content que vous l'avez échappé belle, et ne retournez plus chercher les récompenses de telles folies. Pour vos beaux compagnons j'ai d'autres mesures à garder avec eux."

Sensheim's reply was ineffective, and concerned the manner in which a challenge should be made. But Sir George certainly never intended to fight the baron. One does not cross swords with a man ignorant of how a gentleman should behave. Nevertheless the episode caused more excitement, and the secretary noted " nobody knows where the business between him [Etherege] and Monsieur Sensheim is like to end ; but for fear of the worse Sir George carries a musquetoon in his coach, and each footman has always since a pair of pocket pistols ready charged ".

7

If the year 1686 thus ended in at least a partial triumph for the English envoy, the next year opened badly. To begin with he had sickness to complain of; then there were some changes in the ministry at home, which meant writing courtier's letters; and thirdly the shortage of money was becoming troublesome. He had already grumbled that the Treasury was 'always three quarters in arrear in a place where he had no credit', for it is inconvenient to have to pawn your watch for your *menus plaisirs*. Yet there was no response to the appeal, and as late as May he wrote, "I have not yet had an account of my pension from those I employ to receive it". But still no money arrived, and in June he had to say, "Pray press Mr. Robson to solicit for six months entertainment and not to let my extraordinaries run on farther. I wonder at their not being paid, they being so very reasonable."

One needs philosophy to rest content under such circumstances, and one might think that Sir George's philosophy was just of the sort to sustain a man placed as he was. "The more necessary part of it", he told Dryden, "is better to be learned in the wide world than in the gardens of Epicurus." He had certainly had a fair experience of the wide world and what to expect of it, but maybe that by itself is not enough: we need to know ourselves also. Here again, however, Etherege was well equipped, as may be seen from his letter to Lord Dover: "The life I have led has afforded me little time to turn over books" (though he had a good few) "but I have had leisure sufficient, while I idly rolled about the town, to look into myself." Yet what he found, no doubt, in these moments of introspection was that he needed gaiety, with plenty of action; and, alas! such a life cannot be led without money.

Etherege, however, had worse things to contend with than a shortage of money: somebody at home was blackening his fame. It was said that he gambled, and he found himself forced to write to Middleton 'of speaking in favour of his honour to the Commissioners of the Treasury of the story about his gaming being false'. He could not imagine how such an absurd rumour got about. Here is the whole story as told to Mr. Corbet. "When I was in Holland I won near two hundred pounds and lost near the same sum at my first coming hither, which has given an occasion for an idle report as I am informed from London. I have not played at anything but sixpenny ombre these thirteen months, and am rather a winner than a loser since I saw you. . . ." Sixpenny ombre! What a confession from 'loose, wand'ring Etherege in wild pleasures tost'!

But once tongues are set going there is no end to what they will say. Luckily, as Etherege wrote to Skelton, he had "the testimony of all that are honest here to vindicate me". And in any case "I doubt not but my own word would be taken against whatsoever malicious reports there have been in Holland to the prejudice of, Sir, etc." And to another he wrote defending himself about not doing honour to Skelton, and such little political matters. But he could not understand who had started these things. "I was surprised with what (you tell me) the reports in Holland accuse me withal, I whose conduct ever since I have been in the Empire has been quite contrary." Then, exactly a month later, he saw the whole thing; it was that all who were friendly with the Count de Crécy were regarded with suspicion, and, as he told Mr. Wynne, " this makes me think I ought to be so cautious as to desire nothing may be believed at court to my prejudice, till my answer be heard ".

Perhaps if Sir George had been a little less ruffled than the ironic tone of the letter suggests, he might have seen that the explanation was not sufficient. He soon did see, when he found the true author of his troubles in the Count de Windischgrätz.

This time it was quite plain, and he felt he ought to have guessed it sooner, for the Count had always been against him. " He has endeavoured to play me many mean tricks, as to hinder me from the liberty of coursing, to make my footmen be enrolled by officers, who have made levies here, but I have had the good luck to get the better of him in all." The whole secret was revealed to him by the Count de Lamberg, for whom Etherege had a great esteem, because " he is a gentleman (besides his other merits) knows how to live ". And the Count de Lamberg showed him " a letter from M. de Caunitz to him, in which he owns the Count de Windischgrätz had writ to him concerning me ". It appeared, indeed, that by the middle of June the Count de Windischgrätz confessed to having spread the rumour of Monmouth's success in Paris, London, and Vienna on Etherege's behalf. Although the rebellion had taken place long before Etherege's arrival in Bavaria, the envoy had no doubt that that was how all these things had got abroad. So he instructed his secretary to write to Mr. Petit about " the malicious rumours to embroil him with Mr. Skelton ", and " Sir George has since discovered from whence these falsehoods arise, which is from the mean malice of a great minister here ". It was a queer trick for fate to play, when almost without exception Sir George wrote his own letters, or at least dictated them, and the secretary's face as he wrote the missive must have been interesting to watch. One would think that the calm smile of superior knowledge would have lighted up his dutiful features, but the letter is curiously huffy. Perhaps he did not like to have to use the word 'falsehoods': if it were accepted, all his labours would be lost—and his credit.

But there was some ground for Etherege's suspicions against the king-rook, since truly, on one occasion he had gone too far. For "upon his being lately taxed with having discovered a secret, upon which some say the proposition at Rome is founded, he was pleased to say that if he ever spoke anything of it, it must be to me. . . . As for me, I protest upon my honour, I know of no secret he trusted me with, and in case he should have trusted me with any, I am too honest and too reasonable a man upon a private pique to revenge myself on the whole Empire." This, no doubt, was perfectly true. Gentlemen like Etherege might do all sorts of extravagant things, but they did not confuse issues. They would no more dream of combining private affairs with official matters than they would of coupling affection with physical desire. Whereas here they could not even distinguish between love and ceremony!

Even the secretary gave his master credit for good intentions on that score, but something might have slipped out accidentally. For "Sir George, who has not as yet ten words of Dutch, being forced not only to make use of a Frenchman, but also to interest one or other of his laquays with all his intrigues, was discovered in everything as soon as it was done . . . and although Sir George's servants had been never so silent, yet the stragglers that constantly live upon him and generally such as have the name of Idle Fellows were enough to disclose all his concerns ". It is possible something might have slipped out when the wine had been round a generous number of times.

For His Excellency did drink, and he had none too good a head. Once, according to the secretary, he lay drunk in the streets. Not that he liked being drunk, quite the contrary, but he could not help it sometimes if he was to be at all sociable with the Bavarians. Because, as Etherege wrote to the Duke of Buckingham, " they are such unmerciful pliers of the bottle, so wholly given up to what our sots call good fellowship, that 'tis as great a constraint upon my nature to sit out a night's entertainment with them as it would be to hear half a score of long-winded Presbyterian divines cant successively one after another ".

But a man, especially one of Etherege's mould, does not reach middle years without having some system in these things, and Sir George expounded his with an admirable firmness of touch.

" To unbosom myself frankly and freely to your Grace, I always looked upon drunkenness to be an unpardonable crime in a young fellow who without any of these foreign helps has fire enough in his veins to enable him to do justice to Celia, whenever she demands a tribute of him. For a middle-aged man I consider the bottle only as subservient to the nobler pleasures of love. . . . In old age, indeed, I am of opinion that a little drunkenness discreetly used may as well contribute to our health of body as tranquillity of soul."

And Etherege was not old, he always rebutted the charge, writing to the Lord Chamberlain, " I have always by my way of living taken care to banish age from my thoughts ". Deliberately to become drunk would be to admit age, which he was far from doing, as yet. Besides, he was still granted the nobler pleasures of love.

The description of him somebody gave later on as one who 'spoiled his countenance with drinking', is clearly another of those unfair libels which, not content to harass him in life, pursued him after death. Indeed it was his very sobriety that made it so difficult for him to get on among people "who cannot pretend to any conversation without practising that vice that directly ruins it". The Bavarians went upon 'quite a different scheme of pleasure' from that which Etherege pursued, in this as in other things.

"The best furniture of their parlours instead of innocent china are tall overgrown runners; and they take more care to enlarge their cellars than their patrimonial estates. In short, drinking is the hereditary sin of this country, and that hero of a deputy that can demolish at one sitting the rest of his brother envoys is mentioned with as much applause as the Duke of Lorraine for his noble exploits against the Turk, and may claim a statue erected at the public expense in Germany."

So if under 'these very mortifying circumstances' there did occur one or two lapses in discretion, it is not the English envoy who can be blamed.

However, the whole thing seems to have blown over by the end of June; either Etherege had persuaded their Lordships of his correct behaviour, or else their Lordships were too busy pondering the outcome of the struggle of the Hind and the Panther to concern themselves overmuch with the doings of easy Etherege. Still, it had been rather annoying for him. Doubts thrown upon your character need many explanations to dispel them, and with politicians you have to tread carefully because they have it in their power to use you in short fashion. With your family it is different; for instance, you can write to your wife:

"I beg your pardon for undertaking to advise you. I am so well satisfied by your last letter of your prudence and judgement that I shall never more commit the same error. I wish there were copies of it in London; it might serve for a pattern for modest wives to write to their husbands. You shall find me so careful hereafter how I offend you, that I will no more subscribe myself your loving, since you take it ill, but,

Madame,

Your most dutiful husband, G. E."

The secretary headed the letter, "To my Lady—thus :".

8

In spite of all his efforts to remain young, the English envoy was bound to admit that age was gaining upon him. Thus he wrote to Guy, a jovial solicitor of excise who wrote satirical verses, as one "who as well as myself, have by a long experience of the frailties of the sex, almost acquired a perfect chastity": and he continued, "but while we approach this virtue, let us take care years do not sour us with any of the common vices of age. Let us still preserve our good humour and our good nature to make us welcome near these young people who possess that plentiful [illegible] we have pretty well run out of." There we catch a glimpse of the trait that earned Etherege the title of 'gentle George', though we may guess that it was not the quality of gentleness that obtruded itself upon the vision of his Bavarian friends. Once, however, he charitably comforted a beautiful young widow.

Everybody was 'sensibly afflicted' by the death by drowning of the amiable Herr Hoffman. "But his wife took on so extravagantly that in a short time she was the only talk both of city and country. She refused to admit any visits from her nearest relations; her chamber, her antechamber, and pro-antechamber were hung with black; nay, the very candles, her fans, and tea-table wore the livery of grief. She refused all manner of sustenance and was so averse at the thoughts of living that she talked of nothing but death."

Of what avail in such a case the exhortations of a Lutheran minister who could do nothing but blame the lady for 'downright impiety'? A man of the world was needed here, one whose philosophy had been gathered while he idly rolled about the streets. So Etherege "resolved to attack her ladyship in a more sensible part, and represent to her the great inconvenience, not which her soul, but her body received from this inordinate sorrow". He assured her that he "had heard an eminent physician at Leyden say that tears, having abundant saline particles in them, not only spoiled the complexion, but hastened wrinkles".

After developing this theme for some time, he went on, "Forget the defunct; and in order to bring that about, relieve nature, to which you have been so long unmerciful, with the most exquisite meats and the most generous wines". "Upon condition you will sup with me", cries our afflicted lady, "I will submit to your prescriptions."

"In short we had a fine regale that evening in her bed-chamber, and our good widow pushed the glass so strenuously about that her comforter, meaning myself, could hardly find the way to his coach." One cannot help wondering if in this adventure Etherege hoped to earn the same reward as the hero in Petronius's tale of the widow of Ephesus, to M. de St. Evremond's version of which he referred; but if so, he was disappointed, for, "To conclude this farce, this phoenix of her sex, this pattern of conjugal fidelity two mornings ago was married to a smooth-chinned ensign. . . . I assisted at the ceremony, though I little imagined the lady would take the matrimonial prescription so soon." Is there just a note of pique about the conclusion? Was 'good-nature' the ingredient of youth Sir George most wished to retain?

But howsoever it may have been, he seems to have settled down to an almost pastoral existence, peaceably contenting himself with such life as he could find at Ratisbon, with writing his laborious dispatches and his witty letters. For the rest he enjoyed a little outdoor sport: "I have good greyhounds and coursing is one of my greatest recreations; we have such plenty of game, that now and then I start six brace of hares in a day." He even made friends with those "free-hearted, open sort of gentlemen that compose the Diet". They became so cordial, that on the fourth of November, 'it being very fine weather', the Electoral College let him know they would come and pass the afternoon in his garden. Etherege guessed what that would mean, so he ordered his servant always to fill his glass three parts with water; thus when the others tottered home, he went sober to bed. But virtue has its drawbacks, and the next day Etherege was taken ill of a fever which he could only ascribe to a 'very odd surfeit of Danube water'. This was the first of a series of attacks of tertian ague.

A pastoral Etherege seems an anomaly, but at least he went so far as to translate O *rus, quando te aspiciam?*—'Upon the downs when shall I breathe at ease?' And if Etherege was able to breathe at ease pretty well everywhere so long as he was not upon the downs—those of Epsom apart—he was at least able to wind up spiritedly:

When shall I rest from business, noise, and strife,
Lay down the soldier's and the courtier's life,
And in a little melancholy seat
Begin at last to live, and to forget
The nonsense and the farce of what the fools call great?

Pretty well that for a man who heartily despised the country, where company was so scarce that you " perched up on chairs at a distance in a large parlour, sitting moping like three or four melancholy birds in a spacious volery ", and where nothing was to be heard but the ' hateful noise of rooks '. But, as he himself said, " few of us have the gift to be constant to ourselves ".

We see, then, a rather saddened bird of paradise : yet sometimes the bright feathers would flash, and the rooks would be fluttered in their nests. There was a small business with the queen-rook that was good fun. Sir George one day arranged a little picnic with a certain M. Stocker and Mademoiselle de Vernerin by the fountain in the woods. As luck would have it, the Count and Countess de Windischgrätz passed them on their daily exercise. The latter nearly threw herself out of her carriage the better to see what was going on, " et allongea le cou jusqu'à ce que nous fûmes à perte de vue ". Etherege thought such manners ungraceful, and took an opportunity for revenge which occurred a few days later. It was at a gathering where the Count himself came to call for his wife. The ' crasseux écuyer ' neglecting his duty that evening, Sir George took the Countess by the hand, and although she made every effort to wrench it free, held tightly to it, saying to her in French, that he would never forgive himself if he did not lead a lady of her quality and merit to her coach. The lady scowled, he smiled ; she broke into voluble German, but he ' could not or would not ' understand a word. When one has hold of the hand of a lady like the Gräfin von Windischgrätz, one does not relinquish it without a struggle. And a struggle there was. A few of those present were horrified, but the majority laughed, for the Count was not popular. Finally the Countess was obliged to call for an interpreter to inform Sir George " que cela ne se pouvait faire ".

It might be rather fun, but it begins to smack of senility. Yet what would you have? One is not as lusty as one was. " J'étais péripatétique, et j'aimais la promenade, mais tout d'un coup je suis devenu disciple d'Épicure. Je me tiens dans ma petite retraite et je me suis établi pour maxime que la plus grande volupté consiste dans une parfaite santé. Le transport d'une débauche ne paye pas le mal au cœur qu'on sent le lendemain au matin." The time comes when one must submit.

But the surest sign of all is when the past becomes more important than the present, when reminiscence becomes the most absorbing occupation of the day, and we write to our friends of the things we used to do together in the good time. At that point it is no use pretending any longer.

9

Indeed, Etherege's friends were worth remembering: even now there are people who spend a deal of time thinking about them, some for one reason, some for another. Etherege, a true child of his age, thought about them for both reasons. He liked them because they were brilliant men of letters, and he liked them because they were the first profligates of their time. Charming, graceful people. They performed prodigies of licentiousness, wrote a few delicious verses, and when they died had eulogies pronounced upon them by Dr. Burnet. It was no wonder Etherege felt sad at being out of so well-arranged a world.

What a wonderful companion Rochester had been, and what virile fire had flamed behind his exceedingly fair, girlish complexion: his ardent soul had burned itself out at the age of thirty-one. He had indeed filled the vessel of life to the brim. At eighteen he had stolen his wife, and been put in the Tower for so doing, but he had been afraid of neither God nor man nor Devil, of Dutch cannon balls or Charles II. There could not be any truth in that story Mulgrave spread about Rochester refusing to fight him : or if there were, it was only that he was with amazing moral courage testing his own theory that " every man would be a coward if he durst ". In any case one could forgive him anything for his love of poetry, and his patronage of poets—even if he had sometimes puffed plaguy bad ones like Elkanah Settle—but more especially for his astounding verve. It had been a tremendous spree when he had disguised himself as an astrologer so as to have easier access to the wives of those very hornable cits. He had been undefeatable for quickness, and when those maids of honour, Miss Hobart and Miss Temple, had swapped dresses and walked masked in the Mall on purpose to deceive him, he had not been gulled for a moment. Miss Hobart, memory called her up too : she was that tall, decisive, striking girl, whose fine eyes glowed for her own sex rather than for the other, and whose cupboard was stocked with liqueurs. Moreover Rochester had a wonderfully profound mind ; he was unmatched for scholarship and satire, and even in the middle of a debauch would come out with some pithy, even deep, comment. He was sometimes almost frightening, for he always seemed to be searching beyond the immediate fun, as though he saw something others did not see. In lighter verse too, he was inimitable. That charming song 'I cannot change as others do' : how could the rogue have had the face to write that ? If he did not change as others did, it was only that he changed faster than they.

Burnet said he had died piously, and Flatman the poet, writing of him, had urged the world, " live not like Strephon, but like Strephon die ". Etherege had lived as like Strephon as he possibly could, but he doubted gravely if he would die in the least like him.

Then there was Buckingham, irresistible Buckingham, who had snatched his bride from the Earl of Chesterfield after the banns had been twice called. Poor Chesterfield! he had always been unfortunate in his loves; he was too stiff and solemn and simple. His jealousy of the Duke of York, now his gracious Majesty, had made him the laughing-stock of the whole court. As though a woman could be satisfied with one man any more than a man might be faithful to his wife! But too much could not be said in Buckingham's favour; he had rightly been named 'the first gentleman of person and wit', and he was so wonderfully graceful that everybody's eyes used to follow him as he walked up the banqueting room at Whitehall. Even Dryden's shafts about his being " A man so various that he seemed to be Not one, but all mankind's epitome " were in their way a compliment, if you allowed for personal animus. There was nothing he could not do, and did not do, from glass-making to scribbling *The Rehearsal*. It was good to have him to write to, and wonder why 'the most polished refined epicure of the age' should retire to the country and console himself with a flannel petticoat. But alas! he died in April 1687, just when Etherege most needed the support of his wisdom.

If there had at times been something too sustained, too serious, about Rochester to be quite to Etherege's taste, the same could not be said of Buckhurst (now Lord Dorset), or of Sedley, both so bold, witty, and gay, with such a real turn for verse making. Their sole crime had been to deprive the stage of Nell Gwynn, but they had enjoyed the fruits of their robbery a very short time, and Etherege could not help smiling when he remembered Buckhurst's annoyance on being sent on a sleeveless errand to the Continent by Charles, who had wished to simplify the situation. Nell had been very human and warm-hearted: it was an odd notion to get Charles to build a hospital in the country, at Chelsea, for old soldiers. Then he called to mind Buckhurst's song 'To all you ladies now at land', a song that certainly deserved to live. It had been a good idea to pretend he had written it at sea on the eve of the naval battle against the Dutch. It was almost as good as Wycherley's tale about having written his comedies in his teens, or thereabouts. Nor was Dorset, "The best good man, with the worst-natured muse", as Rochester had called him, a mean hand at satire. Really, he must write to Dorset and remind him of the time "when we carried the two draggle-tailed nymphs one bitter frosty night over the Thames to Lambeth"; and he would ask him for a story, since he was 'so glad of an occasion for laughing here'.

Sedley, it was true, had sometimes a little too much disregarded the ordinary decencies; there were some things one did not do *coram publico*—but then, what a wit he had! He could remember that night at the play when he had talked so brilliantly that no one had paid any attention to what the actors were saying; and how bothered that pompous little secretary to the Admiralty had been—what was his name? Ah yes, of course, Pepys, that was it. Sedley did everything with such marvellous ease. To begin with he possessed

that prevailing gentle art
That can with a resistless charm impart
The loosest wishes to the chastest heart,

though that did not distinguish him from a number of his friends, such as Killigrew. It was a useful gift, no doubt, but not his rarest quality, which was to write verse. How many men of his time, or indeed of any other, could achieve such exquisite lines as " Love still has something of the sea From whence his mother rose " ? It was good to think that he at any rate could still put on his scholarly socks : he had even now just finished an adaptation of Terence. " I have heard ", Etherege wrote, " of the success of the Eunuch [Bellamira] and am very glad the Town has so good a taste to give the same just applause to Sir Charles Sidley's writings which his friends have always done to his conversation." There were not many like him.

Dryden, of course, was his best correspondent ; he would be. There was something more solid about him than about the rest. After all, how lucky he, Etherege, had been to know all those people ; he could thank his good-nature for that. Otherwise he would have had to take sides. As it was he was friends with them all ; with Rochester who had caused Dryden to be given a drubbing (that was certainly monstrous of him—he really had been too queer) ; with Buckingham who had satirized the poet as Bayes, and with Dryden who had castigated the Duke as Zimri. He was the friend of Dorset, who patronized Dryden's enemy Shadwell, but who at the same time was ready to help Dryden. Shadwell had attacked the poet laureate, who had 'immortalized' his foe by belabouring him in the enduring lines of *MacFlecknoe*. Foolish quarrels ! " Dryden finds his *MacFlecknoe* does no good ", Etherege wrote. So why have these differences ? It is so easy for people to live happily together.

Somewhat after that manner must the envoy's memory have wandered over the happy days, mingling with such thoughts visions of those dear actresses, Mrs. Wright, Mrs. Johnson, and Mrs. Barry, the last of whom had borne him a daughter who died young. But memory is no true comforter: the contrasts of the past and present are too painful: one wishes oneself back, joining in it all. "There is not a day", Etherege wrote to Corbet, "but my thoughts dog you from the coffee-house to the play. . . . Some of the ancients have imagined that the greatest torment of the dead was an impatient longing after what they delighted most in while they were living, and I can swear by my damnation in Germany, this hell is no jesting matter."

London! What images the word conjured up, of a friendly city with Wren's churches rising up everywhere—not that one went inside them as one did Wren's new Drury Lane theatre to see Rochester's pupil Mrs. Barry—but how pleasant they would seem after this grim Gothic rigidity. How he sighed after that gay life of movement, from Fleet Street with its naïve signs to Whitehall, from St. James's to the races in Hyde Park. Politics seemed to be rather troublesome at the moment, but all the pother at home was very far away, and he had not found the Popish Plot make much difference to his activities. Above all, how pleasant it would feel to be among people who understood life and the human heart, who lived reasonably and joyously, knowing that "Excess in other things so bad In love's the only measure". Life in any case was an incomprehensible jest, not in very good taste, and had to be defeated by creating an appearance, an image delicate and happy, which must not be looked at too closely lest one should see the horror and the hollowness beneath. The structure had to be composed of gaiety and wit, cemented with much kindliness, made, in fact, with real style, which was certainly not the besotted style of the Empire. Oh, to get the taste of German beer out of his mouth!

The nostalgic note becomes more and more marked as the year wears on. We see how an exile craves for contact with something he knows and loves, for the bygone ways of life, and the old familiar faces. He longs to hear how everything passes, and to feel he is remembered. "Yesterday I received yours of the 27th May with the part of the *Hind and Panther* enclosed. . . . Pray let me know how this poem is approved by the court." Or he writes to Betterton ('the player', Mr. H. H. sees fit to comment) asking for music, and sends his 'humble service to Mrs. Betterton'. Again, "Though I have given over writing plays I should be glad to read a good one—wherefore pray let Will Richards send me Mr. Shadwell's when it is printed that I may know what follies are in fashion." Or, and perhaps this is the most poignant *cri de cœur* of all, "Remember me to all my friends at the Rose, and do not forget the lily at the Bar. I am sorry for the bright nymph who you write me word is under a cloud. I made hay with her I confess, while the sun shined. . . . You may venture to send me the scandal you mention; now I am growing grave, I would not lose any thing which may make me laugh."

Growing grave! they were all doing that. "Sir C[harles] S[edley] sets up for good hours and sobriety. My Lord D[orset] has given over variety, and shuts himself up within my lady's arms." He had indeed reached the horrible state described in one of his own early poems as being 'most miserably wise'. And the feathers drop out of the tail even of a bird of paradise. However much one may take care by ones actions to banish the thought of old age, it will make its inroads. "There is not a maid of honour about Court, no, not my Lady Etherege, who leads a more virtuous life than I do." He evidently found this a telling phrase, for he used it again a fortnight later (February 1688), " To tell the truth I have of late lived as chaste as my Lady Etherege ". A little brutal, we may think now. Still, they used to say ' he was knighted for marrying a fortune ', so there can never have been much delicacy in the marital relation. He was even commiserated at the time of his wedding :

> 'Tis said when George did dragon slay
> He saved a maid from cruel fray.
> But our Sir George (whom knaves do brag on)
> Miss'd of the maid and caught the dragon.

In any case his friends will not have been surprised at the turn of thought, for he was Dorimant, and the Dorimant-Loveit scenes in *The Man of Mode* are not very pretty. And, moreover, the words meant only that since for Etherege chastity implied age, to confess the one was to admit the other. Yes, Etherege was old.

But a man of spirit does not give in without a struggle. There are moments when the old fire burns up bright once more—or at any rate one must make a show that it does when writing to such lusty people as my Lord Middleton. So we read, " Mr. Wynne has sent me the *Hind and Panther*, by which I find John Dryden has a noble ambition to restore poetry to its ancient dignity in wrapping up the mysteries of religion in verse. What a shame it is to me to see him a saint, and remain still the same devil. I must blame the goodness of my constitution which cannot be much altered, since my mind is not much changed." Good psychology ; and a good constitution too one may say on reading : " Our cat the Count de Windisgratz being absent, here is nothing but playing. We maurice dance it all the night till the day peeps in upon us, and sends us home to season us for another meeting." When you are fifty-four and can keep it up till six o'clock in the morning or so, at which time in the month of February, when the letter was written, the day may be said to peep in upon you, you have every right to blame the goodness of your constitution. The envoy seems now and again to have forgotten his Epicurus.

And as though the gods thought so brave a spirit should not be borne into the darkness of time without having one more opportunity to display its powers, the birth was announced, at last, of a Prince of Wales.

10

It was a great event, for now, in spite of fears, the Stuart succession was assured, and all good Tories could rejoice. A fig for the Harringtons and Sidneys, and let caps be flung for Filmer. The baby (descended from Adam, as the last-named writer had proved) would rule by divine right, and all would be well. The news made the inmates of the envoy's house frantic with joy, for no scurrilous Whig doubts as to the authenticity of the babe reached Ratisbon. The servants, 'transported', Sir George declared, opened the cellar, for not being English they no doubt needed something to warm their enthusiasm. But Etherege wished to realize something more symbolic, so he and the Abbot of St. James, after they "had given way to the first motions of their passion, consulted together what was fit to be done . . . in this place on so great an occasion".

What was done was done in the old Roman manner. Sir George wrote the account himself, some of it in his own hand, although he soon reverted to dictation. For what does one keep a secretary? It was, of course, a banquet, preceded by a high mass, since the succession *was* assured, and the Te Deum. Everybody was invited, the plenipotentiaries, margraves, and notables; and to add a further air of distinction, the magistrates were kind enough to send "a company of foot to keep good order", and their cannon, which was 'not very usual'.

Sir George was most careful to record every detail, for the account was to appear in the *Gazette*.

"In the place before my house was erected two large substantial buildings, the one a kitchen where an ox was roasted whole, a thing which is usual here on the coronation of an Emperor, and never otherwise: the other was a triumphal pyramid built triangular, the top being covered with an imperial crown. Beneath was an arbour wrought artificially with branches of trees, in which a concert of oboes played. Below that was a rock out of which three fountains of wine sprung; in the hollows of this the men were placed which were to play the engines and direct the pipes. In the frontispiece were His Majesty's arms, on the side next the house the Prince's, and on the other the four corners of England, Scotland, France and Ireland. In the three corners were erected in carved work two lions and an unicorn as big as the life, as they are in the supporters of the Arms, the wine pouring from the lions' mouths, and the unicorn's horn. The lower part was a representation of an antique palace, the pillars of the Doric order, with cornishes and festoons. On the front was a painted Bacchus presiding at the celebration of a Bacchanal, with this inscription:

> Nunc est bibendum, nunc pede libero
> pulsanda tellus.

On another side a cornucopia was drawn, with beds below, on which the guests lay extended as in the feasts of the ancients, they and their goblets crowned with red and white roses mixed, handsome youths waiting on them, and bringing in jars of wine with this writ:

> Antehac nefas depromere Caecubum
> cellis avitis.

On the third side Mars appeared above, and the drunken combat between the Centaurs and Lapithae was described with the words, likewise out of Horace :

> Natis in usum laetitiae scyphis
> pugnare Thracum est "

as a gentle hint to the guests, perhaps, not to behave like the Centaurs and Lapithae ; though, of course, the company of foot was in reserve.

It must have been a huge success ; there was no end to the letting off of cannon, and " the dinner consisted of three several services, each of fifty-two dishes, loaded with venison, and all manner of fowl which the country could yield for above thirty English miles in circumference ". There were fruit creams, and ice, and wines of all kinds, with drums and trumpets to usher in the courses. Moreover, the tables were adorned with flags representing their Majesties and the Prince as sea deities ; and even Mr. H. H. on this occasion unbent so far as to devise two of these trophies himself.

So much provender is not to be consumed at one sitting, and the feast lasted for three days. It certainly outdid the Count de Windisgratz's celebrations for the victory of Buda, though the king-rook " had (as was computed) thrown out at the window about ten crowns to outdo the Bishop of Passau in munificence ". The Bishop—" a good old man, who loves his quiet without genius or experience "—had only distributed about forty shillings' worth of wine. But Etherege amused the rabble with meat, wine, and bread, as well as with largesse. This last was thrown to the populace, and " while the crowd was scrambling and fighting for money, footmen, who were placed in the windows for that purpose, flung three or four hundred squibs to part them who were most mutinous : this had an admirable effect, and caused much laughter ".

It was well done, and it is this sort of thing which may distinguish one diplomat from another. It is not everybody who can cause to be carved a unicorn ' as big as the life '. It was not for nothing Etherege had some time before written to Buckingham, " Ten years ago I as little thought my stars designed to make a politician of me, and that it would come to my share to debate in public assemblies, and regulate the affairs of Christendom, as the Grand Signor dreamed of losing Hungary ; but my royal master having the charity to believe me master of some qualities of which I never suspected myself, I find that the zeal and alacrity I discover in myself to support a dignity which he thought fit to confer upon me has supplied all other defects, and given me a talent for which, till now, I justly fancied myself incapable ".

II

But this was the final blaze, for the time was coming upon Etherege when he should suffer for his faith. His religion was Shaftesbury's, that which all sensible men hold, but which no sensible man ever speaks of. " I have ever enjoyed a liberty of opinion in matters of religion ; " he wrote, " 'tis indifferent to me whether there be any other in the world who thinks as I do. This makes me have no temptation to talk of the business ; but quietly following the light within me, I leave it to them who were born with the ambition of becoming prophets or legislators." Certainly it was not wise to declare yourself—as Dryden was to find. Obscure parsons might play the Vicar of Bray, but not men of distinction. Unfortunately, however, Etherege did declare himself. Writing of the *Hind and Panther* he had said, " Let them go and turn the churches into what beasts they please. I shall never turn my religion which teaches me to be always obedient and faithful to the King my master."

Then what was to be done when the Revolution came, and with it William III, who was not descended from Adam on his father's side, and so no true king? It was a difficult point for a loyalist, and it is most unlucky that just here the secretary fails in his duty to history. We can only conjecture what happened. It is often said Etherege ' fled ' to Paris, but there is no need to use so strong a term. For his great friend Dorset had welcomed William of Orange when he came, and had helped to smuggle the Princess Anne away from London and her father. He would surely have protected gentle George. Even the secretary only says that he was ' relieved '. We may guess he did not wish to serve William, and being allowed to go where he would, naturally went to a place where, besides being gentlemen, they knew how to live. Thus shaking the dust of the famous ' Street of the Envoys ' off his feet, he journeyed to Paris, leaving behind him his books, his secretary, and his debts.

The rooks then were done with him ; but not so Mr. H. H., who would in some measure repair the insults he had suffered, and settle a certain small question of emoluments. A man of Mr. H. H.'s accomplishments was not with impunity to be treated in any scurvy way. First of all Sir George, when in England, had promised him three-score pounds a year, with his own and his man's diet, but when he came to Ratisbon " would have flinched from his bargain ". Even if your salary is in arrear and you have to pawn your watch, you ought, Mr. H. H. considered, to pay your secretary. As good fortune would have it, after Etherege had left his post, money was sent him, and the secretary " laid an arrest upon it until

I should be paid what he owed to me by his note in writing. After all my fair proposals to be satisfied, he would have shuffled me off, and writ to the magistrates against me, calling me his domestic with other harsh terms, which gave occasion to the following letter I sent him to Paris—"

It is doubtful, however, if Sir George read the letter. It was as long as the longest of his own dispatches, and in Latin. And, we have Dennis's authority, he knew no Latin. True, there were those mottoes at the feast, but anybody can rake up a tag or two from Horace. There was as well the version of *O rus* . . ., but then, with the help of a secretary, anybody can throw off a short translation. But the curious thing is, Mr. H. H. knew that Sir George had no Latin. He had even taken the trouble to record it, in the manly metre of Hudibras. What it was exactly that impelled him to do so it is hard to say ; this time indignation cannot be to blame for the scurrilous lines, most of them unquotable, which compose " An imperfect copy of the most renowned original S. G. E." For indignation, as is well known, is a respectable servant of the muses, even a noble one. However, we learn of the late envoy :

> He play'd oft the philosopher
> Although he was no strict liver,
> And if his Latin had held out
> He would have baffled all ye rout.

To be sure, if Sir George's Latin held out no better than the secretary's powers of versification, his command of latinity cannot have been much to boast of. But if this was the case, why did Mr. H. H. write to him in that tongue? He must have known he would be unlikely to read it. Still, the great thing is to have written a long letter in Latin, and—to send a copy to somebody else.

We have already seen the worthy man was proud of his erudition.

In any case that was the end of His Excellency, and very nearly of Sir George Etherege. For no more is actually known of him than that in 1691 he was 'lately dead'. Rumour had it that he had met his end in Paris, the bottle and a staircase having proved too mighty for the 'sense, judgement, and wit' Buckingham had extolled. But we do not know. His is altogether a mysterious history. He was born perhaps in Oxfordshire, probably in 1636. He died most likely in Paris, maybe in 1690. He appeared with a play in 1663, and disappeared with a Latin letter in 1688. What we know of his intermediate life is contained in a few verses, a reference or an anecdote from Dean Lockier, Dennis, or Pepys, and a statement that Sir Roger de Coverley often supped with him. It is scanty enough; but thanks to the secretary, the period at Ratisbon is perfectly clear. It is not a very grave history, but it disengages for us the whole of the man, and a distinctive if not essential aspect of his time. And that is much. Bishop Wilberforce might even have said, too much.

THE ARCHITECT OF BLENHEIM

"No person ever lived, or died, with so few enemies as Sir John Vanbrug, owing to his pleasant wit and unaffected good humour."—NOBLE, *History of the College of Arms.*

To

Mrs. R. L. Devonshire

PART I

I

Early Years

ENGLAND in the years following the Revolution was the scene of vociferous and embittered strife, to be stilled only when time had hallowed the Hanoverian succession, and the long reign of Walpole had seemed to fix eternally changing elements. Especially were the first thirty years a period of faction, of backstairs intrigue, of rapid change of front, and of almost avowed duplicity. The great heroes of the rebellion were gone, and had given place to men of narrow minds or fierce ambitions; instead of Pym and Hampden, Rochester and Bolingbroke: and yet out of this atmosphere of defamation and virulent libel, with the whip, the prison, and the pillory ever at hand, imperceptibly there arose, almost it would seem by mistake, that august, mysterious, but practical entity, the British Constitution.

Those were gay, bustling days, enlivened by anonymous pamphlets, broadsides, and ballads, days of impeachments, of secret correspondences with St. Germains, of rival clubs and crowding to great trials. A man ever so little in the public eye needed all his wit to keep his head above water, every vigilance over his smallest acts. For it was a robust age, with no room for moral squeamishness. Each had to walk warily, on the look out for traps, with an eye always alert to perceive the implications of what he said or did, otherwise he was sure to be caught somewhere, to be dragged in somehow. And through these sunny but troubled waters that resembled a choppy sea on which the sun shines after the heavy storm is over, sailed John Vanbrugh, quite simply, quite unaffectedly, without seeming to realize what was going on around him, hardly conscious of where his actions might lead. Although very much in the tumult, he was never of it. Kindly, sincere, of not more than average delicacy; in some ways stupid, in others extremely talented, 'honest Van' was carried forward on a tide of great good fortune (his own vigour aiding not a little) until the age to which he belonged by birth but not by temperament, passed gently beyond him. Thus while he subsided on sandy shores, others entered the ports he only just failed to make.

The attention of the clamorous, intriguing world was first drawn to him in a way which did not mark him out for future distinction. Early in February 1692 it was informed by a letter from France that "three English gentlemen, Mr. Vanbrook, Mr. Goddard and Mr. North were clapt up in the Bastile, suspected to be spies",[1] and since there seemed to be nothing else to do, some French merchants were sent to the Tower "to be used as Mr. North and Mr. Vanbroke are in the Bastile".[2] The polite world expressed some concern for Mr. North, a member of its circle, but nobody knew who Mr. Vanbrook might be.

Had they known, the gentlemen of King William's reign would not have been much interested. A prosperous sugar-baker of Chester,[3] now dead, had had nineteen children by Elizabeth, daughter of Sir Dudley Carleton,

[1] Luttrell, i. 387, 11th February 1691–2.

[2] Ibid., 15th March.

[3] Giles, see Swain. The original Dutch name was Van Brugghe. We find it as Vanbrook, Vanbroke, Vanbrug, Vanbruggs, Vanbrugge, Van Brugg, and Brooke. Downes in *Roscius Anglicanus*, spells it Vantbrugg, and on one occasion is careless enough to write 'Mr. Vantbrugg' as playing Ventidius in *All for Love* at St. James's Palace in 1704. Surely he means Verbruggen the actor, as there is no other mention of our Vanbrugh ever acting. The name was probably pronounced Vanbroog.

and the prisoner, the eldest surviving son of the stout old merchant, had been born in 1664. A 'liberal' education at the Chester High School and two years wandering in France to study house-building, had, in 1686, a little strangely led him to a commission in the Earl of Huntingdon's Regiment of Foot.[1] But his military duties had not interfered with his travels, and he had once more gone to France, whence returning in 1690 he had been seized at Calais to be cast into prison. In the next year he was transferred to Vincennes, and now he was promoted to the Bastille among men of importance, an honour neither he nor anybody else was ever able to explain.[2]

The causes of his confinement are obscure, but not beyond conjecture, since for a commissioned officer to amble about France when England was at war with that country might very well lead to untoward incidents. The more so that Vanbrugh appears to have neglected to take out a passport, which the French authorities learned "upon the information of a lady in Paris",[3] or so it was rumoured. Perhaps he thought he might escape notice among the crowd of officers dangling loyally after James, of whom, indeed, his commission would declare him to be the 'trusty and well-beloved' servant. The more popular view, however, is that he was seized on the report of an engineer who had seen him gazing with too much attention at a piece of military architecture,[4] and no doubt it was difficult to explain that his interest was entirely technical or aesthetic. The French, though they understand a devotion to art, are a realistic people.

[1] Afterwards 13th Foot, and E. Somerset Regt.
[2] *D. N. B.*, Ward, Swain. The place of his education is doubtful.
[3] *D. N. B.* [4] T. Cibber.

True or not, the latter tale is characteristic of Vanbrugh's life. His most innocent actions—and what is more natural than for an architect to look at any structure he happens upon?—seemed always to involve him in the violent quarrels of others, and the only dissensions of which he had not the heartiest dislike were those domestic broils he invented to enliven his comedies. Quite unwittingly he was continually thrusting his hand into hornets' nests, and being badly stung. But he always extricated himself in the same manner, and on this occasion, tradition, if not faithful to fact, is still true to character. It is said that while in the Bastille he was constantly cheerful, and amused himself not only with reading French comedies, but by translating them, as well as by sketching out some scenes for an original piece: and that he made himself so agreeable to the gentlemen who visited him there, that it was through their pleading he was released at the end of November 1692. Personal charm! there, at the outset of his career we feel his distinguishing touch, the winning quality of one who liked his fellows, and was ready to take life as he found it. A happy directness of manner, an engaging appearance, and a knack of doing with zest anything which came to his hand to do, were graces ever ready to serve him. And to such as command these, Fate is apt to be generous.

On his release, however, she at first dealt her favours with a niggard hand, in the form of a mean auditorship of the Southern division of Lancaster,[1] probably through his cousin William, who was a treasury official. It was a small enough gift to a man of Vanbrugh's honesty, but the prospects of an architect being poor, doles were not to be scorned. There was, of course, the army, but at twenty-eight the position of an ensign is not very gratify-

[1] Swain.

ing or encouraging, and the pay, as well as being small, was uncertain: for not only was Parliament, through suspicion of William, dilatory in raising funds, but it was not unknown for superior officers to cheat their subalterns. Even the seniors themselves were not very sure of their pay, and on one occasion the secretary of the Treasury needed the stimulus of a bribe to jog his memory as regards arrears.[1]

The army, then, promised no advancement; but it is possible that as a makeshift Vanbrugh joined his brother Dudley, a captain in the Scots Regiment,[2] and who at about the time John was leaving the Bastille, had, while in winter quarters at Ostend, an unfortunate experience. He killed his colonel, one Beveredge, in a duel, the colonel "having used abusive language to the Captain first, and shook him".[3] Dudley was tried by court-martial, but acquitted, the irascible Beveredge having obviously been the aggressor, while his opponent was, like his brother, known to be "always of a peaceable, quiet temper".[4] But whether or no Dudley gave his brother temporary haven, and brought out the pleasanter aspects of the life, it is certain that when in 1696 an opportunity arose for John to take a captain's commission in Bulkeley's Marine Regiment, he found nothing better to do than to accept:[5] and inscribed in the records as John Brooke, he was thenceforth known as Captain Vanbrugh.

It was something to be a captain, and still more to be a marine, for at least the winter was passed at home and not in Holland. And life was not likely to be very arduous, especially as the regiment formed part of the sea force commanded by Carmarthen, who the year

[1] Burnet. [2] There was a Brooke in his company.
[3] Luttrell, quoted by Ward.
[4] *Athenaeum*, 18th August 1894. [5] *D. N. B.*

before had returned under full sail from the Scilly Islands, the distant view of a merchant fleet having made him regard Milford Haven as a more discreet riding. And in 1696 the fleet did no more than burn the buildings on a few islands when returning from the port of Cadiz.[1] This inactivity gave Vanbrugh leisure to find another outlet for his overflowing vitality, and after this brief, inglorious campaign, his military career faded into the background.

[1] So Burnet.

2

Play-writing

It was nevertheless owing to an incident in his soldier life, that Vanbrugh was able to make fruitful the long months spent in the company of the comic muse in the depths of the Bastille.

It so happened that in his early ensign days, 'when his heart was above his income', he had become 'particularly obliged' to a certain Sir Thomas Skipwith, with whom he was billeted. Cheerful and generous, Sir Thomas, as one of the patentees of the Theatre Royal, Drury Lane, took the responsibilities and chances of the position as carelessly as he did everything else. The finances of the theatre were therefore at a low ebb, and now Vanbrugh was inspired with the idea of repaying his obligation by writing a successful comedy.[1] In any case, even if the play did not take enough to repay his benefactor, it would be an amusing thing to do, and might later bring its reward.

A suitable opportunity arose when in January 1696 the Theatre Royal staged Colley Cibber's first play, *Love's Last Shift*, a comedy which, as Congreve said, had a great many things in it that were like wit, but were not really such. Vanbrugh, on his part, did not find it at all satisfactory from the common-sense point of view. In Cibber's play a virtuous wife reclaims a dissolute husband after a separation of eight years, and the conclusion suggests that they lived happily ever after. To Vanbrugh this seemed absurdly contrary to likelihood, certainly at variance with

[1] Cibber, vi.

his own observation of men and women. So as a comment on the moral, as well as to have a good deal of fun of his own, he rapidly wrote a sequel to the play, *The Relapse, or Virtue in Danger*, incidentally raising Sir Novelty Fashion, not only to the peerage, but to a much higher power of comedy. Everybody who read his piece found it highly entertaining, and a more faithful reflection than *Love's Last Shift* not only of the life they knew, but of human nature. However, owing to the lateness of the season—vacation time was near at hand—it was not produced until the end of December, with Cibber in the part of Lord Foppington.

Although the play succeeded by virtue of its raciness and its bold, not to say exaggerated treatment of actuality, rather than by its literary grace, all the wits at once wanted to know the author. They met a large, fair, handsome man, perhaps a trifle heavy, particularly as to the chin, and with eyes that slanted upwards a little towards the temples. But what charmed them especially was the caressing look in his frank eyes, the smile hovering about his full, shapely lips, and his ready, downright wit. Always cheerful and willing to oblige, good-hearted to a fault, with a robust appreciation of the good things of this life, he took men as he found them, without expecting them to be what they were not, and he liked to be accepted on the same terms.

And accepted he was by the great coterie of elegant writers and noble amateurs—an agreeable and distinguished company, in strong contrast with both his military acquaintance, and the struggling quarrelsome band of actors with whom he had recently come into contact. His fortune was evidently taking a turn for the better. He received the compliments even of that very rising politician, Mr. Montague, London's midwife of letters, who would bring any promising babe into the literary world, carefully leaving the troublesome and expensive business of nursing to others. He had read to him some scenes of the play Vanbrugh had scribbled in the Bastille, and scenting perhaps another dedication (a form of writing of which he was inordinately fond) urged him to tack the comedy together, and give it him for Betterton to act in the other theatre at Lincoln's Inn Fields. And from this time onward Captain Vanbrugh was known primarily as a playwright, everybody, himself included, having apparently forgotten he was a soldier. Perhaps, however, since campaigning was only a half-yearly affair, he succeeded in dovetailing professions.

But to be in the public eye, though gratifying, may mean to be misunderstood, and before Vanbrugh had time even to print *The Relapse* he was amazed to find himself the object of attack from certain quarters. Some tiresome people were beginning to mutter dark things about the theatre, and although Vanbrugh was willing enough to admit that the stage shared the dual tincture of the rest of life, he could not imagine why the prudes should set upon him in particular, and accuse him of 'blasphemy and bawdy'. He was genuinely puzzled. Blasphemy and Bawdy? for the life of him he could not 'find 'em out' in his play, in which he had with the utmost innocency of intention portrayed the life of his time. He found himself compelled to write a preface, so as to point out that a lady of *real* reputation might without affront to her prayer-book lay his volume beside it on her shelf. It was not his fault if people chose to read sinister meanings into everyday ejaculations. Surely anybody of sense could see that his sole design in writing this play had been to please the honest gentlemen of the town, and "to divert (if possible) some part of their spleen, in spite of their wives and taxes ". But there were some who were not men of sense, ' friends to nobody ', saints, " thorough-paced ones with screwed faces and wry mouths ", men guilty of that very excess it is the duty as well as the pleasure of every comic writer to belabour. " They make debauches in piety ", Vanbrugh declared roundly, " as sinners do in wine ; and are as quarrelsome in their religion, as other people are in their drink ; so I hope, nobody will mind what they say."

But it is difficult to please every variety of person in a complex community, and if the most thorough-paced saint could find nothing against the play Vanbrugh produced at Drury Lane the following January, the less saintly found *Aesop* tedious. It was choke full of morality from beginning to end, and even duller than Boursault's French original. But Chancellor Montague was still urging him to complete his Bastille play, and Vanbrugh felt this was " a request not to be refused to so eminent a patron of the muses ". So *The Provok'd Wife* was acted in May, and soon afterwards printed. It was as unlike *Aesop* as it is possible to imagine—full of festiveness and frolic, and if not unduly nice as to morality, was no more indecent than the openly lived life of the times. But it had about it an Elizabethan tang, something of that freedom, and even of that wildness, which was disturbing to those who desired a safer, a more sedate world. Vanbrugh, and indeed, most of his contemporaries, thought he was writing plays like Congreve, or any one else ; but once again, quite unconsciously, he had thrust his hand into a hornets' nest. For it appeared that his plays were, after all, not like Congreve's, whose chaste example was, at the end of the year, held up for imitation by the doctor-poet Sir Richard Blackmore, who deprecated the 'obscene and profane pollutions' practised upon the stage by other dramatists. Blackmore set the hornets' nest astir, and early in 1698 Merriton published a work on the "Immorality, Debauchery and Profaneness" of popular amusements. The insects were beginning to sting.

These efforts, however, were mere flea-bitings in comparison with the sulphurous tirade soon afterwards launched into the world under the title of *A Short View of the Profaneness and Immorality of the English Stage, Together with the Sense of Antiquity upon the Argument.* Between its covers ranted Jeremy Collier, breathing famine and fire, slaughter and desolation, wildly hurling all the brickbats of heaven at the unguarded heads of dramatists, particularly those of Vanbrugh and Congreve, between whom the new Prynne could see no effective difference.

In any case it would not have mattered to him if he had: he had at last found a long-sought opportunity. A non-juring parson dissatisfied with the position accorded his merits in the world, he was consumed by a passion half for notoriety, half for martyrdom. An extremist in religion who revelled in the more dramatic aspects of high Anglican ritual, he had at one time delighted to preach rebellion in crazy pamphlets directed against an Erastian government. He longed to suffer for a cause. When arrested in 1692 on suspicion of complicity in a plot, he had barely been prevailed upon by his friends to accept bail.[1] Even now he was under ban of outlawry for absolving two murderous traitors upon the scaffold. He was, however, no fool, and by no means lacking in erudition; but he was ill-balanced, over-emotional, easily precipitated into violence; and once he saw red

[1] Macaulay, *Rest. Dram.*

he became half demented, rushing into extravagance and dishonesty. And now that the hunt was up he blew his tantivy horn, declared himself huntsman, and halloing on his pack, rode himself desperately back into official grace. For after all, martyrdom when too prolonged is apt to lose its point.

His book fell like a thunderbolt into the coffee-houses and drawing-rooms where art was discussed with intelligence, and life lived reasonably according to the manners of the day. Nobody could quite penetrate the design of this squib, with its absurd confusion of issues; a true jeremiad in style, in which to dally with vice seemed the same sort of crime as to trifle with the Aristotelian unities. Congreve, who had been severely handled, was as much bewildered as hurt; Wycherley was growling angrily in the country; while Dryden, who at his age was not going to allow himself to be much bothered, was contemptuously ready to admit anything, since no admission of the kind Collier sought would affect the literary quality of his plays. The actors, for their part, professed themselves quite at a loss. Everybody knew the stage to be a moral instrument, so why should Collier attack it? They were forced to be content with the solution of the actor Haines, who said that "Collier himself was a morality mender, and, you know, two of a trade never agree".[1] Vanbrugh, whose scent seemed to stink hottest in the nose of the pack, could not make head nor tail of all this pother made by one of those very carpers "with plod shoes, a little band, and greasy hair" against whom he had warned the readers of *The Relapse*. He could not understand why he should be singled out above-all others as a monster of depravity. Surely one need not pay much attention; for men of sense would

[1] Cibber.

never think any the worse of a play or of its author on account of the mud-slinging of a man 'who runs amuck at all'. No doubt the affair would soon blow over.

The worst of it was, however, that the book achieved instant and enormous popularity. Edition after edition was called for. Collier was hailed as a great reformer, and the decree of outlawry against him allowed to fall into abeyance. Thousands welcomed the book with that acrimonious delight with which the stupid always greet an attack upon their betters in intellect or sensibility. Perhaps also the citizens saw their chance of retaliating upon the heartless playwrights who always made the 'cit' look a goat, and duly supplied him with horns. No doubt Alderman Fondlewife and Alderman Gripe presented copies to their consorts.

Collier certainly knew his public; and moreover the book was vigorously written, and amusing to read, whatever view of art or morality you might hold. And it soon became clear that it was a dangerous book, for early in May the justices of Middlesex 'presented' the playhouses to be 'nurseries of debauchery and blasphemy', and they also presented Congreve for writing *The Double Dealer*, D'Urfey *Don Quixote*, and Tonson and Briscoe for printing these works. They further declared that "women frequenting the playhouses in masks tended much to debauchery and immorality",[1] a side-issue in which they were probably right. Indeed, Collier's pack yelped so noisily that a drowsy and neglected act of James I against profane swearing,[2] to which the reverend divine had drawn attention, was put into force. Prosecutions were begun for lewdness and blasphemy; and informers stationed in the theatres

[1] Luttrell, 10th and 12th May 1698.

[2] Ward. For text see Courthope, p. 95.

caught the words from the mouths of the actors, and carried them red-hot to the justices. It was evident that this 'young histrio-mastix' would have to be answered.

The play from the other side began on the 17th of May with *A Vindication of the Stage*, perhaps by Wycherley,[1] a light, amusing piece of writing that had no effect whatever. It was followed by a volume of Filmer's, not much to the purpose, being chiefly concerned to show that the Greeks and Romans were not free from the guilt of having written smutty things. On the 6th June, however, there appeared the only considerable answer, by Dennis, the raging critic, who in *The Usefulness of the Stage* laid stress upon Collier's unfair controversial method, and also gave the sense of antiquity upon the argument, turning the tables with some skill. For instance, Collier had quoted the lines of Ovid which Dryden had translated:

> But above all, the Play-House is the Place;
> There's Choice of Quarry in that narrow Chace.
> There take thy Stand, and sharply looking out,
> Soon mayst thou find a Mistress in the Rout . . .

apropos of which Dennis quoted a little more Ovid anent the value of Church Parade for the same purpose, and remarked, "And have we not here a merry person, who brings an authority against going to theatres, which is as direct against going to church? Nay, and upon the very same account too." Such hits were telling, but on the whole the book was too learned, and attacked the question from too high an angle of general philosophic aesthetics, to act as an effective counterblast.

The public, indeed, had small time to digest that work, for two days after its issue there appeared *A Short Vindication of The Relapse and the Provok'd Wife*,

[1] Gosse, *Congreve*; Macaulay, *Rest. Dram.*

of course by Vanbrugh, though like the plays it bore no signature. Collier's ' lampoon ', he declared, although contemptible enough, was " now a thing no farther to be laughed at ", because it had " got credit enough to brand the persons it mentions ". But although it must be answered, it was extremely difficult to do so, because Collier's " play is so wild, I must be content to take the ball as it comes, and return it if I can ". The *Short View* was indeed a slippery thing, for, as Dennis had written with a virulence almost equal to Collier's, the parson was " so far from having shown in his book either the meekness of a Christian, or the humility of an exemplary pastor, that he has neither the reasoning of a man of sense in it, nor the style of a polite man, nor the sincerity of an honest man, nor the humanity of a gentleman or a man of letters ". Vanbrugh could not hope to equal this Jeremiah Collier in invective, nor would he wish to imitate his florid polemics. He could only oppose the common-sense view of a man of the world, and this, unless handled by a master, offers but meagre resistance to fanatical revilings.

So wild indeed was Collier's play, that not only was it sometimes impossible to see into what part of the court he was aiming the ball, but in some places it was beyond the endeavours of man to take him seriously. To do so, to make too vigorous a defence, might even expose a man to ridicule. What could you make of a fellow who said that the characters in *The Relapse* " swore in solitude and cold blood, under thought and deliberation, for business and exercise ", and declared this to be a ' terrible circumstance ', when after all, ' the stretch of the profaneness ' lay in Lord Foppington's ' Gad ! ' and Miss Hoyden's ' Icod ! ' ? " This ", said Vanbrugh, " is all this gentleman's zeal is in such a ferment about." " Now," he continued, " whether such words are entirely justifiable or not, there 's this at least to be said for 'em : that people of the nicest rank both in their religion and their manners throughout Christendom use 'em." That certainly might be a sufficient defence for their use by frail flesh in daily life, but was it applicable to a work of art? If Collier attacked a play as though it were a sermon, Vanbrugh defended it as though it might be a speech in Parliament.

But Vanbrugh had done worse than offend against decorum, he had jested against the holy order of priests, and the Reverend Mr. Collier, taking one or two phrases such as Berinthia's " Mr. Worthy used you like a text, he took you all to pieces ", brought all his turgid eloquence to bear on the assault. " There are few of these last Quotations ", he fumed, " but what are plain Blasphemy, and within the *Law*. They look reeking from Pandaemonium, and almost smell of Fire and Brimstone. This is an Eruption of Hell with a Witness ! I almost wonder the smoke of it has not darken'd the Sun, and turned the air to Plague and Poison ! These are outrageous Provocations ; enough to arm all Nature in Revenge ; to exhaust the Judgements of Heaven, and sink the *Island* in the Sea ! " For a simple-minded gentleman, who has merely designed to divert the spleen of his countrymen, to be accused of nearly bringing the worst horrors of the Apocalypse upon his native land, must be sore trial—when it gets beyond a joke—for how can one answer preposterous fustian? Indeed, at one point Vanbrugh gave up the contest as hopeless, and resorted to burlesque. When Collier accused him of denying revealed light by making Amanda say, " Good Gods, what slippery stuff are men composed of ! Sure the account of the creation's false, and 'twas the woman's rib they were form'd of", the vindicator said, "I'm sorry the gentleman who writ this speech of Amanda's is not here to defend himself; but he being gone away with the Czar, who has made him Poet Laureate of Muscovy . . . &c.", on the principle, no doubt, of answering a fool according to his folly.

Yet Vanbrugh did his best to engage Collier seriously. The divine had laid down that "The business of plays is to recommend virtue and discountenance vice". Vanbrugh had thought it was to counteract the depressing effect of wives and taxes, and to get full houses; but since everybody seemed to admit the truth of that part of Collier's argument, he too must rank himself upon the side of the angels. A little thought made it quite plain that *The Relapse* was a tract. Was not its second title *Virtue in Danger*? Slowly he developed the theme that he had been moved to write this play entirely by the touching and satisfactory conclusion of *Love's Last Shift*. He yearned for the happy couple to remain happy; it would be heartbreaking to think of further conjugal misunderstandings. But on the other hand, they must not live in a fool's paradise. Over confidence might bring temptations. And it was solely to warn them against these temptations, out of a sheer desire for good, that *The Relapse* had been written. Of course the object of plays was to recommend virtue, but how can one discountenance vice without portraying it? "For the business of comedy is to show people what they should do, by representing them on the stage doing what they should not." Could any reply be simpler, more triumphant than that?

We need not farther follow this conflict, at once so entertaining and so sad, in which feelings were screwed up to the height of bitterness, and men of intellect failed to answer fools.[1] A host of scribblers sided with Collier against Congreve, and the parson, not content to look on with his sleek smile and supercilious glance, once more rushed into the fray with *A Defence of the Short View.* Like his opponents, he got in a few shrewd side blows, but they did nothing to better his case. Indeed, it needed no bettering, for it was already judged. When art and morality are forcibly made bed-fellows, it is usually art that has to yield the place. Certainly on this occasion morality remained in the bed, its pillow smoothed by Addison and Steele, its quilt arranged by Cibber. And as for art, it sought refuge first in the satires of Pope and Swift, and then in the novel. But the result was not brought about all at once. Numbers of pamphlets, signed or anonymous, whitened the booksellers' stalls with their idle leaves, and Dryden wrote a few scathing lines in prologues and epilogues. On the one hand sprung up The Society for the Reformation of Manners, while on the other there appeared in 1699 a timid little sheet modestly showing that swearing and references to child-bearing really had been heard upon the stage before the Restoration.

The controversy rumbled on through the eighteenth century, Dr. Blair declaring that the immorality of *The Provok'd Wife* "ought to explode it out of decent society", while William Law in 1726,[2] and later the Reverend Doctor John Witherspoon, not so sure of the ballistic qualities of vice, declared the stage an altogether unchristian amusement. But the immediate battle was not confined to words. In November 1701 information was brought against twelve of the players, including Mrs.

[1] See Aitken's *Life of Steele.*

[2] For an example see Gibbon's *Memoirs of my Life and Writings*, World's Classics, p. 16.

Barry, Mrs. Bracegirdle, Mr. Betterton, and Mr. Verbruggen, " for using indecent expressions in some late plays, particularly *The Provok'd Wife* ",[1] Betterton and Mrs. Barry being actually fined.[2] Yet these measures were not altogether efficacious in cleansing the heart of the people of London, for as late as about 1706 the author of *Hell upon Earth, or the Language of the Playhouse*, confessed that a public was still attracted by ' horrid comedies '. " The more they have been exposed by Mr. Collier and others ", he lamented, " the more they seem to be admir'd."[3] Nevertheless, at the time of Queen Anne's accession the attacks of vexatious busybodies grew so fierce as to endanger the very existence of the theatre, and the Queen herself found it advisable to interfere. She placed the licensing of public shows entirely in the hands of the Master of the Revels, forbade the wearing of masks, and enjoined that " no Person of what Quality soever, Presume to go Behind the Scenes, or come upon the Stage, either before or during the Acting of Any Play ". For which signal service to the drama, though one which must have interfered not a little with the activities of some of the peers, she received the thanks of the Lords.[4]

[1] Luttrell V. iii, 20th November 1701. [2] Baker.
[3] Quoted by Ward.
[4] Ashton, II. xxv, from Luttrell, 20th January 1704.

3

The Kit-Cat

THE rapidity and ease with which Vanbrugh now mounted the steps of Parnassus is, among other things, to be accounted to the excellence of Christopher Catling's pies, and to the sharpness of Jacob Tonson's nose. That organ could smell out not only rich meats, but enriching copy; and if a man was well-bred and good-humoured, had no inconvenient views on the Revolution Settlement, and seemed likely to write saleable matter, he was almost sure to become a member of the Kit-Cat Club, of which the publisher was the father and president.

Jacob Tonson was possessed of one of those sinewy natures for which men feel either a great liking, or a profound, unreasoning antipathy. At this time success had not yet mellowed him enough to earn for him Pope's affectionate title of 'genial Jacob', and the shrewdness of his look, combined with a malformation that gave him the nickname of 'left-legged', made upon many an unpleasant impression. Business came first with him, and although he had some reputation for gallantry, he was able to suppress the promptings of his heart, even when it came to dealing with so famous, beautiful, and witty a lady as Mrs. Aphra Behn.[1] He was credited with a haughty temper, so much so that Dryden was afraid to be left alone with him when verses were overdue,[2] and took his revenge by describing him

> With leering looks, bull-faced and freckled fair;
> With two left legs, and Judas coloured hair,
> And frowzy pores that taint the ambient air.[3]

[1] Summers, Introduction to edition of Behn: Letter.
[2] Johnson's *Dryden*.
[3] Scott's *Dryden*; also *Faction Display'd*.

From a print in the British Museum

Finally, enormous misshapen ears, and a mouth even Kneller could not make into a Cupid's bow, added to the effect but not to his charms.

These were hard things to struggle against in a world where personal grace still counted for much, and it was only by persistence, by culture, and by performing real services to letters and printing, that he achieved the position of being the first of the line of great publishers, from which he could almost patronize the patrons. For he was a stern, honest critic : flatter a lord he might, a paper of verses never.[1] Yet he could not smooth over his angularity ; he " looked like a bookseller seated among lords, yet vice versa he behaved himself like a lord when he came among booksellers ".[2] It was then by virtue of his mind that he lived among the great, becoming in old age " the perfect image and likeness of Bayle's *Dictionary*, so full of matter, secret history, and wit and spirit ".[3] And although to the last a contract with him remained a contract,[4] already at the opening of the century his friends were able to " conceive him the cheerfullest, best, honest fellow living ".[5]

One day in the last decade of the seventeenth century, wandering about Temple Bar he had discovered an ordinary where the mutton-pies were particularly good : and knowing with Addison that eating and drinking " are points wherein most men agree, and in which the learned and illiterate, the philosopher and the buffoon can all of them bear a part ", he instituted a weekly feast at the sign of The Cat and Fiddle. Later, this place being inconveniently hot, the circle of patrons, beaux, and poets moved to the Fountain Tavern within easy distance of

[1] Dunton, *Life and Errors*. [2] E. Ward.
[3] Pope to Oxford, 1730.
[4] See letter from Gay, Add. MSS. 28275, f. 8.
[5] Rowe, *Reconcilement*.

Tonson's bookshop, The Shakespeare Head, over against St. Catherine's Street in the Strand.[1]

It was a brilliant clique, in which everybody had his especial cachet. There was Dorset, 'the grace of courts, the muses' pride'; Lord Keeper Somers, 'the all-accomplished'; Walsh, the member of Parliament and 'the muses' judge and friend'; and Montague, now Lord Halifax, who not only

claim'd the station
To be Maecenas to the nation,

but was granted it by universal consent. There was, of course, another sort of member, requiring epithets of a different kind, such as cross-eyed Mohun, with the face of a cretin, and Lord Carberry, who was supposed to sell Welshmen for slaves in Jamaica, and looked as though he well might. But among thirty-nine members one must have variety.

Though all were Whigs, the aim of the club was not political; it had one colour simply because no man could be very well with another who did not share his views as to the position of the church in the state. Indeed, a Tory Strephon would not bestow a second glance on a Phyllis if it was rumoured she had been kind to a Whig; while if one of the latter interest fell ill, he would as soon think of sending for Dr. Arbuthnot as a Tory would of dispatching his servant to Dr. Garth. Politics, of course, were discussed, as was everything else, from the character of the Elector of Hanover to the degree of each man's *tendre* for the black-eyed, ravishing, but ever-distant Mrs. Bracegirdle; from the Odes of Horace to the latest lampoon. But it was chiefly in current literature that the club pretended to dictate. If it said a poem was good,

[1] As far as can be gathered from Hearne 1705, *Spectator* ix, Blackmore's poems, and E. Ward.

good it was; if it said a play was bad, it was damned; while if they felt well-disposed towards an actor, its members could make his benefit night pay.[1]

Entrenched within such a *cénacle* Vanbrugh could defy the shafts of a Collier, especially as he got on famously in this society. If he chose his firmest friends rather than was chosen by them, it would appear that, like Caesar, he wished to have men about him that were fat. Neither Maecenas nor Jacob were wanting in comfortable covering; Steele's face, like his adaptable morality, was as broad as it was long; while the countenance of Lord Carlisle beamed out from the row of Kneller Kit-Cat portraits with all the rotundity of a cherub's. But these were meaner glories compared with that of the good-natured poet, the sceptical Dr. Garth, who believing in medicine as little as he did in Christianity, practised both with results far above the ordinary, and could lay claim to be the fattest man in London.[2] Such were Vanbrugh's particular friends.

The club was so successful that in 1703 Tonson built a room for it at his house of Barn Elms, at the Upper Flask in Hampstead, and during the summer

> One night in seven at this convenient seat
> Indulgent Bocaj did the muses treat,

not quite, indeed, the muses of the Mermaid, but the best replica of them the early eighteenth century could compass. Congreve, the acknowledged king of letters now Dryden was dead, would rule there, his kindly, modest wit every now and again breaking through his wistfulness; Nicholas Rowe, the tragedian, would laugh merrily all the time at everything and everybody, to the

[1] See Prior, Longleat MSS. 393, Jan. 1700. Quoted by Bickley.

[2] Johnson, and Lady Mary Wortley Montagu. Letter, October 1709.

scandal of Addison,[1] whose grave demeanour induced so deep a mistrust in Tonson that he ever thought him a priest in his heart.[2] But it is unlikely that Addison was very often present, although he duly played his part when they toasted 'old cats and young kits'; for his bashfulness made him prefer societies where the standard of intelligence was not quite so high as his own. It is true that if he would he might seat himself next to Tom D'Urfey, though on the other hand he might find himself face to face with Matt Prior, whose look was uncomfortably realistic, but who, indeed, shortly transferred himself to less Hanoverian surroundings, his mind in this respect marching with Dr. Swift's.

Tonson's 'treating' of the muses was not, of course, merely to indulge his genial nature; he had an eye to the main chance, and even in conviviality was a sound business man. In return for his dinners he got not only patronage and imposing subscription lists, but also the first refusal of literary fruits, especially of those occasional verses which made up his attractive miscellanies. If too bad for publication, the poems he was given were not too good to serve as bottoms for Christopher Catling's pies, thus a customer who bought a penny meat might have two penn'orth of poetry thrown in. It is true that, according to Somers, the coldness of D'Urfey's verse would prevent the dough from baking properly,[3] but since everybody did not share the Lord Keeper's fine palate, either for pies or poetry, the disadvantage was negligible.

Tonson, however, got little from the new member of the Kit-Cat beyond the publication of his later, less successful plays, Vanbrugh's contribution to the *Miscellanies* being only one. The collection of 1704 contained

[1] Johnson's *Rowe*. [2] Spence. [3] Escott.

his reproaches to ' A Lady more Cruel than Fair ', lines which may, but probably do not, record a defeat, for there are some failures to which no man likes to draw attention. But Vanbrugh's poetic sterility was no matter to Tonson, for he had found a lifelong friend. When he quarrelled with Congreve—the only quarrel Congreve is known to have had—Rowe reported him as saying:

> I'm in with Captain Vanbrugh at the present,
> A most sweet-natured gentleman, and pleasant . . .
> For him, so much I dote on him that I
> (If I was sure to go to heaven) would die,[1]

and in with Captain Vanbrugh he remained until the poet's death.

Indeed, they had one important trait in common; ' honest Van ' as little as ' genial Jacob ' was overawed by the company he frequented, and always kept his common-sense acumen about him. Kneller to him was ' that fool ',[2] and even Halifax failed to dazzle. One day, after dining with Maecenas and Congreve he wrote to Tonson in Holland, " My Lord Hallifax desires you will bespeak him a set of all kinds of mathematical instruments, of the largest sort, in ivory, but adorned as curiously as you please, they being more for furniture than for any use he's like to put 'em too; he designs to hang 'em up in his library ".[2] A man who could pierce through pretences in that manner appealed to Tonson, who saw in his friend's acuteness, honesty, disdain of toadyism, and frank good nature, just those very qualities he himself aimed at possessing.

But if Tonson chuckled over such remarks, one may be sure he kept them to himself, for though he got much gain from the poets, he knew that they in their turn

[1] *Reconcilement.*

[2] Letters to Tonson, 13th and 15th July 1703; *Athenaeum*, July 1836.

expected much from the patrons. And not in vain. Congreve got his hackney coaches, his Pipe Office and his Secretaryship of Jamaica ; Rowe collected a number of posts ; including an under-secretaryship ; Addison obtained a Countess and a portfolio ; while Steele got stamps, a Scottish commissionership, a post in the Royal stables, a lord-lieutenancy, and a knighthood. Prior, it is true, obtained his advancement from the other side, but lived to regret his impatience, while D'Urfey had to be content with a disproportionately large gratuity from the Queen for some doggerel verses on the senile Electress of Hanover.[1] And it was not, we may be sure, out of a fatuous love of social glamour that Vanbrugh welcomed his introduction into the Parnassus of the Strand ; and indeed, after Congreve, he was the first to reap a substantial benefit from his ability to consort agreeably with great Whig lords.

[1] Molloy.

4
New Openings

VANBRUGH, in truth, was more than a little in need of some profitable employment, for his heart was still above his income, which for the matter of that was not dazzling. He seemed to have exhausted the possibilities of the two professions he had so far adopted. Playwriting was an uncertain, and in any case a meagrely paid activity, for even Halifax, who was no longer Chancellor, had reduced his rewards of genius to a dinner or two. And now that William had made peace, the army held no prospects. In fact the reverse, for in 1702, Vanbrugh's first regiment, on the lists of which he figured as a captain on half pay, 'being broke', he asked for his arrears, to be met with the statement that he must "apply to ye Collonel".[1]

But he had not forgotten that he was by choice, and to some extent by training, an architect, or surveyor in the term of those days. He thought it worth while to mention this to the Kit-Cats, who no doubt discussed architecture with the knowledge and taste they brought to bear upon most subjects of that nature. Probably, in fact, they were better informed upon that point than upon others, for it was the day of the enthusiastic and successful amateur in building—lords had been known to design their houses themselves, and make no mean show in the art. After all even Inigo Jones had been but a dilettante. Vanbrugh evidently had many interesting and even exhilarating things to say on the subject, for in 1701 the Earl of Carlisle, bowled over by the

[1] *Athenaeum*, 1st September 1894.

magnificence and imaginative quality of Vanbrugh's drawings, employed him to build a gigantic country house in Yorkshire.

And, from having been a target for the moralists, Vanbrugh now became a butt for the wits, for it seemed absurd to them that a man who wrote light comedies should turn his hand to building houses. They forgot that Sir John Denham had been famed as a poet long before he preceded Wren as surveyor-general, and that Wren himself had only in middle age deserted mathematics to build St. Paul's. But the Kit-Cat rallied around him ; while Kneller commissioned him to see to Whitton Hall at Hounslow, 'to receive nobody in' as Vanbrugh gaily remarked.

If no argument could bring the outside world to believe that a comic dramatist might be as good an architect as another man, if the proof of the pudding was really to be in the eating, here was Vanbrugh's chance to display all his powers, and he determined to make the most of it. As a consequence, since his views on architecture were vigorous and original, the copy of *Palladio* in French, 'with the plans of houses in it', he asked Tonson to send him,[1] did more than any other book has done to transform the countryside of England. With a sheet of paper before him he was a very different person to the genial wit of the playhouse. He became titanic ; he took huge masses of masonry and kneaded them into form, abandoning himself to an orgy in true Palladian style, wherein it was the abstract qualities of architecture that counted. Utility was a base matter to be thrown to the winds ; a house had to be conceived as an aesthetic unit in a landscape, and the laying out of the garden was at least as important as the housing of the future inhabi-

[1] 13th July 1703 ; *Gent. Mag.* July 1836.

tants. He aimed at sublimity, and as he designed the fury grew: a sort of megalomania possessed him, and he really felt that Garth was not exaggerating when he compared him with an Apollo at the touch of whose lyre "stones mount in columns, palaces aspire".

Certainly the vastness of his conceptions is visible in the massive pile of Castle Howard, as thought and design are to be seen in every stone. It was the first house Vanbrugh built, and it remains among the most famous of England's noble homes. From 1701 to 1714 it continued to rise up full of picturesque splendour, as solid as it was grand, the structural simplicity enhanced by the striking boldness of the ornament. In the centre was a tremendous portico, two stories high, flanked by long galleries ending in symmetrical advancing wings provided with pavilions. A dome a hundred feet high, yet perfectly in proportion, attracted the gaze of wanderers from a distance of many miles, while the façade toward the garden possessed unexpected grace by reason of its fluted columns.[1] At all events the wooden model sent to Kensington so much pleased the king,[2] himself a distinguished amateur of the art, that he shortly made Vanbrugh a Comptroller of the Board of Works, his readiness to do so being perhaps increased by the Dutch sound of the architect's name.

As early as 1703 the Earl of Carlisle could get a very clear idea of how his house was going to look. He was delighted, and felt that it behoved him to reward the architect beyond the usual measure. Casting about for some suitable, and inexpensive, manner of doing this, it occurred to him that the post of Clarenceux King at

[1] Description largely from Cunningham. Pictures may be seen in *Vitruvius Britannicus*, or more conveniently in Gotch, Statham, and Barman.

[2] Macaulay, *Hist.* IV. 611.

Arms was vacant, while he himself as Deputy Earl Marshal had the gift to all intents and purposes in his hand. If a playwright could make a good architect, why should not an architect make a good herald? Moreover, it would be a splendid jest to give the post to Vanbrugh, because he was notoriously contemptuous of heraldry and all that it involved. He had ridiculed it in *Aesop*, not very violently it was true, but with enough satire to sting the occupants of the College. Vanbrugh also appreciated the jest, especially as it would not be unremunerative, and Whig prospects did not at the moment look very bright. Unfortunately there was one difficulty in the way. Custom ruled that no man could be raised to the office of King at Arms without first being a herald, and all the heralds' posts were already occupied. Luckily the check proved a trifling one, for it occurred to the Earl that he might, without let or hindrance, revive the obsolete office of Carlisle Herald, in which post he proposed, as a preliminary, to install Vanbrugh.

As was only natural, the gentlemen of the College viewed this procedure with indignation. They " felt the slight put upon them in having a total stranger made King at Arms, the more because though he had great abilities, yet he was totally ignorant of the profession of heraldry and genealogy, which he took every occasion to ridicule ".[1] And, of course, it was more than a slight, it was a threat to the interests of their close corporation. The blow was especially felt by Gregory King, Senior Poursuivant, a man of some fifty years of age, who had devoted his whole life to the science, and had been a worthy pupil of the great Sir William Dugdale. With very good reason he himself had expected to become Clarenceux, for, as his epitaph was to state,

[1] Noble.

He was a skilful herald,
A good accomptant, surveyor and mathematician ;
A curious penman,
And well versed in political arithmetic,

to which last quality Macaulay has paid a striking tribute.[1] Smarting from a sense of injustice, he organized " the just remonstrances and protests of the injured, superseded heralds ", a resistance Vanbrugh described as ' a great deal of saucy opposition ', which the Queen was inclined to uphold. But, to quote Vanbrugh again, " my Lord Treasurer set the Queen right, and I have accordingly been soused a Herald Extraordinary to be a King at winter ". Moreover, it was no ordinary sousing, for " Lord Essex was left deputy to the feat, which he did with a whole bowl of wine about my ears instead of half a spoonful ". And since the quarrel had been, as usual, none of Vanbrugh's making, the heralds allowed themselves to be won over by his charm and simplicity. " King was on the spot suspended, which the rest seeing renounced him, owned he drew 'em into rebellion, and declared him the son of a whore." [2]

But Vanbrugh was not yet Clarenceux, and when the time approached for his further elevation, Gregory King returned to the charge, and applied for the post for himself. The Earl Marshal replied that it was his intention to make it over to Vanbrugh. Thereupon King, gallant fighter, once more persuaded some of the heralds to join with him in a ' memorable petition ' [3] against the Lord Marshal's power. The case was heard in council during the month of March, and since it was unanimously decided against the petitioners, on the 29th of the month Vanbrugh was appointed Clarenceux ; an

[1] Macaulay, *Hist.* I. iii.
[2] To Tonson, 13th July 1703 ; *Gent. Mag.* July 1836. The ceremony took place on 21st June 1703.
[3] Add. MSS. 9011, f. 346.

event which made Swift exclaim, " Now Van will be able to *build houses* ".

The point for Vanbrugh, however, was that he would be able to gather in emoluments for a very small outlay of time or energy; and as for his thoughts on the whole procedure, they are perhaps not difficult to guess. A plum had dropped into his mouth. Certainly one looked for plums when one served a nobleman, but this one, besides being juicy, had a joyous flavour about it. Here was a wit, a Kit-Cat, a writer of plays some called scandalous, in any case a jovial man of the world, solemnly made King at Arms over the head of a quill-driving old fogey. Let life be to him who can most enjoy it. And when in 1706 Vanbrugh went abroad in company with Halifax and Addison to present the Garter to Prince George of Hanover,[1] he no doubt performed the two-day ceremony with a great air, and looked vastly well driving about in a six-horsed coach, gorgeous in the robes and insignia of his office.

[1] Beltz.

5

The Italian Opera House

In six years Vanbrugh had sprung from being an altogether inconsiderable captain of marine to being among playwrights comparable with Congreve, among architects the rival of Wren. If time has modified these judgements it is undeniable that he was a person of importance in the management of the pomp of state. But amid all his activities, of which the social life was probably not the least exacting, he did not forget the theatre. For though soldiering had led to playwriting, the stage to architecture, and this last again to heraldry, he knew that fortune, however kindly disposed, has not command of inexhaustible resources, and after a man is of a certain age is more likely to remain constant to him if, while relying partially on her aid, he helps himself. Thus, busy as he was, Vanbrugh had produced *The False Friend* (from Le Sage and Rojas y Zorilla) at Drury Lane in January 1702, and *Squire Trelooby* (from Molière), written in collaboration with Congreve and Walsh, at Lincoln's Inn Fields on the 30th March 1704, the day after his installation as Clarenceux.

At this time it was evident to most beholders, certainly to a Kit-Cat, for whom the question was important, that a strange decay was coming over the stage. The death of Dryden seemed to mark an epoch, not only among writers, but among actors and managers as well. Betterton, whom Pepys had thought the finest actor in the world, was growing old, and his company at Lincoln's Inn Fields producing nothing new of a higher quality than a tragedy by Rowe; while at Drury Lane, Rich, the active patentee, was rattling at breakneck speed down the valley of vulgarity in the hope of attracting audiences. And, as is usual with those who regard the public merely as a financial venture, he gauged the taste of the public too low. But, indeed, there was little to choose between the two houses, which had sunk so far that when one man asked another if he was going to the playhouse that evening, the answering question would be " Who dances there? ' The rival managers strove to outdo each other in scenic effects. If a cornfield was set ablaze at Lincoln's Inn, a barn would be burned down in Drury Lane, while in a farcical version of *Faustus* the theatres competed in reproducing the prodigal blazes of hell. However, it was all to no purpose. The managers were at their wits' end. In vain they tried prologues recited by boys of five, whom they declared with unnecessary emphasis to have " never before appeared in public ", and epilogues spoken by ladies on horseback; the theatres continued to lose.

Rich, however, was in his element: in spite of losses he was enjoying himself hugely, and earning immortality in the couplets of the *Dunciad*. Aided perhaps by Dennis's new stage-thunder, he would sit behind the wings " 'mid snows of paper and fierce hail of pease ", and, in an enviable frenzy, " ride in the whirlwind and direct the storm ". When in the slack season this comfort was denied him, he amused himself with building perfectly useless corridors in his theatre, all pigeon-holed with back-doors and cupboards. These he showed with great pride to his friends, who, however, remained completely bewildered as to their purpose. But what were plays to him? He thought it easier to attract a public with knockabout turns, high kicking, and performing animals. At one time he even thought of introducing an ' extraordinary fine ' elephant on to the stage, a design he was regretfully forced to abandon on being told that if he enlarged the entrance sufficiently to admit this certain draw, the wall would be in danger of collapsing.

Since plays were of small consequence to Rich, those who performed them were of less. Being, moreover, a mean man, he underpaid his actors, and bound them by ferocious contracts. As a result they quarrelled with him and among themselves, while Cibber, who felt his art being debased, one day went into the pit and told all his friends that nothing would induce him to act on such a stage; for which he received as much applause from the audience as he had ever had. In vacation time the actors were forced to open booths at the Bartholomew and May fairs, and produce the strangest spectacles so as to compete successfully with such undeniable attractions as Siamese twins and other monstrosities, performing animals, and the seductive 'girl from Somerset'.[1]

In these circumstances it occurred to some that the only way "to recover the actors to their due estimation" and to raise the drama to its old glory was to build another theatre. The notion may have emanated from Vanbrugh, to whose lot, at any rate, the building of the theatre fell, and who was to share its management with Congreve and Betterton. With the two leading writers of comedy standing godfathers, the scheme appeared promising; and it suited Vanbrugh peculiarly well, for he was eager to establish opera firmly in England, and Congreve loved music even beyond the drama. One hundred pounds was collected from each of thirty patrons, who in return were to be allowed free entry for life. Armed with this capital, Vanbrugh selected a two thousand pound site in the Haymarket, and began operations.[2]

[1] Ashton, Cibber. The lines in *the Dunciad III* are as appropriate to him as to his son.

[2] Baker, Cibber, Thomson.

The outside would not be unlike Drury Lane,[1] but for the rest it would far surpass Wren's antiquated theatre, now some thirty years old. In hubristic vein Vanbrugh wrote to Tonson, " I have drawn a design for the whole disposition of the inside very different from any other house in being ; but I have the good fortune to have it absolutely approved by all that have seen it ",[2] all, no doubt, including many actors, and the members of the Kit-Cat in dining committee assembled. Certainly the laying of the foundation stone was made a Kit-Cat function, and on it was inscribed ' The Little Whig ', in honour of that beautiful toast the Countess of Sunderland, daughter of the Duke of Marlborough.

But the activities of so notorious a subject as Vanbrugh caused great alarm to the members of The Society for the Reformation of Manners, who saw in the erection of this new theatre a grave menace to right living. At the end of 1704 they addressed a letter to Archbishop Tennison describing ' Mr. Vanbrook ' as " a man who has debauched the stage beyond the looseness of all former times " ; but if their object was to put a check to the building, the protest came too late, and the piece of triumphal architecture grew to completion. It was duly opened on Easter Monday, the 9th April 1705.

Since it had been part of the collaborators' ambition to provide a home for the musical form of the drama, the new playhouse was called The Queen's Theatre or Italian Opera House, and the first piece performed was an Englished version of Giacomo Greber's *The Loves of Ergasto*, with a gracefully satirical epilogue by Congreve. With what anxious hopes must Vanbrugh have followed the fortunes of this opera, for the theatre had cost far

[1] An illustration may be seen in Palmer, p. 207.
[2] 13th July 1703 ; *Gent. Mag.* 1836.

Emery Walker

CAPTAIN VANBRUGH

CLARENCEUX KING AT ARMS

(*National Portrait Gallery*)

more than the money subscribed :[1] but alas, " the new set of singers arrived from Italy " proved to be " the worst that e'er came from thence ", and after a very few days, " being liked but indifferently by the gentry, they in a little time marched back to their own country ".[2]

An inauspicious beginning does not preclude final success, but every kind of performance met with much the same fate. Even such an attraction as " *The Indian Emperor, or the Conquest of Mexico by the Spaniards.* The Part of Cortez to be perform'd by Mr. Powel ; with Entertainments of Dancing, as also Singing by the new Italian Boy " failed to draw good houses. Neither did *The Merry Wives of Windsor*, nor Mrs. Centlivre's breezy moralizings on the theme of Regnard's *Gamester* bring the necessary crowds. With affairs looking so black, Vanbrugh rallied to the fray, and at the end of October produced *The Confederacy*, his most dashing and most racy creation, far better than Dancourt's original. But although the same combination of authors had made a success of *The Country House* at Drury Lane in June, here even the talents of Mrs. Barry, who had charmed London since the days of Gramont, and the utmost sparkle of the divine Mrs. Bracegirdle, proved lamentably null. In desperation the associates turned to " the frippery of crucified Molière " ; yet *The Mistake* and *The Cuckold in Conceit* did hardly any better, while the popularity of *The Provok'd Wife* and *Squire Trelooby* was found to have waned almost to nothing.[3]

Was it possible that there was something wrong with the theatre itself? Might it be that, after all, Wren had known what he was about when he built the low ceiling

[1] *Priv. Corr.* July 1708. From Maynwaring.
[2] Downes. He says the play lasted five days ; Cibber says three.
[3] Ashton for succession of plays.

in Drury Lane? For although the massive pillars and gilded cornices, the proscenium arch that sprang to fifteen feet above these, and the vast vault above the pit, were magnificently Palladian; although the design had pleased everybody by its grandeur and its sense of space, these advantages seemed to involve the drawback that nobody in the theatre could hear what was said on the stage. Nine words out of ten were lost, and the actors' voices "sounded like the gabbling of so many people in the lofty aisles in a cathedral". The acoustics were very well for "the tone of a trumpet, or the swell of an Eunuch's holding note", but the application of these instruments is not universal enough for a whole piece. There was no doubt about it: as a place for the performance of stage plays the Italian Opera House would not do.

Perhaps also, Vanbrugh's friends were kind enough to suggest, the site had been wrongly chosen: it was too far out of town. Drury Lane and Lincoln's Inn were handier for the mass of playgoers; and since the theatre no longer subsisted on the patronage of Whitehall and St. James's, little sustenance could be drawn from the immediate rural neighbourhood "unless it were that of milk diet". Congreve, whose distaste for the dustier arenas of life ever made him timid where his income was concerned, was the first to see that the venture was a failure. He withdrew, handing over his share to Vanbrugh. The latter, however, was unable at the most critical moments to give his attention to this business; another, more important fish had come to his hand, and it took nearly all his energy and time to see to the proper frying of it.

PART II

I

Blenheim I

WHEN towards the end of 1704 the Duke of Marlborough came back to England arrayed in the glory of the Blenheim victory, the mass of his countrymen vied with each other in heaping upon him the more dubious benefits of fame. The people huzza'd him in the streets, Parliament voted him thanks, and all the poets set to work to link their names immortally with his. Above all, Mr. Addison gave birth to a thought which the *Tatler* was to declare " one of the noblest that ever entered into the heart of man ", in which the great, but very human soldier, found himself likened to an angel. He certainly seemed so to the once more triumphant Whigs.

But when all is said and done, a national hero expects his highest recompense from his sovereign, and for the matter of that, Anne was not behindhand with her public laudations. More, she wished to do something not only magnificent, but intimate as well, for her close and tried friend Mr. Freeman, as the Duke was known in her correspondence with the Duchess ; so she decided to give him an estate and build him a house. She first whispered the idea privately to him, and since he was not averse to it, began to prepare the way. He in his turn, when he met Vanbrugh, informed him it was his intention to build a house, and that he would like to consult him as to a model.[1] Therefore early the next year [2] the Queen asked Parliament to clear off the encumbrance of two

[1] So Vanbrugh deposed in *Justification*. D'Israeli accepts it.
[2] 17th February 1705.

lives from the Manor of Woodstock and the Hundred of Wootton, so that she might present it to the hero of Blenheim, and erect him a mansion upon it. Within a month Parliament passed the necessary Bill;[1] Anne arranged with Lord Treasurer Godolphin—or, in the familiar circle, Mr. Montgomery, the great personal friend of Mr. and Mrs. Freeman—that the payments for the building should be made through him; and in May a builder named Joyns was granted a warrant as clerk of the works, which empowered him to make contracts for material.

The chief surveyor, or architect, would naturally come from the Board of Works, but why Wren was passed over in favour of Vanbrugh remains a mystery. Perhaps the latter's Whig friends pressed him forward; or, with the Castle Howard designs before him, the Duke thought Wren's art too restrained to express the symbolic intention of the building; or it may have been suggested that the Surveyor General was getting too old. In any case, presumably a comptroller in the Board would know his business, and as the Haymarket Theatre had not yet proved a fiasco, Vanbrugh was set to work.

Here was a double stimulus for him to put forth his most prodigious efforts, for not only would the eye of the nation be upon him, with undying fame to be gained by success, but his genius would have to rise to the occasion of providing a monument for an incomparable hero and a world-shaking victory. To be fitting it must rival the 'wild enormities of ancient magnanimity', and he designed it nobly. Making massiveness the foundation of grandeur, he relieved the transcendent pile with great outstanding blocks—since architecture was a plastic art depending upon light and shadow. The chimneys

[1] 14th March.

resolved themselves into sweeping ornaments, 'Art in curious strokes surprising ',[1] giving not only variety, but unlooked-for splendour to the summit, so that the building seemed to "combine the beauty and magnificence of Grecian architecture, with the picturesqueness of the Gothic, and the solid boldness of a castle ".[2] This 'princely edifice' was so full of imagination, so much in the grand manner, and so "adapted to the martial genius of the patron ",[3] that the Queen ordered the drawings to be placed in Kensington Palace. And there, every day, she feasted her eyes upon a model of the dwelling soon to be occupied by her 'dear, dear Mrs. Freeman' and that lady's glorious lord.[4]

On the 9th June Godolphin accordingly made out a warrant appointing Vanbrugh surveyor,[5] and on the 18th a foundation-stone eight feet square was laid, and duly tapped with a hammer by seven gentlemen, including the architect. After each had thrown down a guinea the appropriate festivities began. "There were several sorts of music; three morris dances; one of young fellows, one of maidens, and one of old beldames. There were about a hundred buckets, bowls, and pans, filled with wine, punch, cakes, and ale." All then went to the Town Hall, where the 'better sort' regaled themselves with punch and claret, while the 'common people' emptied eight barrels of beer, and consumed abundance of cakes.[6]

Vanbrugh now found himself in a position most true Whigs would have envied to greenness, that of being in close and constant touch with their idol the Duke of

[1] *Rosamond.*

[2] Price, quoted by Ward. Also Reynolds, 13th Discourse. Pictures in *Vitruvius Britannicus*, or more conveniently in Lovegrove, or Barman.

[3] *Vitruvius Britannicus.*

[4] *Athenaeum*, 1881, pp. 84–6.

[5] See Appendix I.

[6] Upcott's *Diary*, quoted by Ward.

Marlborough. His Grace was, indeed, an irresistibly charming person, in manner as well as in appearance, who knew how to be friendly without being in the least familiar. He did not ride the high horse, yet nobody was ever known to be pert with him.[1] He was, in fact, what a great man should be. But as time went on Vanbrugh found to his surprise that he was, for a man of his powers of leadership and command, curiously unable to make decisions. He seemed to evade them, as though he feared to commit himself; and although it was in Marlborough's name Vanbrugh made all the contracts, the Duke was extremely averse to signing even the most insignificant paper; in fact, he never once did so. It was difficult for the architect, who was a simple man, to guess that this was the result of delicacy, due to a nice feeling that, as he told his duchess, " it in no way became her or him to be giving orders for the Queen's money ".[2] Besides, it might lead to misinterpretation—on the part of those to whom payment would be due.

But it was with her Grace that Vanbrugh had most to do, for the Duke would on no account allow her to accompany him on his campaigns.[3] The architect was charmed at the prospect of frequently meeting one who Cibber had told him had darted forth " so clear an emanation of beauty ", and possessed " such a commanding grace of aspect ". Even now she was very handsome, her autumnal face vying with the spring beauty of her daughters', and, moreover, she was as famous for her impetuous character as for her wonderful wealth of golden hair. She too seemed very agreeable, just the sort of woman Vanbrugh could like—frank, outspoken, a little bravura in manner perhaps, but that was not unsuitable in so great a lady. It might even be said that she was the greatest lady in

[1] Spence. [2] Add. MSS. 9123, 9th Nov. 1706. [3] Coxe.

the kingdom, not excepting her Majesty, for 'Queen Zarah' was held to rule her mistress. People were beginning to say she was too overbearing, but that was because they allowed themselves to be overawed, and a love of truth which takes the form of never flattering any one makes for popularity even less than other forms of that virtue.

At first the progress made justified the exuberant junketings that marked the laying of the foundation-stone. Vanbrugh got on excellently well with Joyns, as he did with the workmen; and with such harmony between all the parties it seemed likely that the building would very soon be completed. This was very much to Marlborough's liking, for, as he wrote to his wife in August, "I own to you I have a very great desire to have that work at Woodstock finished; and if I can be so happy as to live some years in quietness there with my dear soul, I shall think myself fully recompensed for all the vexations and troubles I am now obliged to undergo".[1] The Duchess also had her vexations, for the Queen had been thoughtless enough to give the neighbouring estate of Cornbury to her uncle, the Earl of Rochester, and although Mrs. Freeman had bluntly told Mrs. Morley that without possessing this estate also she could not go on with the work at Woodstock, the royal *commère* obstinately refused to revoke the gift.[2] Nevertheless the work at Woodstock went on.

But already towards the end of the first year there were signs that the building might not be finished so soon as the 'patron' hoped. As winter drew on it was found that the stone of which the house was being built would not weather: it cracked with the frost, and it was feared that the foundations would have to be replaced.

[1] Coxe, i. 264; 24th Aug. 1705.

[2] Hearne, 31st Oct. 1705.

Indeed, by March it was found that some of the walls would have to be pulled down. Such an occurrence was looked upon as a bad omen. Those of the Tory faction shook their heads, and remembered that sacrilege had been committed when building the park in the time of Henry I, and that in the Civil War the chapel had been 'strangely abused'. During the Commonwealth stone-throwing ghosts had manifested their dislike of surveyors, and had even beaten one with his own scabbard.[1] It was darkly hinted that if the old Manor House was tampered with, as had been rumoured was to be done, the Duke and his heirs would have no luck in the place.[2] However, these skyey influences did not prevent his Grace from hugely enjoying his winter conferences with Vanbrugh about the laying out of the grounds and gardens, which were designed to be the most magnificent in England, the latter being, as Lady Wentworth wrote it, 'fower myles about'.[3]

Nevertheless, little by little, Vanbrugh began to find that the building of Blenheim was not such a paradisal occupation as its inception had seemed to augur. He had at first been delighted at the great interest the Duchess took in the operations, and at the practical good sense that she showed. But by imperceptible degrees he came to feel that she was taking too much interest, and that though her good sense was very well, her taste left something to be desired. And, unfortunately, she could not abide having her suggestions disregarded. She began to behave as though an architect—a Crown surveyor—was to be ordered about like any undertaker,[4] and Vanbrugh

[1] Aubrey, p. 84. [2] Hearne, 1st Nov. 1705 and 9th March 1706.
[3] *Wentworth Papers*, 8th Sept. 1705.
[4] Contractor. As this word will often occur in the correspondence to be quoted, I shall use it throughout in its old, proper, unspecialized sense, of one who undertakes.

disliked being interfered with in his art. By the autumn of 1706 he had come to the conclusion that the Duchess's masculine directness was but a specious form of the meddlesome instincts of an old woman. He was huffed, and could not hide the fact from Godolphin, who wrote of it to the Duke in Flanders. "My Lady Marlborough is extremely prying into . . .", he said; "I am apt to think she has made Mr. Vanbrugh a little—— "[1]

The Duke accordingly wrote a humble remonstrance, suggesting, no doubt, that a man should be left to do his job in his own way: he knew what interference was. But the Duchess could deal with her husband on a little point like that; indeed, she had always been able to deal with him on every point except two—the conduct of his campaigns, and one or two trifling political appointments: there he showed disconcerting firmness. For the rest he was clay in her hands. Once and for all she had established her moral superiority when, just before their marriage, he had ill-advisedly been attracted towards a lady with a fortune superior to her own. So on this occasion she replied, "I must say it is a great trouble to me to find you have so little confidence in my real kindness and esteem for you, as that you could be uneasy at anything that could pass between such men as Mr. Vanbrugh and myself".[2] Had the Duke interpreted Mr. Montgomery's dash altogether rightly?

Her Grace, then, continued to be extremely prying into, in spite of the fact that it in no way became her to give orders for the disposal of the Queen's gift. Although she again and again insisted that the money spent was not hers, and that she had no say in the matter, she was continually taking exception to the contracts Vanbrugh made. For instance, she objected that $7\frac{1}{2}d.$ a bushel was

[1] Add. MSS. 9123, 25th Sept. 1706. [2] Ibid., 9th Nov. 1706.

too much to pay for lime, especially as it was made in the park itself; and, moreover, she suspected the measure.[1] So great a lady, Vanbrugh must have thought, should not concern herself with such mean matters.

So the perfect harmony was disturbed—but, indeed, the disagreements were far more fundamental than a mere haggling over odd ha'pence. Her Grace and the architect did not see eye to eye in the matter of Blenheim. The former wanted a house to live in, and that quickly, for her husband was writing to her: "I have bespoke the hangings, for one of my greatest pleasures is doing all that in me lies, that we may as soon as possible enjoy that happy time of being quietly together, which I think of with pleasure, as often as I have my thoughts free to myself."[2] All Vanbrugh, on the other hand, seemed to care about, was the construction of a colossal and immortal work of art, regardless of expense or time. The Duchess found poor satisfaction in the prospect of her lord being thus pyramidally extant, instead of enjoying the comforts of a home.

Indeed, there was some need to confine the scheme within the smallest possible limits, for the money was running short. Already in May the Duke had written to his wife about the danger of having to turn off workmen,[3] and by July Vanbrugh was aware of the difficulty. He wrote to the Earl of Manchester,[4] "There being so much required for the public good this year, . . . my Lord Treasurer can't afford us at Blenheim half what we want. However," he added, "there will be a great deal done, and two summers more will finish it. My Lady Duchess was there lately, and returned to Windsor

[1] Add. MSS. 9123, Sept. 1706.
[2] Thomson, ii. 129: 1707 or 1708.
[3] *Priv. Corr.*, 30th May 1707.
[4] *Athenaeum*, 1861.

so entirely pleased, that she told me she should live to beg my pardon for ever having quarrelled with me." This, it is true, was only a conditional apology, but Vanbrugh's charm was evidently still dominant over the termagant temper of Atossa. In November he wrote to his staff at Woodstock, "both my Lord Duke and my Lady Duchess are in perfect good humour with the account I have given them of what we have done and are doing ".[1]

The worst difficulty, however, was that of getting stone, and if in 1707 the problem was a trying one,[2] in the next year it became so acute as to cause a turn in the flow of the Duchess's forgiving tide. Vanbrugh proposed to pay a penny a foot more, but her Grace would not hear of it. "My Lady Duchess ", the harassed architect wrote, "is determined not to raise the price for the carriage of stone of any kind : so that you must acquaint those that go with the carriages that there is positive orders rather to let the work stand still than give anything more than sixpence a foot."[3] If only the Duke were at home! His Grace did not like the workmen to be ground down : he had known a place spoiled because of it.[4]

The Duke, however, was occupied, first in gaining the somewhat sterile victory of Oudenarde, then in besieging Lille, and Vanbrugh had to face the Duchess single-handed. And as he found himself forced to comply with many of her wishes, he began, though it took his simple, kindly nature an unconscionable time, to find out what her Grace was really like. He came to learn that she was relentless in friendship, implacable in hatred ; that she ruled all about her with a rod of some brittle material

[1] Add. MSS. 19605, 11th Nov. 1707. [2] Ibid., 18th Nov. 1707.
[3] Ibid., 9th and 24th June 1708. [4] *Justification.*

that might indeed break, but could never bend. He discovered that the form of her life was modelled into marble by two ideas—one a passion, the other a faith, the former a lust of domination, the latter an unshakable belief that she was always in the right. At first these qualities had shown themselves on the one hand only as an engaging, an almost tomboyish frankness; and on the other as a readiness to apologise *if* she should be in the wrong. It was a long time before Vanbrugh understood that she was never in the wrong, and that an 'inferior not dependant' was a worse offence to her than one who presumed to be her equal. And was even the Queen her equal? The worst was, however, that her sense of dignity was not consistent; at all events it did not seem to extend to money matters, and she was always nagging at her architect to get things done more cheaply, until the subject, with her an obsession, became a sore trial to him. When at Blenheim he would " avoid all company, and haunt the building like a ghost from the time the workmen leave off at six o'clock, till 'tis quite dark . . . studying how to make this the cheapest as well as (if possible) the best house in Europe ".[1]

But in spite of all his efforts, the position became ever more strained. Since she had never before found anything so obdurately resistant to her will, a suspicion began to grow in the Duchess's mind that the house was not nearing completion with the rapidity that matched her desires because of a deliberate malignity on Vanbrugh's part. Surely he could have finished it had he wished! So in September " My Lord Godolphin thought proper to add another person to Mr. Joyns, one Mr. Boulter (a creature of her Grace's), and to make them joint comptrollers as well as clerks of the works. And after

[1] Add. MSS. 9123, 8th July 1708.

that again, the Duchess of Marlborough (beginning not to love me so well as I could have wished because I was ordered to do what she did not like) procured another warrant to empower the comptrollers to make and sign all contracts with me." [1] The bitterness of wording belongs to a later period, when the passage was written, but the new appointment cannot have served to make things run more smoothly. A flavour of tartness is perceptible in the relations of the architect with the lady who had chosen the name of Mrs. Freeman as a descriptive pseudonym.

And into this tense atmosphere a note of pathos was wafted from across the sea, where the Duke was engaged in a struggle more weighty, perhaps, but no more acid, and less prolonged. "I am obliged", he wrote to his wife, "for your kind expressions concerning Woodstock; it is certainly a pleasure to me when I hear the work goes on, for it is there I must be happy with you. The greatest pleasure I have, when I am alone, is the thinking of this, and flattering myself that we may then live so as to anger neither God nor men, if the latter be reasonable; but if they are otherways, I shall not much care if *you* are pleased." [2]

The Duchess was certainly doing her utmost to make the work go on, but the appointment of Boulter at a charge of four hundred pounds a year produced little change to her purpose, for never once did Vanbrugh disagree with him over a contract. Indeed, the result

[1] *Justification.* In the British Museum copy the long phrase in brackets is deleted, but not so as to render the print indecipherable. I suspect, from other deletions, and from one marginal word that is to my eye almost certainly in Vanbrugh's hand, that this is Vanbrugh's proof copy, especially as there are several blank pages at the end. If so, the phrase will not have appeared in the published pamphlet, but I have been unable to compare this copy with any other.

[2] Thomson, ii. 129, 1707 or 1708.

was one she had not foreseen—a demand from the architect upon her private purse.

For in this year Vanbrugh was in a precarious way, so much so that he feared the same fate might befall him as had overtaken another, and greater, comic dramatist, Wycherley, who had languished some years in a debtors' prison. He had lost heavily by the opera,[1] the playhouse had cost far more to build than had been subscribed, and, as the Duchess's confidant Maynwaring wrote to her in exoneration of his 'good and tractable' friend, the theatrical furnishers and hangers-on generally were clamouring for payment.[2] His work at Blenheim gave him little time to attend to other business, so that, as he wrote to the Duchess, he was "under such uneasiness that he was scarce fit for service now, having only a short reprieve from what he expected would have immediately fallen upon him". Therefore he asked to be put upon some paid work, for instance "in the position of Mr. Boulter".[3] Only financially, of course, for as he was careful to point out at some length, a surveyor was not at all the same thing as a controller, the latter being employed merely to check the former, as a slow horse might be harnessed to a high-spirited animal to subdue his speed.

It was a grave question, for, of course, Vanbrugh being already a paid Crown servant, the money would have to come out of the Marlborough pocket. The Duke, when consulted, agreed with the Duchess's reasons against giving him a 'pension', adding that "it is more to his interest to have patience till something happens which may be lasting".[4] Vanbrugh had naturally hoped for 'something lasting' from so great a patron. If an Earl

[1] Letter to Earl of Manchester, 7th July 1708. Quoted by Palmer, p. 208.
[2] *Priv. Corr.*, i. 140, July 1708.
[3] Add. MSS. 9123, Sept. 1708.
[4] *Priv. Corr.*, 1st July 1708.

of Carlisle could get him made King at Arms, what might not a Duke of Marlborough do? After all, one did not work as he had done at Blenheim for the mere official pittance. But was the position of the Duke quite so secure as it had been? Was not in this case a bird in the hand worth a considerable number in the bush? And besides, would so great a man allow a meagre four hundred a year to prejudice his chances of getting other plums? In any case, only the rich can afford time for their capital to develop, and Vanbrugh continued to press the Duchess. The latter at last consented,[1] perhaps because she felt that now at any rate she could claim this ' inferior ' as ' dependant ', and he would no longer be able to argue that he was a Crown functionary. It might be worth four hundred a year.

But so far no money was saved, nor was the question of stone smoothed over, for in September there was trouble with the workmen, in which Vanbrugh had to use all his tact and good nature to mend quarrels, and break up what looked dangerously like a combination.[2] And through it all the relations of the Duchess with her architect were strained. The building still hung fire, desire still continued to outrun performance, while all the time Vanbrugh excused his slowness on the ground of difficulties as to material, and trials with the men. Her Grace knew she was in the right, but there was no point on which she could indubitably show it. It was vexing.

[1] Inferred from Vanbrugh's letter, and the Lord Chancellor's summing up of the ' Case ', *c.* June 1721.

[2] Add. MSS. 9123, 8th July and Sept. 1708.

2

Blenheim II

THE next year, however, brought a clear issue.

The ancient Manor of Woodstock stood on a little hill not far from the Palace of Blenheim itself. Vanbrugh found it a difficulty in his scheme, for unless carefully treated it would spoil the effect of the grand approach to the new house. But since he loved the place as much for its old associations as for its picturesque dignity, he set himself to fit it into his design, and prepared a plan which would, for a very trifling sum, actually enhance the appearance of the Duke of Marlborough's dwelling.

But at this time no sum seemed trifling to the Duchess: she was losing, indeed had lost, her hold upon her 'poor, unfortunate, faithful Morley', who had been seduced by the infamous Mrs. Masham, while her lord was being betrayed by the monster Harley (whom she had always mistrusted), although both the wretches had been launched by the Marlboroughs themselves. The whole position was becoming very insecure. Why then spend money on such rubbish as an old, half-ruined house? She could not conceive why Vanbrugh wanted to preserve it; for her own part she would do away with 'this extraordinary place' as ruthlessly as she had destroyed the offspring of the Boscobel oak planted by Charles II in the garden of Marlborough House. She had not suspected 'common-sense Van' of such absurd sentimentality. There must be something else behind it. Then the whole sinister design flashed upon her: Vanbrugh had all along determined to play the parasite; that was why the

From Houbraken's engraving of a painting by Kneller

building was so delayed—and as to the Manor House, he wanted it restored so as to live in it himself! There was no other possible explanation.

She complained to Godolphin, and made him raise the question with Vanbrugh, who argued the case valiantly. He declared that the improvements in the Manor House had only cost eleven hundred pounds, and not three thousand as her Grace had said; that some of the building had already been taken down; and as for the rest of it, his scheme was the cheapest way not to make the Manor a fault in the approach: he even enclosed a drawing to convince the Lord Treasurer. And as to his desire to live in the house himself, this was a charge he repudiated indignantly, declaring himself "much discouraged to find I can be suspected of so poor a contrivance for so worthless a thing". When this letter came into the Duchess's hands she endorsed it, "All that Sir J. V. says in this letter is false". The drawing also was 'false'. This time she would not be fooled.

It is possible that in the sincere desire of a conscious artist to preserve a beautiful building, Vanbrugh had a little exaggerated the possibilities of the Manor as a part of the new design—it would be a pardonable falsehood; but in any case he put too much faith in her Grace's artistic perceptions. For the drawing he sent her in the next few days, 'to plead in silent paint', had not the least effect. The Duchess was convinced there was something queer about it all. It was true that Vanbrugh had another house in the park already, and that "Mr. Travers, who calls himself the superintendent-in-chief of the Blenheim works", could so little conceive that the architect wanted the Manor to live in that he had asked for it for himself—but what could the reason be for wanting to spend money on it when even

Mr. Travers, as surveyor to the Crown, complained of the expense? [1]

So the Duchess, in her most Atossian mood, was blind to silent paint, and equally deaf to honest Van's "Reasons Offer'd for Preserving some part of the Old Manor", which he addressed to her in June.[2] "As I believe", he wrote in the dignified prose he could use when he was angry,

> "it cannot be doubted, but if travellers many ages hence shall be shown the very house in which so great a man dwelt, as they will then read the Duke of Marlborough in story; and that they shall be told it was not only his favourite habitation, but was erected for him by the bounty of the Queen, and with the approbation of the people, as a monument of the greatest services and honours that any subject has ever done his country—I believe, though they may not find enough in the builder to make them admire the beauty of the fabric, they will find wonder enough in the story to make 'em pleased with the sight of it. . . . It cannot indeed be said that [Woodstock] was erected on so noble nor on so justifiable an occasion, but it was raised by one of the bravest and most warlike of the English kings; and though it has not been famed as a monument of his arms, it has been tenderly regarded as the scene of his affections. Nor amongst the multitude of people who come daily to view what is raising to the memory of the great Battle of Blenheim, are there any that do not run eagerly to see what ancient remains may be found of Rosamund's Bower. It may perhaps be some little reflection upon what may be said, if the very footsteps of it are no more to be found."

But the Duchess was a strong-minded woman, and her endorsement runs, "This paper has something ridiculous in it—to preserve the house for himself . . . but I think

[1] Add. MSS. 9123, May, June, July 1709.
[2] Ibid., 11th June 1709.

there is something material in it concerning the occasion of building Blenheim". So evident was it, that Vanbrugh's flattery was wasted—swallowed as part of her due nourishment—and she would not budge an inch. Nor was she going to allow herself to be taken in by Vanbrugh's argument that his scheme would take only two hundred pounds to finish, whereas thousands would not make the hill look well if the building was destroyed. The artifice was too transparent, and the Lord Treasurer was appealed to, being made to journey to Woodstock 'to see the trick'. Godolphin was a shrewd judge of horseflesh, a frequenter of Newmarket, and would pronounce a good opinion upon a main of cocks,[1] so he found no difficulty in deciding this question. He cared nothing for either art or literature, but he could put a thing graphically. Of course the old ruin must go: there was no more doubt about it, he said, than there would be in removing a disfiguring wen from a man's face. Thus the battle of Woodstock Manor was lost, and Vanbrugh began regretfully, and very slowly indeed, to pull down the gracious and historic abode of sovereigns.

Atossa had now lost all confidence in her architect. She warned the Duke that she suspected Vanbrugh of sending him false reports as to progress. The Duke replied that he was sending no reports at all, but was he not perhaps too eager to lay the foundations of new portions of the building when it would be better to finish the old?[2] Undoubtedly; but the Duchess had no help, for her 'creature' Boulter was dead, and had been replaced by one Bobart, with whom Vanbrugh seemed on the best of terms. Why could not others see through the latter as she did? It was most annoying, and when the question of stone again arose, she thoroughly lost her

[1] Macaulay, Addison.

[2] *Priv. Corr.*, 11th July 1709.

temper. Vanbrugh wrote that he was afraid it would not come in time because the quarries were farther away, so that " the carters don't find it worth their while to go thither at the price now allowed 'em ", and he actually had the effrontery once more to suggest a higher rate, which would only cost another hundred pounds.[1]

Only ! when the estimate had already been outrageously exceeded. She flew at him ; it was all his fault. In vain Vanbrugh pleaded that " there happened a great disappointment ; the freestone in the park quarry not proving good " ; that the house had been raised six feet higher ; and that certain courts and gardens had not been included in the original estimate. She closed on that point. Who had approved those extra courts ? It was by no means clear that they had been sanctioned at all. It was all very well for Vanbrugh to swear that he had shown the Duke plans, the Duke was not there to verify the statement. The angry architect retorted that in future he would take care to have everything signed :[2] it was obviously poor policy to trust to honour in verbal dealings.

And everything Vanbrugh wrote only served to infuriate the Duchess more, for he could not see what terrible stabs he was inflicting on her when he wrote such things as, " I believe that when the whole is done, both the Queen, yourself, and everybody (except your personal enemies) will easily forgive me laying out fifty thousand pounds too much, than if I had laid out a hundred thousand too little ".[3] If only he had known in what relation her Grace stood to the Queen he would have seen that to expend even a thousand pounds too much would be unforgivable. For she was no longer Mrs. Freeman,

[1] Add. MSS. 9123, June and July 1709. [2] Ibid.
[3] Thomson, ii. 592, July 1709.

as was made only too clear when in the autumn the Queen—not Mrs. Morley—wrote to her, " It is impossible for you to recover my former kindness, but I shall know how to behave myself to you as the Duke of Marlborough's wife, and as my Groom of the Stole ".[1] The world was full of ungrateful and stupid people ; not one was dependable. And peace was in sight, yet where was the home in which the Duke might pass his honoured old age ? It was a race to see which would be finished first, Blenheim or the Queen's patience, while Vanbrugh was dallying, and talking blithely about spending ' fifty thousand pounds too much ' !

The peace, however, was not concluded, and in the spring the weary struggle at Woodstock continued, with the Duchess more vigilant than ever ; as she had need to be in the increasing shakiness of her position. She had tried to clear it up, had made every effort to regain the Queen's confidence, but in vain. Time after time she had asked for an interview, time after time she had been fobbed off with some lame excuse. It was plain that her Majesty wanted nothing from the Duchess but to be left alone : she had written as much to the Duke the year before, saying, " I desire nothing but that she would leave off teasing and tormenting me, and behave herself with the decency she ought, both to her friend and Queen, and this I hope you will make her do ".[2] A vain hope, for in such things the Duke was powerless. So all the Queen could do was to avoid her, and refuse an interview, even when the Duchess wrote to say she would not expect an answer, but merely wished to be told what the charges against her were. There were, of course, no charges beyond that of being an intolerable bully ; so when at last the Queen was trapped at Kensington one day in

[1] Molloy, ii. 444, 26th Oct. 1709. [2] Ibid., 441.

April 1710, she resorted to her favourite practice of entrenching herself behind a phrase. To everything the Duchess said she replied, "You desired no answer and you shall have none". Finally, in the Duchess's own words, "The Queen offered to go out of the room, I following her, begging leave to clear myself; and the Queen repeating over and over again '*You desired no answer and you shall have none*'. When she came to the door I fell into a great disorder; streams of tears flowed down against my will, and prevented my speaking for some time." At last the formidable Atossa, the domineering Mrs. Freeman, completely broken, humbled herself abjectly, and stammered out that she had heard 'things were laid to her charge of which she was wholly incapable'. But still the only return was "'*You desired no answer and you shall have none*'. I then begged to know if her Majesty would see me some other time? '*You desired no answer and you shall have none*'." It was to no purpose that her Grace continued her attempt to batter down this staggering obstinacy, and begged the Queen to admit "whether she did not know me to be of a temper incapable of disowning anything I knew to be true". Although here she did not belie her character, her Majesty still intoned the maddening refrain, "You desired no answer and you shall have none".[1]

This amazing and terrible scene closed the old intimacy for ever, and—it was the Queen who was paying for the building! It was true that Marlborough was still Captain-General; that his wife was still Groom of the Stole, Keeper of the Privy Purse, and Ranger of Windsor Park; that her daughters still held most of the lucrative posts in the household; and that Godolphin, their great friend, the father-in-law of one of their daughters, was

[1] *Conduct*, pp. 238–244.

still Lord High Treasurer. But the Queen's ineradicable Toryism—Jacobitism, one might say—was asserting itself; that wicked Abigail Hill was favourite, and Harley was sneaking up the backstairs every evening to see his sovereign. The country was tiring of the war, Godolphin's character was being bandied about under the name of Volpone, and Sacheverell had been only nominally punished, to the joy of an exuberant mob. Who could say what would happen? Indeed, very shortly afterwards the Queen appointed a new Lord Chamberlain, the Duke of Shrewsbury, thus making people expect a complete change of ministers.

These things had their repercussion at Blenheim; every penny was important to the Duchess, harried between the Queen and her surveyor. She blazed out at the latter when he gave more per foot than before for iron railings. And yet he had the face to say that they were "the cheapest that has been done in that kind", although the year before a contract had been made at a lower rate with the same man for precisely the same article.[1] Once more Vanbrugh was piling up expenses when all the world was tottering, was beginning indeed to disintegrate, for in June, her son-in-law, Lord Sunderland, a Whig of Whigs, was dismissed the ministry.[2] What faith could be put in the Queen's promise to the Governors of the Bank of England that she would for the present, out of regard for the stability of credit, make no more changes? Even the workmen and contractors at Blenheim appreciated the situation, and were much alarmed, as Vanbrugh wrote to inform her Grace.[3] Thus when in July the money began to run short, and Vanbrugh asked for further supplies,

[1] Add. MSS. 9123, July 1710. The transaction probably took place in June.
[2] Burnet. Not December 1708, as is often stated.
[3] Add. MSS. 9123, 24th June 1710.

discretion caused her to stop all building operations, and await events with what calm she could muster.

The blow was not long in falling. In August Godolphin was dismissed, and Harley and St. John rode triumphant. There was no going on with the work now, especially as the Duchess suspected the new ministry would try to saddle her husband with the debt.[1] His wisdom in refraining from signing the least scrap of paper was only too apparent. However, if progress was stopped, Vanbrugh was anxious at least to get covered the work that had been done; frosts might do untold harm, and the memory of the great hurricane of 1703 was still fresh in men's minds. So in October he went down to Blenheim to see to it.

But when he arrived there Joyns and Bobart told him they had received a letter from my Lady Marlborough ordering them " to put a stop at once to all sorts of work " until the Duke came over, and not to employ a single man a day longer. Vanbrugh at once saw the gravity of the situation, and harangued his lieutenants at great length. They seemed curiously uneasy during his discourse. ' Unspeakable mischiefs ', he explained, might be done the whole summer's work by the frosts, but there were weightier reasons for not discharging the workmen " in so surprising a manner without a farthing ". It was all very well for the big men, who ' work by the great ', such as masons and carpenters, who would no doubt have faith in the promises they had been made ; but with labourers, carters, and such-like, it was different. They were used to being regularly paid, but were now in arrear ; many were far from their families ; they would consider their money lost ; they would hold a meeting, and " the building might feel the effects of it ". Indeed, he knew " there

[1] Coxe, ii. 409.

were people not far off who would be glad to put 'em upon it ", and moreover he had already " observed 'em grown very insolent ", and only kept quiet by assurances of payment. Yet Joyns and Bobart showed a strange reluctance to move in the matter, even under such urgent circumstances. At last they were forced to explain. They showed Vanbrugh a postscript to the Duchess's letter, in which she strictly forbade ' any regard to what he might say or do '.

This was hitting below the belt. There was only one thing a man could do, and Vanbrugh did it. He wrote to the Duke relating the affair,[1] and added :

" Your Grace won't blame me if, ashamed to continue there any longer upon such a foot, as well as seeing it was not in my power to do your Grace any farther service, I immediately came away . . . I shall, notwithstanding all this cruel usage from the Duchess of Marlborough, receive, and with pleasure obey, any commands your Grace may please to lay upon me, being, with the deference I ever was,

Your Grace's most humble
And most obedient servant,
J. VANBRUGH."

Travers, however, saw how serious matters were, and went so far as to pay five hundred pounds to some of the poorer workmen out of his own credit. The Duke appreciated the ' cruelty ' of his consort's behaviour, and asked Vanbrugh to see to the protection of the house, which task he loyally performed. As soon as the 10th October he was back, and able to report " I am glad to find little mischief has happen'd to the building, which I know there was a good deal of reason to apprehend how light soever my Lady Duchess might make of it ",[2] and

[1] Thomson, ii. 522. Vanbrugh to Marlborough, 3rd Oct. 1710.
[2] Add. MSS. 19605, 10th Oct. 1710.

assured his subordinates that the Treasury would allow money for protection.

Nevertheless it was a dismal situation, and feeling it as such the Duchess early in the next month made the nearest approach to an apology she ever was guilty of. There is something pathetic in this letter to Vanbrugh, as though, seeing her world dissolving around her, she was feeling out desperately towards some one who had much of her own bluntness and frank outspokenness. Perhaps, for once, her husband had exercised sweet persuasion, but if so, she carried it off with a high hand, her pen running as fast and as vigorously as ever it had, with all the old breeziness and tomboy slap-dash. Yet through it all there runs a feeling of fatality, as though the curse the Tories had remembered were really coming true—as indeed part of it had already been fulfilled in the death of her only son, the Marquis of Blandford—while the end is almost valedictory.

" Every word in your letter ", she wrote, " concerning the payment of the carters is reasonable, and if I had known all these particulars sooner, I had certainly found some way of ordering the money, and you are in the right, for they should be the first people to be paid, for the reasons you give : . . ."

And after repeating his arguments, she hopes no damage has been caused by weather, for it had been ' extreamly good '. And then, with a fine waiving of all their differences, she thanked him for the interest he had taken, and for his hard work, and suggested that when it was all over he would get a worthy reward,

" for though you have vexed me extremely, in forcing me to things against my inclination ; yet I shall always think myself obliged to you, and will always be endeavouring to be out of your debt ; because I know, that what I did not like, as well as what I did approve of, you intended for the best; and though it is said in the world there is no perfection, you are not the only architect that thinks 'tis impossible they can err; I believe it is the opinion of all that science, which makes it more reasonable for me to forgive you, and I hope you will do the same to your humble servant

S. MARLBOROUGH."[1]

Honest Van may have wondered what it was the Duchess had to forgive him, but it is probable that the letter, with all its gaucherie, touched him. There was, after all, something admirable about the Duchess, in spite of her rapacity, her lack of affection, her exaggerated opinion of herself, and her desire to dominate. She was passionately wilful, but she never spared herself, and was whole-hearted in what she did. She had no meanness except as to money, and just as in this last she never cheated anybody, so she had no subterfuges. She was direct and open; she would admit everything, and if her fury sometimes carried her beyond the barriers social amenity has directed are not to be passed, she would not lie about her reasons. If she struck hard, she bravely supported the blows inflicted upon her. She had need at this juncture, for in January poor Atossa was dismissed all her posts except her Rangership: her influence at Court was gone, and who knew how long her husband's would survive?

Once the world had seemed so fair, so secure. Only six years ago the Queen had written—the Duchess still had the letter from her 'faithful Morley'—"I will never forsake your dear self, dear Mr. Freeman, nor Mr. Montgomery, but always be your constant and faithful friend; and we must never part until death mows us

[1] *Justification.* Dated only 2nd Nov., but it has every appearance of belonging to this year.

down with his impartial hand ".[1] Where were these promises now? Mrs. Freeman was dismissed, Mr. Montgomery had broken his white rod of office in a rage, and her Majesty had been furious at Mr. Freeman's harmless suggestion that he should be made Captain-General for the period of their joint lives!

As matters stood, would the great house be proceeded with? For although Parliament had sanctioned the grant, it was not the same Parliament now, and the royal promises were apparently writ in water. Yet in January Vanbrugh was able to go on with the work, having obtained a balance of seven thousand pounds due on a warrant of Godolphin's; and Harley, shortly to be Lord Oxford, who in spite of St. John's clearer view, still hoped to conciliate both parties, asked for an estimate to complete the building. The amount must have astonished him, for although Godolphin had spent ninety-five thousand pounds in excess of the original estimate of a hundred thousand, Vanbrugh considered another eighty-seven thousand pounds would be required to finish the house and grounds.[2] Would the Queen be willing to pay all this out of her own pocket for people whom she no longer either loved or trusted?

It seemed unlikely in view of another ugly incident between her Majesty and her late Groom of the Stole. The latter was asked to remove from her quarters in St. James's to make room for Lord, lately Lord Chancellor, Cowper, and the manner of the asking appears to have been unfortunate, for the Duchess wrote to Mr. Craggs, " The message the Queen sent me that I might take a lodging for ten shillings a week to put my Lord Marlborough's goods in, sufficiently shows what a good education and understanding the wolf has, who was certainly

[1] Molloy, i. 326, 1704.

[2] Coxe, iii, pp. 409 seq.

the person who gave that advice ".[1] Mrs. Masham was not behaving generously, but after all she was only an underling, and the Duchess consented to go with a good enough grace ; the more so that the Queen admitted they had been a part of Lady Marlborough's appointments, thus raising the matter out of the realm of the personal. And being of a careful disposition, when she went she took her fixtures with her.

To her amazement she a little later received a letter from her friend Mr. Maynwaring, which ran :

" 285 was two hours with 199 who began to tell him how concerned he was that 42 would do nothing towards the building at Woodstock. 285 said he was in hopes the matter had been over, having heard so much of it. 199 answered, so it was till the late bustle about the lodgings. 'What was that pray?' said 285. 'Come, come,' replied 199, 'you must have heard what 240 has done, and the message sent by Mr Cowper.' In short 42 is so angry, that she says she will build no house for 39 when 240 has pulled hers to pieces, taken away the very slabs out of the chimneys, thrown away the keys and said they might buy more for ten shillings." [2]

In reading of this bitter, if somewhat vulgar, quarrel between numbers, we feel as Alice must have felt when she realized that all the angry people thronging around her were nothing but a pack of cards. It all seems absurd, far away, marionette-like. But to the Duchess it was far different. She knew that she was 240 ; that the Duke was 39 ; Mr. Craggs 285 [3] ; Harley 199, and the infuriated 42 the Queen herself. So ! On these farcical grounds her Majesty had refused to sign a warrant Lord Oxford had presented her for more money for Woodstock. The Duchess, enraged and hurt, sent for the steward, and,

[1] Add. MSS. 751. *c.* April 1711. [2] *Priv. Corr.*, July 1711.
[3] Craggs, afterwards Secretary, Pope's friend.

conscious of her innocence, had an inventory made which proved the accusation unfounded. Mr. Craggs went of himself to my Lord Oxford, now Lord Treasurer, to say that the Duchess's behaviour had been, to say the least of it, misrepresented. But his lordship replied there could be no mistake. Had not the Queen herself, in spite of her obesity and her gout, gone to view the apartment, and "been much displeased at the taking away of the brass locks, which she believed *were mostly her own*"? [1] It seemed that Blenheim would be spoiled for the sake of a few pieces of ironmongery her Majesty believed were peculiarly hers. But perhaps she saw that the affair was tending to the unbecomingly burlesque; that to vent the accumulated fury of years on this account, to erect brass locks to symbolic heights was absurd; in any case the matter was allowed to drop.

"In the conclusion his lordship [Oxford] was so good as to say that he was sorry anything should happen to put the Queen out of humour, and the best way was to say no more of it, for he had prevailed with her Majesty to sign a warrant for twenty thousand pounds to go on with Blenheim." [2]

This, however, was not until the 17th July, and though Lord Oxford said he would procure a further grant as soon as possible, Vanbrugh disposed warily of the money. "I acquainted the chief undertakers with what has passed at the Treasury; upon which encouragement they went on with the work, without insisting that all the money then issued should go to the discharge of the debt, which otherwise they would have done." [3] However, in the late summer he was given enough to finish off the work of the building season,[4] and it looked as though all would be well.

[1] Molloy, ii. [2] Thomson, ii, Appendix. [3] Coxe, iii, pp. 409 seq.
[4] Add. MSS. 9123, 10th Aug. 1711, and *Journal to Stella*, 19th Aug. 1711.

But on the last day of the year the great Duke was ignominiously dismissed all his posts, and in the following spring the Queen ordered the work at Blenheim to cease. The Duke was about to shoulder the burden himself, and went so far as to ask Vanbrugh for an estimate of the year's work,[1] but he shortly afterwards went abroad: not, it has been suggested, without a hint from Oxford that he held certain papers relating to that old old story of the proposed attack upon Brest. A little later he was followed by his wife, who left Abigail Hill, now Lady Masham, to reign in her stead; and although the new favourite did so discreetly ("Som says the Queen has order'd her to live very privatly that she may not get the envy of the Peaple like the Duchess of Marlborough" Lady Strafford commented)[2] she was the more secure.

It seemed as though all were over, that the great house would remain unfinished, to decay perhaps into oblivion, or be known as Queen Anne's Folly. The architect's vision of fame and place faded away with the great soldier's dream of a noble fireside by which he would spend the remainder of his days in company with his beloved wife. A glorious age seemed to be passing away, while the glamour of a family and the stones of a splendid edifice crumbled together into forgetfulness to the sound of malicious laughter. But if there was nothing to hope for the future of the man who had once swayed the destinies of Europe, for the Prince of the Empire, for the man to whom more than to any other the monarch owed her throne, the highest posts in two minor departments of the Crown were still within sight for the man who, in his own phrase, had begun life in the Bastille, and with whom nobody, not even the Duchess of Marlborough, could successfully quarrel.

[1] Add. MSS. 19605, 15th June 1712. [2] *Wentworth Papers*, p. 285.

3

On the Sea of Events

1705-1714

If, once Blenheim was begun, Vanbrugh was too busy to write plays, he had still to attend to his official duties. As Crown surveyor even a famous architect had to carry out the meanest works, and it surprised nobody that the creator of St. Paul's, not to mention of dozens of gems of architecture, should be haled before the Lords to explain why the scaffolding for the Sacheverell trial would not allow for each peer to have as many seats as usual.[1] The Board of Works, no doubt, had plenty of humdrum tasks for Vanbrugh to do, such as that of erecting the water-works in Kensington, which he did in what Leigh Hunt called his ' no nonsense ' style, though such cannot have been congenial to one who loved to " hew jests and humours out of stone ".[2] And amid all his duties, with such time as he could snatch from his plaguy troubles at Woodstock, or official heraldic journeys to Hanover (which must have come as a blessed respite), he was building Castle Howard, finishing Whitton Hall, and restoring Kimbolton Castle. Nor was this all. For in 1706 he found himself, with a certain Williamson and his old enemy Gregory King, appointed commissioner to settle all King William's debts, military and civil.[3] This can have been no mean labour, though it may have been some satisfaction to him if his application to ' ye Collonel ' some years previously had been unfruitful.

Yet in spite of this immense and varied activity,

[1] *Wentworth Papers*, p. 110.
[2] Nichols.
[3] Luttrell, 10th June 1706.

Vanbrugh had time to build for himself. Finding his domicile at Greenwich not central enough for so busy a man, he decided to construct a small, but snug, bachelor's *pied-à-terre*, upon a portion of that site of Whitehall left bare by the great fire of 1698. It was quite unpretentious, but in spite of that, or perhaps because of it, it proved an irresistible temptation to the wits. Swift, to whom Vanbrugh's versatility was an offence, diverted himself hugely with both it and the multifariousness of its builder. " Van ", he wrote in 1706,

> Van, (for 'tis fit the reader know it)
> Is both a herald and a poet ;
> No wonder, then, if nicely skilled
> In both capacities to build.
> As Herald, he can in a day
> Repair a house gone to decay ;
> Or by achievement, arms, device,
> Erect a new one in a trice :
>
> [He was determined not to let *that* pun be wasted.]
>
> And as a poet he has skill
> To build in speculation still.
> " Great Jove ! " he cried, " the art restore
> To build by verse as heretofore,
> And make my muse the architect ;
> What palaces we shall erect !
> No longer shall forsaken Thames
> Lament his old Whitehall in flames ;
> A pile shall from its ashes rise
> Fit to invade, or prop, the skies " . . .

Jove consents to bestow this gift, and Vanbrugh, hoping the ruler of Olympus will not notice, steals a French farce which he proceeds to transcribe ; and

> The building, as the poet writ
> Rose in proportion to his wit,

each act producing a corresponding portion of the house,

even the epilogue having its usual, if impolite, counterpart in stone and mortar. At last all was finished, and,

> . . . Poets from all quarters ran
> To see the house of brother Van :
> Look'd high and low, walk'd often round
> But no such house was to be found.
> One asks the waterman hard by
> " Where may the poet's palace lie? "
> Another of the Thames enquires
> If he has seen its gilded spires?
> At length they in the rubbish spy
> A place resembling a goose pie . . .

Brother Van did not at all care for those verses ; he was beginning to have a sense of his own dignity. It was true that he had borrowed pretty freely from the French, and perhaps a very large palace would not correspond with his muse ; but if the literary criticism was fair, was it altogether fitting to treat the architect of Castle Howard —not to mention the Clarenceux King of Arms—in quite so flippant a manner? Swift might be allowed to say these things, but the worst of it was that others of less wit, even the Duchess of Marlborough, used to tease him with those lines. It rankled ; he quarrelled with the author, and even four years later when he met Dr. Swift at dinner, they were ' very civil and cold '.[1]

But this had not been the irrepressible satirist's only offence. In 1708, still unable to swallow the fact of Vanbrugh's architectural knowledge, and immensely tickled by the contrast of the builder of Blenheim being also the designer of the ridiculously tiny house by the Thames, he had written,

> Van's genius, without thought or lecture
> Is hugely turned to architecture,

[1] *Stella*, 7th Nov. 1710.

which was unfair and not true. He further insisted that Vanbrugh's mind had been thus 'turned' both by seeing 'Miss' build a house of cards, and small boys dabbling with mud pies. Thus he had been incited to build a real house,

> Taller than Miss's by two yards,
> Not a sham thing of clay or cards.
> And so he did, for in a while
> He built up such a monstrous pile
> That no two chairmen could be found
> Able to lift it from the ground . . .

Can it be that the prosaic Goose-Pie House was the germ from which sprang the wild conception of Lilliput?

But Vanbrugh had much more insistent troubles to contend with than the gibes of a man who at that time was nothing more than a scheming rhymster. He was, as we have seen, in debt over that infernal Haymarket Theatre. Discreet Mr. Congreve had withdrawn himself from the probable complications, but there was nobody to whom Vanbrugh could in his turn hand over his share. Besides, it was he who had paid out the money. However, in 1706 he discovered a man who declared himself bold enough to try his luck. This was Owen Swiney, a queer, jolly fellow, with a habit Vanbrugh liked of speaking his mind. He was himself a minor playwright, loved the stage and music, and offered to pay five pounds every acting day—the whole not to exceed seven hundred pounds per annum.[1] Vanbrugh accepted the deal. But even though Swiney seemed to be doing his best for the house, and even wrote two operas himself,[2] the number of five pounds did not reach Vanbrugh's expectations. It was even hinted that there was something peculiar in Swiney's relations with Rich, who looked upon the theatre

[1] Cibber. [2] Boswell.

with no friendly eye. Thus in February 1708 the architect bought Swiney out, and retained him only as a manager. But he lost a great deal by his musical ventures, and though he was confident that the opera would some day settle in London, he was in May glad to take advantage of his manager's obliging disposition—or Rich's machinations—to part with the whole concern to him. In any case, with the building season in full swing, there was small time to devote to theatrical matters. Atossa was becoming too prying. At the same time these transactions did not make him free of debt.[1]

Luckily at this period, as he wrote to the Earl of Manchester, " all the world were running mad after building as far as they could reach ",[2] and for his part he was approached in the year 1710 by a Mr. Pelham, who with such bewildering rapidity became Mr. Pelham-Holles, Lord Pelham, and then the Earl of Clare, that for convenience sake he will here, until his further elevation, be referred to by the last title. Vanbrugh possessed a little place near Esher, which Lord Clare thought would suit him very well, if the architect would remodel the house and lay out the grounds to the best advantage. The suggestion came most opportunely, and just as Blenheim was about to fail as a source of income, the house around which ' nature was to borrow dress from Vanbrook's art ', and which was to become famous as Claremont, came to the rescue.

But in the next year the calm which had reigned in the Heralds' College since 1704 was disturbed by another outsider, who, flying higher even than Vanbrugh had done, threatened to usurp the place of Garter King of Arms itself, to which Clarenceux hoped to succeed. This was

[1] Letters to Earl of Manchester, May-July 1708: *Athenaeum*, 1861, and Palmer, p. 208.

[2] 27th July 1708: *Athenaeum*, 1861.

one Anstis, who asked permission of the Queen to pass a reversion with the then Garter for the place when it should become vacant. Gregory King, filled with a jealous love of his calling—and the hope that if Vanbrugh was elevated he would be preferred to the post of Clarenceux—combated this fresh indignity with all the eloquence at his command.

" The honour I have of being in some measure known to you ", he wrote to Harley,[1] " encourages me to represent to your honour the hardships which will lie upon the Society of Heralds in general (though chiefly on myself in particular) should such a step be made as to enabling a stranger to our corporation to pass a Patent jointly with the present Garter King of Arms for the place of Garter, and to the longer liver.

" As to the Heralds in general, there being only two places of Garter and Clarenceux of tolerable profit, what a discouragement must it be to learning and industry in our faculty to have those places always filled up with strangers, when some of the society have spent the prime of their days and a number of years in qualifying themselves for those employments, beside the consequence to the public to have the heads of a society ignorant of their faculty, and a coadjutor himself to want a coadjutor.

" As to myself though by right of seniority I ought to have been Clarenceux, yet if I had not . . ."

but the tale of his training, qualifications, and accomplishments reads a little sadly. It was all so ineffective. We do not know what answer he got. Perhaps none. Mr. Harley was very busy over his clandestine meetings with the Queen, and over his evening paper of verses for what was afterwards known as the Scriblerus Club. Vanbrugh, however, was assured that the place of Garter would be his ; but it served King no whit, for in 1712 he died.

Both Harley and the Queen had, after all, more

[1] Add. MSS. 4253, No. 15 : 2nd Jan. 1710/11.

important matters to attend to than the complaints of a poursuivant. At about this time the great struggle for power, in which Electors and Pretenders were mere pawns in the game, was centering amid seething excitement about the trial of Sacheverell. Nobody could talk or think of anything else. The Queen herself, who at last saw a prospect of breaking free of the Marlburian tyranny, declared her intention of being present. On the result would depend her power to make that change of ministers she so ardently desired. None cared for Sacheverell, but all realized that through him would be decided the issues of peace and war, not to mention the more important matter of social leadership. And owing to the latter consideration the ladies were as eager as the men to witness the historic scene. Peter Wentworth wrote that they were " making their advances to the Lords to get tickets for them to see and be seen at the Tryal, for that reason the Young Lords make a bustle to have their full number of ticket, 8 a peace " ; while Lady Wentworth, diverted from her attention to her lapdogs, declared " Sacheverell will make all the Ladys turn good huswivs, they goe att seven every mornin ".[1] During the trial the crowd outside roared ominously, damping the rhetorical fire of the Whig orators within the hall ; and as her Majesty drove to the scene in her coach, they clamoured about the wheels and cried, " God save the Queen and Dr. Sacheverell ". What they meant was, " Devil take the Duke of Marlborough " : the great deeds they had once so loudly cheered time had already claimed as alms for oblivion.

Then began such pamphleteering as has never since been seen, a time when men of letters throve because of the fear their pens inspired—and, indeed, some wrote in

[1] *Wentwarth Papers*, pp. 112, 113 : February and March 1710.

venom rather than in ink. If one can sum up in a phrase the characteristics of that period, one would say they were an unscrupulous love of power and a healthy distrust of idealisms. Bolingbroke could without self-condemnation intrigue with St. Germains, and be honestly surprised that the Pretender would not change his religion for the sake of the throne of Great Britain. This was to have "all the superstition of a capuchin . . . but no tincture of the religion of a prince".[1] Walpole, with his blunt actuality, would refer to the commendable sentiments of young men as 'schoolboy flights'; and when they mentioned 'patriotism' or 'virtue' would good-naturedly say that they "would soon come off that and grow wiser".[2] Ballad-makers and pamphleteers had their chance, and when great men fell, rhymed couplets pursued them to their retreats.

During 1711 Vanbrugh cannot have been left unperturbed by the screams of faction and the revilings of political sects. Whether in retreat at Maze Hill or The Bastille at Greenwich, or doing what little he could at Blenheim; building the Clarendon Printing House with Hawkesmoor; or, as it fell to his lot to do in August, burying his mother, his ears and his eyes must have been assailed by such productions as the scurrilous *Secret History of Queen Zarah and the Zarazians*, so popular in France; or he would read the bitter attacks of Swift—'strenui pro virili libertatis vindicis'![3]—in *The Examiner* or in *The Conduct of the Allies*. The Whig cause seemed doomed, and with it all his friends and possible patrons. Steele put up a gallant fight, but how ineffectual were Addison's exhortations to be good! Even the traditional 17th November Pope-roasting demonstration prepared by

[1] Bolingbroke, p. 269.
[2] Green.
[3] As he describes himself in his epitaph.

the Whigs, with so fine a procession including a figure of Harley as the devil (the property of Dr. Garth), was raided by the police and came to nothing.

Indeed, there was in the air a feverish feeling, a massing of forces, a wild pandemonium of battle-cries, in expectation of an inevitable event. Some day, perhaps soon, the Queen would die, and what would happen then? It was felt that there was no time to waste. Thus pamphlet poured out after ballad, and ballad after broadside. Every occurrence was seized as a pretext for slander or defamation. When certain high-spirited young gentlemen played rough pranks about the town, there appeared a ballad headed ' O Wicked Whigs ', declaring,

> You sent your Mohocks all abroad
> With razors armed and knives,
> Who on night walkers made inroads
> And scar'd our maids and wives,[1]

and, they might have added, Dr. Swift. To some the turmoil seemed ominous of cosmic disaster. A ' Reverend Divine ' took " from the Mouth of the Spirit of a Person, who was lately slain by one of the Mohocks ", " An Argument proving from History, Reason, and Scripture, That the present Mohocks and Hawkubites are the Gog and Magog mentioned in the Revelations, and therefore this vain and transition World will Shortly be brought to its final Dissolution ".[2]

But the denizens of this vain and transition world continued to behave in the faith of futurity—especially those who attacked the Marlboroughs. Nearly every week there appeared something in the manner of *No Queen, No General*, or *The Duke and Duchess of Marlborough's Loss* of income (an unworthy stab in the back), or *A Bill of Roman Gratitude* (£994 11*s.* 10*d.*)

[1] *Broadsides and Ballads*, B. M. 1876, No. 15.
[2] *Rariora*, p. 128.

contrasted with *A Bill of British Ingratitude* (£540,000). And if a Whig partisan wrote,

> Wheneas Q—— A—— of great renown
> Great Britain's sceptre swayed,
> Besides the church she dearly loved
> A dirty chamber-maid,[1]

the friend of Abigail Masham would retort with,

> A widow kept a favourite cat
> At first a gentle creature,
> But when he was grown sleek and fat,
> With many a mouse and many a rat,
> He soon disclosed his nature,[2]

or would reel off *A Fable of the Housewife and her Cock*, on the same lines.

Vanbrugh's good nature was warm enough to make him sore at the way the Duke was being harried by these hired bravoes of the quill, and perhaps, in spite of everything, he had kindly thoughts of the Duchess in her downfall. He did not care about politics, except as epistolary matter wherewith to entertain his great Whig friends when they were out of town. But this sort of thing he could not stand; he thought it grossly unfair, and allowed himself on one occasion to comment upon it. Writing on the 25th January 1713 to the mayor of Woodstock about paving the market-place, he said he believed the Duke would have done it " ere now but for the *continual plague and bitter persecution he has most barbarously been followed with* for two years past ". This was indiscreet; it was no quarrel of his, and the hornets into whose nest he was now blundering were mighty big ones, and could sting. The letter came to the notice of the people he was reproaching, and since it amounted to a government servant passing judgement on his sovereign, the sovereign took umbrage. At last Vanbrugh had been caught into

[1] *Ballads and Broadsides*, B. M. 1876, No. 9. [2] Ashton.

the whirlpool of events: his post at the Board of Works was taken from him, his dismissal to date from the 15th April.[1] And even before this took effect, his letter was published in *The Post Boy* of the 24th March, with the offending phrase italicized as above, and prefaced by the comment, "The Gentleman who writ the following letter to the Mayor of Woodstock, having met with the chastisement he deserves for, 'tis to be hoped that those, who by the extreme lenity of the present Administration, are yet suffered to enjoy those offices they obtained under another, will take warning, and keep themselves within the bounds they ought". *The Post Boy*, rather meanly, rubbed salt into the smart by printing the postscript—"I have lately received some very good hopes that the Treasury will pay the Blenheim debt . . ."[2]

After this blow Vanbrugh was very glad to be offered some work at King's Weston, for at this time it was not at all certain he would obtain much employment as a private architect. Doubts were beginning to be expressed, not as to the picturesque, but as to the utilitarian, value of his houses. They looked monstrous well, but were they comfortable to live in? Was it not probable that the man who had failed to combine art and morality in his plays would find it difficult to resolve the conflicting claims of art and convenience in his buildings? Verses upon Blenheim were being written, after the style of:

'tis very fine,
But where d'ye sleep, or where d'ye dine?
I find, by all you have been telling,
That 'tis a house, but not a dwelling.[3]

The architect vehemently combated such ignoble, spiteful aspersions; he was getting tired of this sort of ignorant criticism. So once, when he was writing about King's

[1] *Athenaeum*, Aug. 1894. [2] Reprinted *Gent. Mag.*, 1804, i. 411.
[3] Printed in Pope's works, but perhaps by Dr. Abel Evans.

Weston, he took occasion to say of Castle Howard that in cold weather every room was like an oven, and that " in corridors 200 ft. long there is not air enough in motion to stir the flame of a candle ".[1]

Castle Howard was now, in fact, very habitable, and towards the end of the year its architect went to join the Earl of Carlisle's house-party in " the top seat and garden of England ". He needed relaxation ; indeed, he seems to have felt he needed consolation, escape from the consideration of his troubles. For in York he would contrive to meet a lady (of some thirty-seven summers),[2] who had just that sympathetic knowledge of the world that can comfort a man of fifty ; and he was not afraid to allow his pleasure to be visible even to the unsentimental eyes of sweet and twenty. Certainly it did not escape those of sprightly Lady Mary Wortley, who wrote to her sister-in-law :

" I can't forbear entertaining you with our York lovers (strange monsters, you'll think, love being as much forced up here as melons). In the first form of these creatures is even Mr Vanbrugh. Heaven, no doubt, compassionating our dulness, has inspired him with a passion that makes us all ready to die with laughing. . . . He keeps Mondays and Thursday market (*assembly*-day) constantly ; and . . . there's extraordinary choice indeed. I believe last Monday there were two hundred pieces of women's flesh (fat and lean) : but you know Van's taste was always odd : his inclination to ruins has given him a fancy for Mrs Yarborough : he sighs and ogles so, that it would do your heart good to see him." [3]

We need not inquire whether the attraction was a purely Platonic one ; in any case there was no danger, for Mrs. Yarburgh's husband was still alive.

[1] To Southwell, 23rd Oct. 1713 : *Gent. Mag.* 1837, i. 479.
[2] See Appendix II.
[3] Montagu, *Letters.*

Dalliance, however, is but an episode; one can hope it gave Vanbrugh refreshment, for in May 1714 he had to face a fresh blow. "The Queen", he wrote to the Duke of Marlborough, "has at last passed a patent . . . to Mr. Anstis for the reversion of the Garter. She said she had been under an obligation to me not to consent to it; but my behaviour had been such in writing that letter to Woodstock, that now she had done with me—That was her expression."[1] It was a sad outlook for the College, for Anstis was a disagreeable fellow. In 1711 Le Neve, Norroy, had written to Lord Oxford to complain of Anstis's behaviour in borrowing some books. When the manuscripts were sent for, Anstis had declared "the office was made up of a parcel of fools and knaves, and the knaves had sent the fools of their errand: that when he should be made Garter, which would be shortly in spite of all their teeth . . . he would make them all stink"[2]. And now he had the reversion. Thus it was in vain that Vanbrugh, as though finally to conciliate the heralds, had had his arms proved on the 15th April of that very year: he would never be Garter King of Arms.

Thus, owing to his loyalty, his last hope of advancement was gone. What chance was there now for a Whig, however self-effacing and quiet he might be? The elections had brought back an almost wholly Tory Parliament, the Schism Act followed the sinister Occasional Conformity Bill, and Dick Steele was expelled the House for defending the Hanoverian succession. So at least it seemed to ardent Whigs—for surely to exclude the author of *The Crisis* on the ground of 'sedition and irreligion' was too transparent a trick. The world had finally toppled, and it is difficult for a man of fifty to begin life over again.

[1] Add. MSS. 9123: 14th May 1714.
[2] Add. MSS. 7125: 28th June 1711.

PART III

I

New Reign: New Hopes

ALL at once the whole aspect of things changed. A sudden storm swept away the lowering clouds, and a bright midday sun flooded the landscape. In dismissing Oxford—once again Lady Masham had proved ungrateful—the Queen had so overwrought herself, that she fell into an apoplectic stupor. Every day it became more certain that she had done, not only with John Vanbrugh, but with everybody else. Bolingbroke was in despair: he was touching the crown of triumph, but could not get it into his hand. For five days the country held its breath in tense expectation. The militia was up, the guards at the royal palaces were strengthened, and men tightened their belts against another civil war. The French were on the alert, and the net of persuasion was flung towards the Dutch. Bolingbroke prepared a Jacobite ministry, but the cunning of Shrewsbury proved too subtle for the craft of Henry St. John, so that when the Queen died, on Sunday, the 1st August, all that the brilliant intriguer could do was to write to Swift " What a world this is, and how does fortune banter us ".[1]

And by a strange coincidence, on the day the Queen died the Duke and Duchess of Marlborough landed in England. Their progress was almost a triumph, only marred by one slight, inexplicable flaw—the Duke had not been appointed one of the Regents. No matter: in spite of a little Tory restlessness in the country, and

[1] Morley.

strange rumours from Scotland, all was well: and when on the 20th September the new sovereign entered London, it was observed that "the Duke of Marlborough was more huzza'd . . . than King George, and that the acclamation *God save the Duke of Marlborough!* was more frequently repeated than *God save the King!*"[1] The Whigs were up, more up than they had ever been before. Vanbrugh's personal friends Lords Carlisle and Halifax succeeded one another in the Exchequer, while Townshend, with his brother-in-law Walpole in the background, formed a ministry. Moreover, Marlborough was again Captain-General.

The immediate result for Vanbrugh was an honour procured him by the Duke as a recompense for the troubles consequent upon that unfortunate Woodstock letter; he stood sponsor for him to the King, and a disgruntled Tory at Oxford noted that "The first knight that King George made is one Vanbrugh, a silly fellow, who is the architect of Woodstock".[1] Such a promising beginning put the 'silly fellow' into great fettle, visible in the high glee with which he wrote of current affairs to Lord Clare:

"I wish you much joy of your elections, and of a good Parliament in general, for it will be a rare one. And I find our friends dispos'd to make good use on't, Hang, Whip, Pillory, etc: I wish they could love one another, tho' they can't. At least I think they're all resolved to hate Soups [?] The storm thickens against him daily, but he cocks still, and thrusts his little belly amongst 'em; but I'm afraid they'll give it a squeeze at last."[2]

Events continued gratifying, for not only was he on the 15th June 1715 restored to his post at the Board of Works, but in the same year he was made architect at Greenwich Hospital, at an extra salary of two hundred

[1] Hearne, 25th Sept. 1714. [2] *Athenaeum*, 1861: 5th Feb. 1715.

pounds a year. It was thought that Wren was too slow. He had confronted the Inigo Jones wing with an admirable replica at the other side of the court, and had built the colonnade blocks with their graceful domes, but he was unbearably dilatory in finishing the façade towards the park. This Vanbrugh did, altering the design to please himself, and making innovations his contemporaries found a little startling.[1] It was even offered to displace Wren, in his favour, from the post of Surveyor-General, but respect for the genius and years of Sir Christopher caused him to decline the promotion. And without this, Vanbrugh certainly had enough to do: not only did Lord Clare urge him to finish Claremont, but he employed him to refit a house in Lincoln Fields and a castle at Nottingham. Besides these, Vanbrugh in 1716 set to work upon Oulton Hall in Cheshire, and Eastbury in Dorset, for the world was still running mad after building as far as it could reach.

Above all there was Blenheim. The work there had not quite stood still, for the trifling sum of ten thousand pounds had been granted in 1713, and in 1714 Thornhill had painted a ceiling. To Vanbrugh's idea he had charged a great deal too much, no less than twenty-five shillings a square yard, "a higher price than anything of that bigness was given for Rubens or Titian".[2] But he should have remembered that if he himself was 'the Palladio of the age', Sir James Thornhill was 'the modern Apelles', and it was fitting that the latter should adorn the former's masterpiece, cost what it might. He was gravely afraid, however, that the Duchess would quarrel about the price; but she did not, and took great credit to herself for her restraint. Indeed, the bargain was not a bad one, for Thornhill was charging ten

[1] For illustrations, Barman. [2] Add. MSS. 9123, f. 94.

shillings less per square yard than he did for similar work in St. Paul's.[1]

And the very day the Duke landed in England he sent for his architect to meet him at Woodstock, which he was as eager as ever to inhabit with his ' dear soul '. He told Vanbrugh he proposed to go on with the house at his own expense, as soon as Parliament should have voted the paying off of the debt, and he asked for an estimate to complete. He learned it would cost him exactly fifty-four thousand, five hundred and twenty pounds, four shillings and two pence.[2] On the 12th May Vanbrugh wrote to Joyns that the Blenheim affair was " now in motion in the House of Commons ",[3] and eventually it was directed that all the old debts for materials and work should be cleared off. Claims were put in for forty-five thousand pounds, of which about a third was at once paid, and a little later nine thousand pounds more.[2] This was enough for Marlborough. The work was begun again, and was soon in full swing, Vanbrugh watching the work, and the Duchess watching Vanbrugh. It was understood that they had forgiven one another everything, and it felt exactly like the good old times come back again.

In fact it was soon clear that it was a great deal too much like the good old times ; there were, almost at once, the same troubles with the workmen. The masons, for instance, were not at all easy people to manage, and in 1716 showed a tendency to combine. Vanbrugh believed " (if your Grace pleases) ", the best way was " to employ several of them, so as to make emulation ".[4] And, under pressure, Sir John did succeed in reducing prices, although he found it very difficult, because his old workers and contractors expected the same profits as they had had

[1] Ashton, ii. 43.
[2] Coxe, iii, pp. 409 seq.
[3] Add. MSS. 19605.
[4] Add. MSS. 9123 : April 1716.

before. He was reduced to the expedient of making one Strong foreman, and getting him " to do the work because he thought it dangerous to take lower prices in his own name ".[1] At least that was the Duchess's view of the procedure, but as Vanbrugh was at this time very busy with other duties, such as attending to Hampton Court the personage good Whigs called the Prince of Wales, he probably had not much time to attend to details.

Besides, there were his heraldic duties, and these were not always a matter of mere routine. For instance, on the 26th July 1716 it fell to his lot to degrade the Duke of Ormond from his knighthood of the Garter, since he had been guilty of high treason in the rebellion of '15.

" In virtue of the Sovereign's warrant to Garter King of Arms, at Windsor, after morning prayers, in the presence of the dean, prebendaries, choir and poor knights, and of a great number of spectators. . . . Clarencieux king of arms, exercising the office of Garter, read the sovereign's warrant at the brazen desk. The achievements of the degraded knight were then severally thrown down by the heralds, and spurned out of the choir and West door of the chapel, where the soldiers of the garrison were under arms. Clarencieux concluded the ceremony by pulling the plate of arms from the stall." [2]

The Duchess of Marlborough could allow for official frivolities of this kind taking her architect away from Blenheim, but what really raised her ire was to find that not only was a portion of the ancient Manor House of Woodstock still in being, but that Vanbrugh was actually living in it. She had always known it! She was never in the wrong. It was all very well for him to say, that

[1] Duchess's endorsement of letter of June 1716. Add. MSS. 9123.

[2] Beltz.

Travers having given up all idea of living there, Godolphin had given him leave to do so ; Godolphin was dead. In any case that did not excuse Sir John : and to say that he had made the place habitable at his own expense only made the circumstance worse, for she had given him strict orders to pull it down. And on the top of it all he had the cool effrontery to write, " but if your Grace has any reason against my being there, I'll remove ".[1] This was perilously near adding insult to injury.

Still, that was a thing easily settled. But to her horror the Duchess found there was a much worse abomination being perpetrated. At a certain point in the approach there was across the road a little ditch anybody could jump. Instead of treating this as a negligible affair, Vanbrugh was actually erecting over it a most preposterous bridge that looked like a piece of operatic scenery. To give himself an excuse he had gone so far as to convert the ditch into a rivulet. Men of letters always turned out to be fools or philosophers,[2] but that this one should be so much the former as to think it necessary to waste money on a bridge which spanned a hundred and three yards, and carried an immense superstructure of rooms,[3] was enough to drive any woman mad.

And the architect's attitude only exacerbated her feelings more ; he wrote to her about it almost in a spirit of banter.

" I hope you will ", he had the hardihood to say, " in almost every article of the estimate for finishing this great design, find the expense less than is there allowed. Even that frightful bridge will, I believe, at last be kindlier looked upon, if it is to be found (instead of £12,000 more) not to cost above three ; and I will venture my whole

[1] Add. MSS. 9123 : July 1716. [2] Strachey, p. 116.
[3] *Wentworth Papers*, 345 ; Hearne, 29th May 1717.

prophetic skill in this one point, that if I lived to see that extravagant project complete, I shall have the satisfaction to see your Grace fonder of it than of any part whatsoever of the house, gardens, or park. . . . And if at last there is a house found in that bridge, your Grace will go and live in it." [1]

Was that the tone in which to speak to Atossa? She answered. Her pen flew vigorously over the paper, and she accused Vanbrugh of being fantastically whimsical—the Manor House episode had proved it, though that, as a comfortable habitation for him, had gone beyond a whim. More, she charged him with deliberately throwing dust in her eyes about this absurd causeway. She had latterly, since an illness of the Duke's, signed the orders for everything, but this had been cunningly kept secret from her.[2]

Vanbrugh was 'much surprised' at this attack, indeed more than a little hurt, and in his reply showed he was fully conscious of the fact that he was now Sir John, and Lady Marlborough no longer greater than any other Duchess. The Duke, he said, had most certainly given orders for the causeway,

"in such a manner, as could not possibly be mistaken because it was not upon a short word or two, but a great deal of plain intelligible talk, and that not in a crowd or hurry, but quietly in a room alone with only Mr. Wise and I . . . and this was when he was very well, at least said nothing of being otherwise . . .

"As to what your Grace may say", he continued, determined not to be browbeat, "of the design of this causeway never having been understood, I know no one thing about the building that was so much considered and so cautiously determined. The Duke of Marlborough, your Grace my late Lord Godolphin, the Duke of

[1] Thomson, ii. 524: 27th July 1716.

[2] Endorsement of letter from Vanbrugh about to be quoted.

Shrewsbury, the late Duke of Montague "—the names pile up like a thundercloud—" Sir Christopher Wren, and several others were thoroughly consulted in this matter, and several meetings there were upon it at Kensington, Montague House, etc., where the models were inspected, and that of Sir Christopher Wren's, stuck full of pins, by which he pretended to lessen the charge, was quite rejected, and that I proposed was resolved on . . ." [1]

And since the Duchess had apologized in her usual manner, Vanbrugh showed that he too could apologize—in the same manner, a little threateningly, and with precisely the same openness of thought. He continued :

" I am so far from disliking the plainness with which your Grace writes, that I am very glad you do so . . . but I have often seen you *heated* by wrong informations or misconceptions ; and not make any difficulty of owning your *mistake* when you have found it, so I shall be very disappointed if when I wait upon you at Blenheim, I do not find you very well satisfied with my defence about this causeway . . ."

He maintained none of his doings were ' whimsey ', for everything had been done by order, and protested he had never kept anything from the Duchess.

" If you do not believe me in this I hope you will Madam, when I declare (which I do now) very truly and positively that I will make no secret to you of anything, and by consequence, if I do must be (what by God I am not) a very lying Rascal." [2]

But if the likeness of character of the two antagonists was in one respect striking, the differences were too fundamental to be adjusted by a spirited outburst of

[1] This was perfectly true, as may be seen from a letter of Godolphin to Marlborough, 19th April 1706 : Add. MSS. 9123, f. 11.

[2] Add. MSS. 9123 : 3rd Aug. 1716.

temper. Sir John was getting on the Duchess's nerves. Although in letter after letter he argued how cheaply he was finishing Blenheim, the old suspicion tugged insistently at her mind, telling her that he was determined to ruin the Marlboroughs, deliberately and through malice. Where, after all this fret, was the homely dwelling for herself and her husband? In bitterness of spirit she wrote to her friend Mrs. Clayton:

"As to the affair of this building, I will state it to you as I can; the public has and are to pay £365,000 for it. The Duke of Marlborough has paid and owes above £9,000 since 1712, and we have yet nothing like a habitation for it. Of this great sum £38,000 was paid, with the increase of the debts after the Earl of Godolphin went out, before the building was quite stopped . . ."

Here she indulged in a description of the 'chaos' to be seen at Blenheim; and then:

"It will cost an immense sum to complete the causeway, and that ridiculous bridge, in which I counted 33 rooms. Four houses are to be at each corner of the bridge; but that which makes it so much prettier than London Bridge is, that you may sit in six rooms and look out at window into the high arch, while the coaches are driving over your head. But notwithstanding all this, Sir John has given Lord Marlborough an estimate in which he tells him all is to be complete for £54,381; and because I can't believe that such a sum will do all, when 38,000 so lately did nothing, I am thought by him very troublesome and quite stupid." [1]

The Duchess was evidently making up her mind that Vanbrugh must go. Unfortunately, there was a complicating circumstance.

[1] Coxe, iii. 414: 1716. Coxe dates it 'probably Nov. 1st–10th'. It seems more probably about September. It does not much matter.

2

The Newcastle Marriage

THOUGH she accompanied her husband into exile at Antwerp, my lady Duchess did not allow her family affairs at home to stand still; and among other things, she kept her eyes open for a suitable match for her grand-daughter, the Lady Harriet Godolphin. And a little before her return in 1714 it struck her that young Lord Pelham—whom we will continue here to call Lord Clare—would do very well. He was vastly rich, having inherited a large part of the estates of his uncle, the Duke of Newcastle, as well as his father's considerable wealth, had Whig principles, and was reported to be "very silly and good-natured . . . and easily persuaded to anything".[1] If he took the bait another Whig peer would be added to the Marlborough connexions, and there would be none of the political or financial difficulties that had arisen in the case of her son-in-law, the Earl of Sunderland.

The Duchess, however, who had latterly had enough of rebuffs, did not wish to make the suggestion herself, or perhaps she by now had a glimpse of the fact that her methods were a little too abrupt for a delicate affair. Besides, she was abroad, and such matters need the personal touch, apart from the fact that letters are not only liable to misconstruction, but are regrettably permanent. She knew, on the other hand, that Vanbrugh was employed by Lord Clare in his house in Surrey; and as the former was always as much the friend as the servant of the noblemen for whom he worked, she decided

[1] Montagu, Aug. or Sept. 1714.

that he was the intermediary fit for her purpose. He had a fine working knowledge of the ways of the world and of the great, and bore about him a certain air of genial authority which would certainly impress a young man of twenty-one who was 'very silly and good-natured'. She felt, now that she had apologized, that he could be counted upon to perform this little office for her.

Vanbrugh agreed to do so. He said he felt he would, in bringing about this match, do my Lord Clare as great a service as my Lady Harriet.[1] Incidentally, though he did not say so, he thought he might be doing himself a service; it might, indeed, lead to 'something lasting' from Lord Clare, an opportunity not to be missed, for he was still in debt, held no office in the Board of Works, and had only an infinitesimal chance of ever being Garter King. It might also be amusing. Accordingly, after consulting Mr. Walpole, who was now by no means to be neglected in a Whig affair of state—and an alliance of this sort was very nearly such—he posted off to Claremont to see his Lordship.

But at the moment his Lordship was not in a fit condition to have a proposal of marriage broached to him; he was not well. Vanbrugh would have to walk delicately, especially as he had agreed with the Duchess to put the matter in such a way as not to give Lord Clare the 'uneasiness' of sending her Grace any message in the event of his not falling in with the suggestion. So, without appearing to have any design in the matter, the ambassador would, either during their strolls about the garden which was in the making, or over their mulled claret in the evening, carelessly turn the conversation to the subject of women—a topic which is not apt to startle. And then, no doubt in

[1] Add. MSS. 9123, 16th Jan. 1715, until the next reference to the same.

honest Van's open manner, they would discuss the characteristics of the sex, and how short its members fell of what they could wish. With so many illustrations from real life to hand, one may be certain that the creator of Berinthia and Lady Fancyfull had a great many entertaining things to say. There was, for instance, the Duchess of Buckingham, who always kept the anniversary of Charles I's death as a day of deep mourning, so as to remind the world of her left-handed royal parentage; or the eccentric Duchess of Montague, who had only married the Duke after he had sworn to her that he was the Emperor of China. And was there not a third Duchess who would provide many illustrations?—of course in the friendliest way. It is even not too much to suppose that a copy of *The Secret History of Queen Zarah and the Zarazians* might be taken from the bookshelf, and its leaves turned over in search of mirthful matter. But on every occasion, with never-failing regularity, Vanbrugh would in the end veer the talk round to the shining antipodes of these ladies, the Lady Harriet Godolphin, and enlarge upon her virtues, her understanding, indeed all the charming qualities of her mind and heart.

Soon Lord Clare began to see what was meant, and Vanbrugh had to redouble his carefulness. For his Lordship had notions that seemed to the more experienced man very unusual in one of his quality and fortune. He was romantic, one might even say idealistic. He was unduly hard on the ladies of the court and of the town, and made many observations on their 'bad education and wrong manners'. He "owned he should think of marriage with much more pleasure than he did if he could find a woman (fit for him to marry) that had such a turn of understanding, temper and behaviour as might make her a useful friend as well as an agreeable companion, but of such a one he seemed almost to despair ". Again Vanbrugh pointed to the Lady Harriet, who was certainly of the class ' fit for him to marry ', and had all the qualifications his lordship had mentioned.

Lord Clare was tempted. It certainly would be gratifying to have a posterity descended from the great Duke of Marlborough ; and no doubt there would be money, of which, although already enormously rich, he could not have enough. For he was not like his skinflint uncle, who had amassed wealth for its own sake ; he was going to do a great deal with his.[1] But although he was prepared to believe that Lady Harriet was in nearly every way a suitable bride for him, he found it in him to wish, in spite of his idealism, that she was better-looking. Here certainly was a difficulty ; one cannot argue evident facts as one can spiritual suppositions, and Vanbrugh could not say she was handsome. He declared, however, that though he " did not believe she would ever have a beautiful face, he could plainly see it would prove a very agreeable one, which he thought infinitely more valuable ". She would have, he asserted, what was called a ' good countenance ', and maintained that no one expression in a face was more agreeable than that. And had Lord Clare ever considered her figure ? For himself, he was sure it would be ' perfectly well '. He even went so far as to stake all his skill " (which had used to be a good deal employed in these kind of observations) that in two years time no woman in town would be better liked ". Lord Clare wavered ; he did not contradict ; he even allowed that Vanbrugh ' might very probably be right '.[2]

So far all was well. But on consulting with his friends,

[1] See Pope, *Moral Essays*, Ep. III, ll. 177 seq. : Cotta.
[2] Add. MSS. 9123 : 16th Jan. 1715.

Lord Clare decided that if he took the Lady Harriet to wife, he ought to take forty thousand pounds with her. The Duchess, who, as Vanbrugh said later, " as well as in all her other traffic, so in a husband for her grand-daughter, she would fain have him good and cheap ",[1] was outraged. Lady Harriet, she retorted, was " neither a citizen nor a monster " that any one should require such an unheard of fortune with her. She could only conclude that this demand was the way Lord Clare and his friends had chosen to decline the match.

Her Grace, therefore, thought no more of the matter; but by 1716, Clare, in whom the title of the Duke of Newcastle had been revived, had found no other woman so well fitted to companion him in life as the Lady Harriet Godolphin. He was ' almost in despair '. So at the end of the summer he wrote to Vanbrugh saying he was " come to an absolute resolution to marry somewhere before the winter was over ", and would be obliged for some further accounts of the Lady Harriet. Had Vanbrugh anything new to say? How was she behaving at the Bath?[2] This last would indeed be a test of worth.

Thus the matter was reopened; several letters passed between the Duchess and Vanbrugh, in which the former " thought fit to express her extreme satisfaction to find a thing revived she so much desired, though for some time past had retained little hopes of ". Vanbrugh himself pressed the matter with the Duchess—being now, not her's, but the young man's emissary. He even explained how well the Duke of Marlborough's money would be laid out " to compass the best match in England for the only daughter of his next heir ".[3] Her Grace showed how willing she was. She was that summer

[1] Add. MSS. 33064: 15th Nov. 1716. [2] Thomson, ii, Appendix.
[3] Add. MSS. 9123: 27th Sept. 1716.

staying at Bath (which she hated on account of the noise which would not allow her to sleep), for the sake of her husband, who was there recovering from his first attack of palsy, and, detractors said, saving sixpenny chair fares by walking home of nights. Her granddaughter was with her, and had already attracted one suitor, with a fortune as great as the Duke of Newcastle's, and with whom her Grace might " have had her own conditions ". But on hearing from Vanbrugh, she threw over the fresh suitor, thereby showing, as she did not fail to point out, that money, with her, was ever a minor consideration.

Except, of course, where Blenheim was concerned. She was at the moment not at all pleased with Mr. Surveyor Vanbrugh, however grateful she might have cause to be with the negotiator of marriages; the more so as in August she received a letter from Bobart to say that new work was going on at the Manor, and that Vanbrugh was planting fruit-trees at his own expense! But if she dismissed the architect, could she retain his services in another capacity? What would become of the marriage? It was a difficult, a delicate situation. So when by chance she met at Bath a certain Mr. Walter, whom she found to be a friend of the Duke of Newcastle, she unbosomed herself to him with respect to her granddaughter's future. Mr. Walter seemed an agreeable, understanding man, who might very well carry messages; and moreover there seemed to be one great advantage in making use of him rather than of Sir John; he would not run and blab out the whole affair to that upstarting, ill-bred, Norfolk sheep-breeding squire, Robert Walpole.

Thus when in the autumn she went to Woodstock with her husband to see the progress made there, she was very circumspect in her behaviour. First she visited the Manor House, and found that what Bobart had said was quite true. There was a new wall begun, and walks! To her eye the walls at the palace compared unfavourably with those here, the park "having none but what you may kick down with your foot, nor the fine garden but what must be pulled down again, being done with a stone the undertakers must know would not hold".[1] Certainly Vanbrugh must go: and so during her visit she was careful never to be alone with him, so that he should not raise the question of the marriage. He on his side made no attempt to bring it forward, "and being to see the Duke of Newcastle before there could be anything new to speak upon, did not wonder she said nothing to him of that matter". Once more brother Van was too simple.

When, however, he went to Claremont, he found the Duke of Newcastle full of eager impatience to know what the Duchess had said. Vanbrugh, surprised, answered that she had said nothing, no doubt because there was nothing new to say. The Duke was yet more surprised, because during Sir John's visit to Blenheim he had been called upon by Mr. Walter, who had had a good deal to say about the marriage. He was even then in the house; would Vanbrugh like to see him? The two negotiators were thereupon introduced to one another, and Vanbrugh was more surprised than ever. Then, as he thought upon the situation, his feeling turned to anger; he was greatly annoyed that he, Sir John Vanbrugh, the creator of Blenheim, Clarenceux King of Arms, the friend of all the wits and many of nobility, a man of mature years, should have been shelved in so shabby a way by this Mr. Walter of whom nobody had even so much as heard. Like another 'pitiful goer-between' he had found the

[1] Add. MSS. 9123. Letter from Vanbrugh 1709, endorsed by Duchess later, endorsement beginning "In August 1716 . . ."

task thankless, and, again like the other, would not "meddle nor make no more i' the matter". He at once wrote to the Duchess a letter glinting with cold indignation, in which he simply set forth the history of the whole affair and his labours therein, and in which he also declared his wonder at her silence during their last meeting at Blenheim. But as he wrote a warmer feeling rose up in him, and the indignation became less cold. "I don't say this, madam," he flamed up suddenly,

"to court being farther employed in this matter; for a Match-maker is a damned trade, and I was never fond of meddling in other people's affairs. But as in this, on your own motion and your own desire, I had taken a good deal of hearty pains to serve you, and I think with a good deal of hearty success, I cannot but wonder (though not be sorry) you should not think it right to continue your commands upon

Your obedient humble servant

J. VANBRUGH."[1]

Such a letter was, of course, all the Duchess could desire. Sir John had sent in his resignation as far as the marriage question was concerned. Nevertheless she wrote him a letter in her usual disarmingly frank style, setting forth her view, and innocently supposing nobody could see anything in the least unnatural in her approaches to Mr. Walter, once she had found him to be an intimate of the Duke of Newcastle. And as to not having raised the question at Blenheim, she remarked blandly, "I think it was your turn to speak after what I had written, and not at all reasonable for you to find fault with what passed between Mr. Walter and me at the Bath". Indeed, *her* surprise was unbounded; but in her character of the injured person she magnanimously concluded:

[1] Add. MSS. 9125; also *Athenaeum*, 1890.

" I have now written a very true relation of this whole proceeding, and if any third person will say that I have done anything wrong to you in it, I shall be very sorry for it, and very ready to ask your pardon ; but at present I have the ease and satisfaction to believe there is no sort of complaint against

Your most humble servant

S. MARLBOROUGH.[1]

"[P.S.] I have two letters of yours concerning the building of this place, which I will not trouble you to answer after so long a letter as this ; besides, after the trial I made when you were last here, [Blenheim] 'tis plain we can never agree upon that matter."

But the Duchess knew there was no need to answer those two letters, because she had shot another bolt. Indeed, the only explanation of the one just quoted is her need, in this case not without malice, to prove herself in the right, at any rate to herself. For when Vanbrugh got back to town after his visit to the Duke of Newcastle, a certain Brigadier Richards, a building contractor, showed him a screed [2] in which the Duchess had " given herself the trouble in twenty or thirty sides of paper ", Vanbrugh told Newcastle, " to draw up a charge against me, beginning from the time this building was first ordered by the Queen, and concluding upon the whole that I had brought the Duke of Marlborough into this unhappy difficulty, Either to leave the thing unfinished, and by consequence useless to him and his posterity, or by finishing it, to distress his fortune, and deprive his grandchildren of the provision he inclined to make for them ". At last the Duchess had formulated the dark suspicions she had always had of Vanbrugh. He had always hated the Duke—perhaps he had always been secretly a Tory agent !

[1] Thomson, ii, Appendix. [2] Add. MSS. 9123.

Vanbrugh's anger exploded. He wrote to the Duchess at white heat, and let her see she had for once met her match for straight talk.

" When I writ to your Grace on Tuesday last ", he wrote on the Thursday, " I was much at a loss what could be the ground of your having dropped me in the service I had been endeavouring to do you and your family with the Duke of Newcastle, upon your sole motion and desire. But having since been shown, by Mr. Richards, a large packet of building papers sent him by your Grace, I find the reason was that you had resolved to use me so ill in respect of Blenheim, as must make it impracticable to employ me in any other branch of your service.

" These papers, madam, are so full of far-fetched, laboured accusations, mistaken facts, wrong inferences, groundless jealousies and strained constructions, that I should put a very great affront upon your understanding if I supposed it possible you could mean anything in earnest by them, but to put a stop to my troubling you any more. You have your end, madam, for I will never trouble you more, unless the Duke of Marlborough recovers so far as to shelter me from such intolerable treatment."

For the sake of effect, and even of dignity, the letter should have ended there. But Vanbrugh's temper was, in the rare state of being aroused, far beyond caring for dignity, which, as La Rochefoucauld has observed, is a social cloak. Besides, the temptation must have been irresistible to try to sting one who in all her personal dealings had shown herself so little capable of feeling. So he continued, opening an old wound with cruel point :

" I shall in the mean time have only this concern on his account (for whom I shall ever retain the greatest veneration) that your Grace, having like the [late] Queen, thought fit to get rid of a faithful servant, the

Tories will have the pleasure to see your Glass-maker Moor [Hawkesmoor?] make such an end of the Duke's building as her Minister Harley did of his victories, for which it was erected.

I am your Grace's
Most obedient servant
J. VANBRUGH." [1]

But it is plain he was no longer, even formally, her humble servant, and he did not forbear to make one more thrust, probably a reference to the Duchess's threat to publish Mrs. Morley's letters (1711), and he added a postscript:

"If your Grace will give me leave to print your papers, I'll do it very exactly, and without any answer or remark but this short letter attached to the tail of them, that the world may know I desired they might be published."

The Duchess certainly 'had her end', for Sir John had no more to do with the building of Blenheim, and she had managed it in such a way as to clear herself of all blame. Had not the resignation come from him, thus proving her in the right? All the same Vanbrugh's letter stung her, for when, in after years, her own epistle to him explaining the Walter affair fell into her hands, she endorsed it: [2]

"Upon receiving that very insolent letter upon the same month, 'tis easy to imagine that I wished to have had the civility I expressed in this letter back again, and was sorry I had fouled my fingers in writing to such a fellow."

[1] Add. MSS. 9125: Nov. 1716.

[2] So I believe, both from the obvious inference, and from the appearance of the MSS. Previous critics have given it as a second PS. to her letter—but if she had not sent it, why should she want the civility she expressed in it *back again*? If she did not want to express civility, why did she send the letter? Besides, though her epistolary style is downright, it is not downright rude.

BLENHEIM

THE GARDEN SIDE

From Vitruvius Britannicus

Vanbrugh, on his part, wrote an account of the whole thing to the Duke of Newcastle :

" I need make no remarks to your Grace ", he said, prefatory to making them, " upon this abominable woman's proceeding ; which shall not, however, lessen my regard to my Lord Duke, nor good opinion of his grand-daughter, who I do not think has one grain of this wicked woman's temper in her ; if I did, I would not advise you to take her, though with the allay of a million." [1] " She [the Duchess] ", he wrote five days later, " comes off sadly . . . in saying it was my turn to speak, for it was nobody's turn to speak, but those who had something new to say, which I had not, not having seen your Grace ; but she had, having employed Mr. Walter to you . . . She 's not a fool, though she 's a —— worse thing." [2]

The Duke of Newcastle, in fact, was not deterred. Had he not come to an absolute resolution to marry before the winter was over ? Perhaps, too, he remembered that Lady Harriet's other grandmother had been the saintly Margaret Blagge, to whose praise John Evelyn had devoted a whole book.[3] So the negotiations proceeded, resolving themselves into a haggling for terms. The Duchess, however, was not prepared to increase her bid for this particular grandson-in-law, although, according to Vanbrugh, she was " much disposed to persuade the Duke to part with his money, and was only for saving her own ".[4] She had expressly warned the Duke of Newcastle, through Mr. Walter, that she would not now be able to give as much as would have been possible when the proposal was first made, since she now had her Spencer (Sunderland) grandchildren to look after.

And to make matters more complicated, at this most exciting juncture the Duke of Marlborough had a severe

[1] Add. MSS. 33064 : 10th Nov. 1716. [2] Ibid., 15th Nov. 1716.
[3] *Margaret Godolphin.* [4] Add. MSS. 33064 : 15th Nov. 1716.

relapse. It was feared that he would die, and all the members of his family gathered around him. If he did die, of course the whole question of the dowry would be different. The Duke of Newcastle was perplexed. He sent an emissary to both Mr. Walter and Sir John. The latter advised that the suitor should bide his time, for the Duchess would never give what was asked, or anything near it ; " but if my Lord Godolphin should have what is expected he will, [on the Duke's death] then everything might be much easier adjusted than it can be now." [1] But the Duke of Marlborough did not die ; the bargaining went on, and a little later Vanbrugh, after seeing the young woman's father, wrote that the latter approved the match, but ' could not judge what other folks would do ' : " But he is of opinion nobody can help the Birth forward with the Great Lady, but that she must be left to her own throws, and we must wait a little to see what that will bring forth." [2]

The Great Lady did eventually bring forth twenty-two thousand pounds, with which, and the prospect of having a posterity descended from the famous Duke of Marlborough, the bridegroom had to be content. The marriage took place on the 2nd April of the next year ; but the bargain proved bad. The Duchess of Newcastle never bore her lord any children.

If the negotiations brought no material benefit to Vanbrugh, at least he was finally enlightened as to the true character of her Grace of Marlborough, and earned the everlasting gratitude of the Duke of Newcastle. The kindly Duke of Marlborough was, for his part, surprised at no more seeing the good fellow of an architect he had been used to meet at Blenheim and discuss the grounds

[1] Add. MSS. 33064 : 24th Nov. 1716.
[2] Ibid., 27th Nov. 1716.

with so pleasantly. His wife told him he had thrown up the job. And he soon accustomed himself to the change in architects, especially as he was rapidly becoming less and less capable of doing business, preferring to rest himself at St. Albans, and watch his grandchildren acting *All for Love*, with old Mr. Jennings, his father-in-law, in the part of Ventidius.[1]

[1] Molloy, ii. 584.

3

Troubles, and—an Antidote

THE comedy of Blenheim was at an end, but the last act of the Heralds' College farce was yet to be played. It had not been by chance that in the ceremony of degrading the Duke of Ormond, Clarenceux had performed the part of Garter. It was because, the last holder of the place having died, Anstis had been unable to step into it. He was in prison, on suspicion of complicity in the rebellion of '15. But when in 1718 he had cleared himself of the charge, Vanbrugh thought it worth while to fight the old battle over again with him, and spent many hours with the officials concerned, "settling the Windsor point, as to whether Anstis should be allowed to perform any part of Garter's duties".[1] It all seemed to turn on a legal quibble. Vanbrugh urged that in a contest in the time of Charles II, the King had given up the right of nomination, but Anstis contended that Charles had merely waived the right.[2] Waiving beat; so after the 20th April 1718 Vanbrugh had an unpleasant Tory fellow over his head, and one who had threatened to make all the heralds stink.

A few days later he had another disappointment. Sir Christopher Wren, now in the eighty-sixth year of his age, was summarily dismissed his post, "through the intrigues of faction, and the dullness of the first sovereign of the house of Brunswick".[3] But instead of Vanbrugh getting the place, as he had every reason to expect after

[1] Add. MSS. 33064: To Newcastle, f. 137. [2] *D. N. B.*
[3] *Gent. Mag.*, April 1831.

having been offered it in 1716, it was given to a man called Benson, who had "written a pamphlet about politicks", and was 'a very ignorant fellow'.[1] Architecture may not have been his strong point, but he had the merit of being a confirmed Miltono-maniac. He spent his time in erecting monuments, striking coins, setting up busts, and procuring translations of Milton, until, thirsting for further achievements, he conceived a passion for the version of the Psalms by Arthur Johnston, a Scottish physician, and printed many fine editions of it.[2] Vanbrugh's opinion of his new superiors may be clearly gathered from a postscript to a letter he wrote to the Duke of Newcastle, which runs,

"I have writ to Lord Stanhope, to desire he'll speak to our new Earl Marshall, not to let Anstis put any tricks upon me; which he has already attempted in a very Benson-like manner. I have damned luck to have two such fellows get over me." [3]

Altogether that was a terrible spring, in which one blow came huddling on another with scarce an interval, and the third of these was——Blenheim! If the comedy was over, it was to have an epilogue, one indeed, almost as long, and much more rancorous than the play itself. In the Easter Term of 1718 certain workmen at Blenheim, not having yet been paid the whole of the balance owed them by the Treasury, sued the Duke of Marlborough for the sum of seven thousand, three hundred and fourteen pounds, sixteen shillings, and fourpence, together with the interest from the year 1710, making in all some eight thousand pounds. Moreover, since Vanbrugh had signed the contracts as for the Duke,[4] they bracketed his

[1] Hearne, 8th May 1718. [2] *Dunciad*, and Warburton's notes.
[3] Add. MSS. 33064: Dec. 1718.
[4] See Add. MSS. 19591: copies of contracts. They are signed by Vanbrugh in Marlborough's name.

name with his Grace's. Once more he was involved in a quarrel which was none of his. The Duke fought the case, not that it would have much inconvenienced him to pay the sum, but he considered the debt was not his; it was the late Queen's. The Court of Exchequer, however, decided against him, and when he appealed to the Lords, his appeal was rejected.[1]

But the Duchess, in whose hands the Duke's affairs virtually rested, was not to be so easily defeated. She forgot her old promise to Vanbrugh that she would always be endeavouring to be out of his debt, and tried to make him responsible for hers! The enraged architect, who considered that on the other hand it was the Duchess who owed him money, wrote thus of the affair to Tonson:

"I have the . . . misfortune of losing (for I now see little hope of ever getting it) near £2,000 due to me for many years service, plague and trouble, at Blenheim, which that wicked woman of Marlborough is so far from paying me, that the Duke being sued by some of the workmen for work done there, she has tried to turn the debt due to them on to me, for which I think she ought to be hanged."[2]

Her Grace's contention was that the work being charged for was unauthorized—she would not easily forget, or forgive, those walks at the Manor House—but Vanbrugh indignantly replied,

"I made no steps without the Duke's knowledge while he was well; and I made none without the Duchess's after he fell ill; and was so far, I thought, from being in her ill opinion, that even the last time I waited on her and my Lord Duke at Blenheim, she showed no sort of dissatisfaction at anything I had done."[3]

[1] Coxe, III. cxvi.

[2] 29th Nov. 1719: *Gent. Mag.* 1837, i.

[3] Ward.

No; but she had had up her sleeve that packet of twenty or thirty sides of paper to send to Brigadier Richards.

The most galling part of the affair for the Duchess was that the courts would not view the affair as she did, and refusing to see Vanbrugh as a monster, declined to saddle him with the debt. So to show the world that, as always, she was in the right, in 1721 she composed, and had privately printed, *The Case of the Duke of Marlborough and Sir John Vanbrugh*, of which she gave copies to Lord Chancellor Macclesfield 'to distribute as he pleased'.[1] In it she developed the theme of the faultiness of the warrant, an idea the Lord Chancellor had given her, namely that "the manner in which my Lord Godolphin who was a better Treasurer than a lawyer, thought fit to put this matter, has occasioned all this difficulty".[2] Besides saying that Vanbrugh had not looked carefully enough into contracts, she declared he had tricked Godolphin into giving him the calamitous warrant, of which, until that moment, nobody had ever heard. The Duke, she swore, had known nothing about it, and Vanbrugh had taken devilish good care not to show it him. Finally she boldly taxed the creator of Blenheim with ingratitude. "And if at last", she said, "the charge run into by Order of the Crown, must lie upon [the Duke]; yet the Infamy of it must lie upon another, who was perhaps the only architect in the world capable of building such a house, and the only friend in the world capable of contriving to lay the Debt upon one to whom he was so highly obliged."[3] Her Grace was not strong in sense of humour.

Now it happened that while Atossa was scribbling her

[1] Add. MSS. 9123: 28th April 1721.

[2] Ibid. Not dated, simply June, but put among 1723/4 papers.

[3] *Case*, quoted by Ward. I have so far been unable to obtain a copy of the case even at the British Museum.

Case at top speed, Vanbrugh was in more considered manner preparing his *Justification of what he Depos'd in the Duchess of Marlborough's late Tryall*;[1] the Duchess's, for he could not believe that this fiend's work was that of the poor, sick Duke, who, whatever his faults, was a gentleman. It was " thought fit ", he said,

"(by those who since his Grace's indisposition have taken upon them the conduct of his affairs) to try, if it might not be possible to make a short end with those people [the plaintiffs] by (Gallantly) turning the debt upon me ; it was found necessary (and therefore resolved) to declare false what the late Lord Godolphin, has under his honest hand, in the plainest, fullest, and most express terms, declared to be true, viz. . . ."

And here follows the warrant in full.[2]

He went on to state what everybody knew, that the money was a gift from the Queen, and that only Marlborough could dispose of it—and then came the illuminating statement, " yet he would neither sign any order for the issuing of money, nor have the method altered by which it was issued to him without account ". And he continued :

" If there be something *odd* in this, 'tis not from any inconsistencies of *mine*. What I have said to facts is *true*. But why his Grace did not *call* the money his, and yet was willing the Queen and my Lord Treasurer should go on in the same method of *making* it his——I hope I am not to account for . . ."

This was clever ; intelligent people would ' smoke '. But it was obviously inadequate as a counterblast to the sort of thing the Duchess was saying about him, and luckily a copy of her pamphlet came into his hands before his own had gone to press. This was no occasion for

[1] *D. N. B.* says 1718. Surely it must be later. The title was changed to ' Duke '.

[2] See Appendix I.

gallantry : clearly the gloves were off, and he too would use the naked fist. So away he went again.

" Since I writ the precedent paper, I heard there was a sort of Case handed privately about, relating to the Blenheim affair, in which my name was pretty much used.

" I have at last got a sight of it, and find so much decent language in it, fair stating of facts, and right reasoning from them, that one would almost swear it had been writ by a woman. Some answer, however, it shall have."

It did indeed. First Vanbrugh cleared himself of the charge of having allowed, almost connived at, excessive prices. He went into detail of how he had persistently done his best to reduce them, and concluded :

" The Duchess of Marlborough (who so much complains of them), being pleased to build a house at St. James' [Marlborough House] . . . not only employed Mr. Strong and another of the Blenheim masons, but paid them much better prices than we had allowed them there."

That was a damaging statement, and Vanbrugh increased its force by adding what seemed a reservation his known honesty compelled him to make : " 'Tis true she would have gone to law with them, but the Duke would not let her."

He then went into the question of warrants. He pointed out that they sprouted everywhere like mushrooms—that Joyns had one, that Boulter had had one, that Bobart had one—and that the Duchess herself had procured yet another to empower the controllers to sign contracts with the surveyor. " And now will anyone say, my Lord Godolphin was trick't into the warrant he signed to me ? " On the face of it, the whole thing was an absurd, frivolous, not to say clumsy machination.

"Will anyone be so weak as to think (whatever they may resolve to say) That in so many years, and on so many fresh occasions, to pass warrants upon warrants, the Duke never heard what situation, a thing of so near an affection to him, was in?

"Will anyone believe, that in so many quiet, fireside, evening conferences, as happen'd between these two great Lords and her Grace; the manner and method of receiving in, and laying out, these hundreds of thousands of pounds, should never be part of the amusement? Sure, there's some great forgetfulness in this matter.

"But, I am ask't, Why I did not myself, tell my Lord Marlborough of this warrant?

"Why, truly, because the warrant told me, he knew it already? Besides, it was filed in the office with all the other papers."

The Duchess's effusion was easier to answer than Collier's diatribe had been; there were facts. But when Vanbrugh came to treat of the charge of ingratitude, he did so with a burning pen, in the form of *A Letter from a Gentleman in the Town, to a friend in the country.* The subject, of course, is himself.

". . . After having had the misfortune of being turned out of his place of comptroller of the works, and losing that of Garter by offending the Queen on the Duke's account; the state he finds himself in at last is this,

"That without one court favour obtained by the Duke for him in this long tract of years,

"Or any allowance from his Grace ever made him (except a trifle I believe he would not have him name) he has been left to stand upon his own bottom at the tedious treasury for a recompence for his services; where, through a tiresome application of many years, he has to this hour prevailed for little more than his neccessary expenses; and indeed, instead of any reward from the Duke, finds his authority for acting in his service disclaimed, and himself thrown among the workmen, to be torn in pieces for what his Grace possesses and enjoys in the midst of an immense fortune.

" These (and no other) are the Friendships and obligations laid by the Duke of Marlborough upon his faithful and zealous servant

JOHN VANBRUGH."

That was good plain dealing, and the candid exposition of his maltreatment seems to have caused Vanbrugh's friends to rally around him ; for very shortly we find him working for Lord Cobham at Stowe (1718), in the gardens of which, Peterborough was later to tell Pope, " Immensity and Van Brugh appear in the whole " ; altering the stables at Audley End for Lord Braybrooke (1721) and building Grimsthorpe in Lincolnshire for the Earl of Ancaster (1721–4). And this last house, according to some, is his best ;[1] for a little modifying his conceptions of the plastic purpose of architecture, adopting rather Bacon's maxim that " Houses are built to live in, and not to look on ", he made, although still a noble pile, the most habitable of all his dwellings.

In the meantime the Duke took the case into Chancery, for adjustment, upon hearing of which Vanbrugh arranged a private meeting with Joyns and Bobart to prepare their statement, in case they should have forgotten anything.[2]

These reliefs, however, came later, and at the end of 1718, Vanbrugh found himself looking back upon a life of fifty-five years, during which much strenuous and varied activity had not brought him even ease of circumstance. In nearly every venture optimism and simplicity had played him false. In every phase of his life he had inadvertently fallen into a pit, from which it is true, his charm had usually extricated him, but each time only after a severe jar. He was not made for intrigues. At the beginning of 1705 and again in 1715 the stars in their

[1] Blomfield. Also picture. [2] Add. MSS. 9123 : 18th Nov. 1721.

courses had seemed to fight for him, but in the end not even the patronage of the greatest nobles of England had brought him place or fortune. In no single instance had he really gathered the reward of his labours, and in one, fate itself, rather than persons, had conspired to cheat him of it.

This was the theatre. To him, who had written the best comedies of the century, who had built a playhouse, and who had encouraged opera, it had never meant anything but a clogging burden of debt. Others had reaped the benefit of his courage. Swiney, it is true, had lost, and had had to fly the country,[1] but his successor, a member of Parliament of the sinister name of Collier, who had got the thing into his hands by means of some equivocal transactions with the Lord Chamberlain, had made a comfortable haul.[2] It was true that a new ceiling had been put on the theatre, which may have contributed to his success, but in any case, soon after Vanbrugh's retirement music had become popular. Nicolini drew large crowds and a large salary; the *Tatler* went into raptures over him, for while he sang "there was scarce a beautiful posture in an old statue, which he did not put himself in", and Mrs. Tofts, her 'fine-proportioned figure', coupled with the 'exquisitely sweet, silver tone of her voice' created a furore which did not abate until she went off her head.[3] There were, besides, Valentini and Madame de l'Épine, and all these performed at concerts in Vanbrugh's theatre, and were perhaps supported by Signor Conti, playing upon his great theorbo. Sometimes Congreve would initiate a performance, and then only the very best people would be admitted, while Mr. White of the Chocolate House would provide refreshments. Vanbrugh had no doubt beheld with pleasure the growth of a music-loving public and

[1] Boswell. [2] Cibber. [3] No. 115.

the increasing vigour of the opera—the 'silly diversion of the nobility'—which finally anchored itself in the public favour when, in 1709, Handel appeared with *Rinaldo* and seemed to bring back the times of Henry Purcell.[1] But he had only been a spectator, and had never got a penny out of it. When this was added to his other disappointments in surveying, heraldry, and Blenheim, it did not seem as though fortune had fulfilled the promises due to charm, ability, and solid good temper.

True, he had gathered to himself great friends; but if to them he was 'Van', for him they were 'my Lord'. Certainly there was Tonson, with whom success had so well agreed, but he was very busy, often abroad, and was seldom to be met in the houses where Vanbrugh was a constant guest. So it is not to be wondered at that in the midst of his troubles his reveries should have led him to consider the balm of having some one near him who would give something more intimate, more warm, than the fellowship of dukes and earls, some one who would be permanently on his side—in fact, of having a wife. In spite of the uncertainties, in defiance of the mockery that would fall upon one who had always set up for so argumentatively confirmed a bachelor, would not marriage be worth while?

For his old flame Mrs. Yarburgh was dead: no more would he interchange ideas or dilate upon his troubles with that understanding lady. But when, spending the Christmas of 1718 with the Earl of Carlisle at Castle Howard he once more met her daughter Henrietta,[2] very charming in the mourning she wore for her mother, he felt that the gift of sympathy was hereditary. And moreover the young woman would need protection now, and yet at twenty-five was old enough to be helpful and sensible. He wavered a moment, reasoned. It would be

[1] Gosse, Ashton. [2] See Appendix II.

such a difficult thing to announce; he would have to guard himself with jokes and excuses, treat it all lightly, be the first to make the witty remark, and throw it all off as an affair of no moment. On Christmas Day he wrote to the Duke of Newcastle—as a sounder—" In short, 'tis so bloody cold, I have almost a mind to marry to keep myself warm ".[1] One must not forget one has been a writer of comedies, and has set up for cynicism. And on the 14th January married he was.

Ten days later he found he had to write to the Duke about his castle at Nottingham, to enlarge upon what he had said in a previous letter about its ' stairing you in the face with a pretty impudent countenance ' until you got used to it.[2] And when he had done that, he confessed the fact of his marriage. He spoke of his wife, saying that her " principal merit in my eyes has been some small distant shadow of those valuable qualifications in her your Grace has formerly with so much pleasure heard me talk of . . .", and as the Duke had himself fallen to those very qualifications, he would not after that be able to say much. And the point was driven home

" The honour she likewise has of being pretty nearly related to the Duchess [was not her grandmother also a Blagge, if not the saintly Margaret Godolphin, at all events her sister?] [3] gives me more hopes I may not have been mistaken. If I am, 'tis better however to make a blunder towards the end of our life, than at the beginning of it. [At any rate I was not so foolhardy as you!] But I hope all will be well; it can't at least be worse than most of my neighbours which every modest man ought to be content with. And so I am easy.[4]

" P.S. Jacob [Tonson] will be frightened out of his Witt, and his religion too, when he hears I'm gone at

[1] Add. MSS. 33064: 25th Dec. 1718.
[2] Ibid., 17th Dec. 1718.
[3] Robinson.
[4] Add. MSS. 33064: 24th Jan. 1719.

last. If he is still in France, he'll certainly give himself to God, for fear he should be ravished by a gentlewoman. I was the last man left between him and ruin."

The jest was carried forward in the postscript to the next letter; "I have just now an account that a gentleman arrived from Paris saw friend Jacob in a Frock".

Certainly it was Tonson of whom he was most afraid, widower Tonson, to whom he had sworn an oath of perpetual celibacy, and who was full of such caustic jokes upon matrimony. It was more than six months before he dared open his heart to him, and by that time he was tolerably sure he had not made a 'blunder'. In this letter he spoke first of their common friends who had died, leading deftly from this sorrowful theme to that of his own felicity. And we no longer have the sense of a slightly ludicrous old gentleman, rather like the Heartwell of Congreve, or his own Heartfree, terrified of horns and ironic laughter, but rather of a man who is almost a propagandist.

"Here has been such a slaughter of old friends since you went", he wrote, "I wish those who are left may share enough in your affections to incline you to think of England with any pleasure. I don't know whether you'll reckon me amongst the first or last, since I have taken that leap in the dark—marriage. But though you should date me with the former, I know at least you would be glad to know how 'tis in this (perhaps) your future state; for you have not forgot it was ever agreed, if I fell, you'd tremble. Don't be too much dismayed, however. After six months I have not repented. Thus far 'tis possible you may believe me; if I offer at more 'tis like you won't, so I have done." [1]

Thus gaily, at fifty-five, Vanbrugh embarked upon yet another hazardous adventure.

[1] 1st July 1719: *Gent. Mag.*, July 1836.

4

Fuga

And since he never did repent, it comes about that the tale of the last years of Vanbrugh's life reads like a three-part fugue. In it the melodies, cheerful or tinged with gloom, interweave rapidly, making in the main an harmonious whole. It is not a perfect piece ; there are one or two discords, a passage now and again that does not seem quite relevant ; but then, we are dealing with life and not with a work of art. Moreover, if the composition is not one in which passion has fused all the elements to a single issue, it is because we have to do with a simple, generous man, who liked to take life as he found it, and who sometimes, half humorously, lost his temper.

The principal theme is a broad one, and serene—the domestic happiness of a man for whom ecstatic self-surrender must be, by the nature of things, a far-away memory. And, as should be in a good fugue, it recurs constantly, and seems to include the whole, while the other themes, though formally opposed, are made to harmonize. Some of the ideas used in earlier portions of the suite recur here, either developed and enriched, or fleetingly suggested. Of the two remaining contrapuntal subjects, friendship has grown stronger, bolder, and more secure ; the duel with the Duchess of Marlborough more plangent. Now and again we are reminded that Vanbrugh built the first Haymarket theatre, that he helped to establish opera in England, or that he is a herald and a playwright. All the time we are conscious that the fugue is written for a rich, mellow instrument, from which the

J. Richardson pinx. 1725 · J. Faber fecit 1727

Sr. John Vanbrugh Knt.

Comptroller of His Majties Works & Clarenceux King of Arms.

OB. 26 March 1726 Æt. 60.

notes ring in clear and manly fashion, not admitting, it is true, of much subtlety, but of a full and endearing tone.

Although with his engaging candour, his transparent honesty, and his simplicity, Vanbrugh had a few remarkable successes in the difficult art of human relationships, his very qualities told against him in the outer commerce of the world. In his later years the daily traffic with men seemed to him increasingly hard. In the old days it had all seemed so easy. He had with his wit stormed the citadel of the *literati*; he had charmed away the opposition of the heralds; had refused to quarrel with a man set up against him, Boulter; and had, on occasion, temporarily won over even the Duchess of Marlborough. But by the end of 1719 there were few of the old circle left. Rowe no more lay abed all day for his ease and sat up all night for his pleasure; nor would Addison ever again in this world frown upon any man's laughter. Garth, who such a short ten years ago had raced the next fattest man in London, the Duke of Grafton, for three hundred yards along the Mall and 'to his immortal glory beat',[1] had quietly departed, saying that life was not worth the daily trouble of tying one's shoelaces. Congreve, who with Tonson seemed one of the last links with Dryden—unless one should include his old rival, Elkanah Settle, 'poet to my Lord Mayor's show'—was lapped in retirement, submerged by obesity, cataract, and gout. Walsh was eleven years dead. Even the adversaries had gone. Swift was in Dublin, eating out his ambitious heart, and Prior, after for a short time bearing on his shoulders the whole opprobrium of the Treaty of Utrecht, had retired to the country. In the place of the old lions there was an unlicked whelp called Pope, who wrote spiteful verses about Blenheim, and a

[1] Montagu, Oct. 1709.

young protégé of Tory Lords called Gay. The Kit-Cat, in Vanbrugh's estimation 'the best club that ever was', existed no more, and the brilliant weekly assembly at the Fountain Tavern had given place to a solemn symposium of freemasons.

And although the Whigs were in power the sense of security in their patronage was gone; they did not seem able to protect their friends. They were not of the old race who gambled in crowns; they speculated instead in Mississippi and South Sea Stock. The worst of all signs of the times, however, were the upstart underlings who did not know Vanbrugh, and the members of the new dynasty who were guilty of the same ignorance. The world seemed, indeed, composed of Bensons and Anstises of all grades, and on one occasion Vanbrugh felt so oppressed by this new atmosphere of scrambling contention, that he wrote to the Duke of Newcastle, "I thought twenty times yesterday I must have dropped down dead".[1]

The most humiliating circumstance was that King George had no great opinion of Sir John Vanbrugh. Perhaps he had heard adverse opinions upon Blenheim such as Pope held—there was nothing of the grotto about Blenheim—or had spoken about it with Lord Berkeley of Stratton, who thought it looked "like a great college with a church in the middle, for the hall looks like one".[2] The house, as yet uninhabited, was much visited in those days, and Hearne, aroused from his contemplation of 'rare monkish manuscripts', found it "grand, but a sad, irregular, confused piece of work . . ." In the house he found "nothing convenient, most of the rooms being small, pitifull, dark things, as if designed for——", and here he enumerated persons of a scandalous,

[1] Add. MSS. 33064, f. 137. [2] *Wentworth Papers*, p. 344.

and articles of an intimate nature. " By this work ", he concluded, " we sufficiently see the genius of Vanbrugg." [1] Nevertheless, Vanbrugh had hopes of the King. After all he had knighted him, and the Prince of Wales made him attend him to Hampton Court. Surely if one is in favour with the king's son, one could not be very low in the estimation of the king. But what if the king and his son are not upon speaking terms?

At any rate his Majesty found Vanbrugh too extravagant an architect, and the latter had to beg the Duke of Newcastle to inform the King that he was really not so, as he might judge from the extremely reasonable cost of Lord Chetwind's building. But to indicate that the matter was really of no moment, he added in a postscript, " 'Twas unlucky your Grace was not at the back stairs yesterday, for neither king nor ministers had a word to say to one another ".[2] No doubt they had run out of their stock of bad Latin, in which, for want of a modern language in common, they were forced to converse. But in December 1718 the Treasury was put on the track, and ordered the state of the Board of Works to be examined. But lest their account should be too technically arranged, and accounts are always liable to confuse laymen, Vanbrugh prepared " a plain intelligible paper for [the King] by which he'll see that if the contract had gone on with Benson he had not saved him one shilling; so wildly did that Gent: impose upon the Treasury by giving in false accounts of everything ".[3]

But either the King was not impressed by the plainness of the paper, or it was not intelligible enough for his Majesty; for although Benson was suspended for incompetence, Vanbrugh's plea that he had saved ten

[1] Hearne, 29th May 1717. [2] Add. MSS. 33064. f. 135.
[3] Ibid., f. 175.

thousand pounds a year was not accepted in face of the auditor's report. Not only did he not succeed to the once more vacant place of Surveyor, but he lost the King's work, and the pill was 'a little bitter'. "I don't however", he said, "blame anybody, nor think them wanting." [1]

Still, when one is well over fifty, and knows oneself to be one of the most distinguished men of the time, it is hard to put up with slights, and to remain comparatively poor. And so, in spite of the shake of the shoulders that shows the powerful old brute can yet stand a good deal, there is every now and then a note of complaint in his letters. But this is immediately drowned in the grand fugal theme of domestic happiness, for to balance all ills he has 'a good humoured wife, a quiet house', and finds himself for all that state of matrimony which had 'done so much mischief to many a one' known to himself and Tonson, 'as much disposed to be a friend and servant to a good old acquaintance as ever'. It may not be the pinnacle of ambition, but it is much. So, after once more defending marriage, and declaring that when Tonson's 'old mistress Barnes' twitted him he 'supported her as he did all the other disagreeables', he brought out the theme *fortissimo*:

"I desire to make no such correction in your manners as to stifle one of your jokes upon matrimony; for tho' the chain should happen to hang a little easy about me (by a sort of Messissipy good fortune!) I shall always think of my neighbours as I used to do. And if I should chance at last, to come in for a share of their disappointments, I don't know whether I could not rouse up a little, give the matter a new turn, and reckon when my joke was thrown into the fund I had a better title to a little merriment upon the stock, than before. At least that I always thought I could do, or I had never wed. But more of that if it

[1] Add. MSS. 33064, f. 185.

comes to the trial. I have only to tell you how my wife returns your compliments. She says she is sorry she has not a sister for you ; but she knows them that have. And if you will give her a commission, she'll answer to provide at least as well for you as she has for me . . ."

And here Dame Vanbrugh, tired perhaps of her husband's sentimental vein, or perhaps not altogether relishing the spice of shrewdness behind it all, took up the pen and wrote in her own hand :

" And if you will make one at cards, as I understand you have often done with much finer ladies than I am, I give you my word I will neither cheat nor wrangle.

Your servant

HARRIET V."

Then the letter goes on in Vanbrugh's hand once more :

" I'm much obliged for the advice you give me, to dispose of some money, where you have succeeded so well, [Mississippi or South Sea] and 'tis not out of fear I do not follow it. But to tell you the truth, I have no money to dispose of. I have been many years at hard labour, to work through the cruel difficulties that Haymarket undertaking involved me in, notwithstanding the aid of a large subscription ; nor are these difficulties quite at an end yet, though within, I think, a tolerable view.

" I have likewise had a very hard disappointment of not being made surveyor of the works ; which I believe you remember I might have had formerly, but refused it out of tenderness to Sir Chr. Wren . . .

He tells his old friend of the unscrupulous attacks of ' that wicked woman of Marlborough ', a passage we have already quoted ; then he ends with a magnificent shake, like a lion rousing himself from sleep :

" But I have been so long used to attacks of fortune of these kinds ; and found myself able to bear up against them, that I think I can do so still, though they cost me some oaths and curses . . ." [1]

And the curses come intermittently, for Vanbrugh is on the choppy seas, the winds buffet him, and the tide will not set in the right direction. About his early days there is a feeling of attack ; he seemed to be assaulting the elements—the social elements—but now there is a sense of standing still, of being on the defensive, almost, one would say, of bravely keeping afloat. " I wish I may find a means to change my place in the Board of Works for something else ", he wrote to Tonson at the end of 1719, " being very uneasy in it, from the unparallelled ingratitude of the present surveyor Hewet, who owes his coming entirely to me ; and that in so known a manner, that he has not the confidence to deny it to anybody ; but he 's the son of a w——, and I'll trouble you no more about him." So he squared his shoulders, and entertained Jacob with a few remarks on " the lowering venom that hangs in the countenance of the male-content Whiggs ".[2]

A few weeks later, however, there was a gleam. Steele, with the magnificent recklessness usual with him where his political opinions were concerned, finally cooked his goose by too vehement an opposition to the Peerage Bill. One could be too Whig even for the Whigs. By his *Plebeian* he offended the Lord Chamberlain, none other than his patron the Duke of Newcastle, who saw no objection to the number of peers being limited, and who, by an unjustifiable abuse of arbitrary power, revoked Steele's Drury Lane licence. In Vanbrugh's words, the unfortunate Sir Richard ' work'd a quarrel so high with my Lord Chamberlain ' that his actors were forbidden

[1] 29th Nov. 1719 : *Gent. Mag.* 1837, i. 243.
[2] 31st Dec. 1719 : ibid., i. 479.

to play, and so the patent 'ended in a joke'. A grim one for Steele. The theatre was then handed over to Cibber, Wilks, and Booth.[1] "I take hold of this", Vanbrugh told Tonson, "to call upon those three gentlemen about the stock they had of mine, and think they will be ready to come to some tolerable composition." Indeed he felt he had a right to a little something now, for the opera was flourishing, and "in spite of all the misfortunes and losses that have occasioned more crying and wailing than I believe was ever known before . . . the fine gentlemen of the buskin in Drury Lane, ride about in their coaches".[2]

If crying and wailing make a man absurd, an occasional discreet mention of your troubles to a patron is quite another thing: as long as one does not seem to expect too much. Thus Vanbrugh wrote to the Duke of Newcastle:[3]

"What I mentioned of my hard luck was far from being meant any sort of complaint, either of your Grace, or those others you name, who, I am entirely satisfied, do bear me all good will, and do neither trick me or neglect me. There is nothing your Grace has said, in stating my small affairs, but what is just and true; and I have (in my own thoughts) never once stated them otherwise, so that I have no other meaning, in what I say about them, but to set forth my ill-fortune by way of a little ease. But I am not one of those who drop their spirits, on every rebuff; if I were, I had been under ground long ago. I shall therefore go on, in hopes fortune will one day or other let those help me, who have a mind to it."

No one, however, seemed to have a mind to help

[1] Berguer, Aitken, Cibber.
[2] 18th Feb. 1720: *Gent. Mag.* 1837, i. 479.
[3] August 1720; Palmer, p. 218.

Vanbrugh very substantially. He was made welcome in certain circles in the politest world, but that was all. He would take a party of peers to visit Claremont, and perhaps his brother would be of the party ;[1] sometimes his wife would accompany him, for he records having gone there "not en famille, a bit of a girl popping into the world three months before its time, and so the business is all to do over again" ;[2] or he would join in the revelry at Castle Howard, and write lively accounts of young Lord Wharton's exuberant gaieties.[3] But such distractions are apt to lead to expense, and one can ill afford such things when one is "two boys strong in the nursery" as he in due course was. One then has responsibilities, and has to think of the future. This he did in some measure by obtaining the Earl of Carlisle as godfather to his eldest son ; a gem of the old rock, evidently, for Vanbrugh told the youngster's godfather, "he talks everything, is much given to rhyming, and has a great turn for dry joking. What the seeds may grow to, God knows, they being of a kind that may do his business up hill or down hill, so perhaps on the whole he were as well without them."[4] As things turned out his father need not have been afraid. What 'did his business' was a bullet at Tournay in 1745, when he was not much over twenty years of age.

But if Vanbrugh got little for himself, he was never afraid to ask small benefits for others, and once this caused some friction with his very good friend the Duke of Newcastle. Vanbrugh was really angry at the way his Grace had treated him, and felt constrained to write an upbraiding letter to the young man, in terms which, for

[1] Add. MSS. 33064 : 15th Sept. 1720. [2] Ibid., 1719.
[3] Palmer, p. 217.
[4] 1722 ; Palmer, p. 221.

sheer dignity, might have served Johnson as models for his famous remarks to Chesterfield :

" MY LORD DUKE ", he wrote,

" I never was more surprised at any disagreeable thing, has happen'd to me in my life ; than to find (a day or two ago) your Grace had thrown aside a small domestic, of mine, to make way for another in the King's music.

" When I asked your favour for him, I was so far from designing to press you, if I had found the least unwillingness ; that if you had not granted it to me (as you did) in an easy kind way, at this first word, you had never heard any more of it.

" I thought, after this, there was no need of my troubling your Grace with more talk about the matter ; especially when I observed, you so well remembered, what you had promised ; that a year afterwards (on your own movement, without one word from me) you told Coll. Pelham, while I stood by, I was to have the second vacancy. And that no mistake might happen, you made him minute it down, that moment.

" I must own, my Lord, I did think I had as much pretention to your favour and friendship, as almost any humble servant you had ; and that which made me think so, was, that you used to tell me so. How I therefore come to fall so low in your regards, I can't conceive ; because, I am quite sure I have done nothing to forfeit them.

" If your Grace has been solicited, by greater men than me, for this small matter ; and that your deference to them, has been the reason for passing me by ; I'm sorry there has not been a better ; for I am much of opinion That no Great Man who was enough your friend, to entitle him to ask a favour from you, would have pressed you to grant him this on such terms. Or if he had ; I am sure he had given you a very good reason to refuse him.

" As I could not forbear saying something to your Grace on this occasion, and had not a mind to say very much, I rather chose to do it by writing than otherwise ; and I shall be very glad if your Grace pleases, that we may never have any sort of discussion about it.

I am
Your Grace's
most humble and
obdt servant
J. VANBRUGH." [1]

Significantly there is no postscript.

There is little of the humble courtier there, and such a letter can have only one of two answers—a formal break, or an abject apology. And the Lord Chamberlain seems to have had the grace to make the latter ; indeed, after all that had passed between them only a low dog could have withheld it : for in July 1723 Vanbrugh was not afraid to plead in a postscript for the Duke's late enemy Steele, from whom the characteristic ebullience had departed.

"Happening to meet with Sr Richd Steel tother day at Mr. Walpole's, in Town, he seem'd to be (at least) in the declining way I had heard he was. If it should go otherwise than well with him, your Grace will give me leave to remind you, of what you told me not long since, of your favourable intentions towards me, for that sinecure, the Reversion of which, I now take the liberty to ask of you." [2]

The appeal did not produce the sinecure, but this did not prevent Vanbrugh a few weeks later recommending for a living a ' true Whig clergyman '.

But in the year 1724 it was for himself he had to ask succour, for the trouble at the Board of Works had become acute.

"I have now reason to believe", he told the Lord Chamberlain, " the King has had such an unfair account given him secretly of my management both of his house

[1] Add. MSS. 33064 : 11th Feb. 1722.
[2] Ibid., 30th July 1723.

and gardens ; as must make me appear a very bad officer in the employment he has been pleased to trust me with.

"And I am informed, this representation has been followed with an attempt to have me removed from his service. And that this attempt is in a way of succeeding.

"All I beg is, That my Lord Sunderland will please to obtain his direction to the Treasury, To examine into the truth of my conduct ; and to make an impartial report to him how they find it.

J. VANBRUGH." [1]

There is weariness here, and one misses the usual gay signature 'Van' written with a tremendous arabesque flourish. And though his letters themselves are clear of complaints, the invariable postscripts bear the burden. He will not, he says, ask his friends to get him promoted surveyor, but he would like to be made secure in his present place for life, since

"it must be a cruel reflection upon me in the world, if, in putting another into that station, I have not some mark of the King's favour, to shew, his not being inclin'd to make me his surveyor, does not proceed from any general dissatisfaction with me . . .

"And that the person he thinks to make surveyor may make me some compensation by money, which, I have been honest enough in my station, to stand very much in need of."

Certainly one must live, and at sixty, live well ; but "I apprehend being more out of humour, at this rascally Board of Works than ever".[2] He had come to feel that the world was not treating him rightly ; he had reposed too much trust in the honesty of men, whom he had always expected to be as simple-hearted as himself : and in spite of innumerable instances he would never admit

[1] Ibid., 1724.
[2] Ibid., successive letters to Newcastle, 1724.

that they were not. At the same time he was now a little wounded in his dignity.

If others had always behaved towards him with the generosity he showed his own friends in a lower station of life, all would have been different. Through all his own vicissitudes he was, as we have already seen, eager to help others, and this was especially the case as to his old fellow-workers at Blenheim. It was only because of Benson—who was not above dismissing Hawkesmoor to make room for his own brother [1]—that he had not been able to get Joyns a place in the Board of Works.[2] Thus when in 1723 Joyns was attacked by the Duchess of Marlborough, the builder asked leave to send his solicitor to see Vanbrugh, excusing himself from coming in person on the score of gout.[3] Again, Vanbrugh was delighted to let his house in the country [Greenwich] to Travers, whom he said he would rather have as a tenant than any one else. And when in 1724 Strong brought a case against the Duchess, " The Reply of Sir John Vanbrugh on behalf of the workmen employed in the building of Blenheim, humbly presented to the King's most excellent Majesty ", set forth the case so clearly that Strong won his action.

Yet all his chats to Tonson about the South Sea stock (in which he was like to lose two thousand pounds) ; [4] all his reports to Carlisle about the progress either of the opera or the Paving Bill ; all his accounts of his doings to Newcastle, are tinctured with the memory of the wrongs he suffered at the hands of the outrageous Atossa. Disguise it as he might, his heart was always heavy about Blenheim, his best loved child, the fruit of

[1] Add. MSS. 9123 : April 1722.
[2] Ibid., 19605 : 12th May 1715. [3] Ibid., 20th Oct. 1723.
[4] *Hist. Comm.* xii, App. 6 : To Carlisle, 25th March 1721.

his most arduous labours. Thus in 1719 he wrote to Tonson that he had been to Stowe, " and took Blenheim in my way back, not with any affection (for I am thoroughly wearied) but out of curiosity, the Duchess of Marlborough having taken a run at last to finish it in earnest. . . . He [the Duke] is in point of health much as usual, and, I doubt, not likely ever to grow better. She is likewise, in point of vigour, as she used to be, and not likely to grow worse." [1] This was, however, before the *Case* had reached its full acerbity; but when in 1721 there was talk of Marlborough resigning the Captain-Generalship, he wrote in a slightly different tone to Carlisle.

" This point of Lord Marlborough's quitting has hung these two days, upon her Grace's opposing it, purely I believe for the money; and so I suppose she will haggle for a pension to support the poor old officer and his wife." [2]

The poor old officer did not need support for long, for in the next year he died, without having done more for Vanbrugh than sue him for a debt for which he was not responsible. Even the Duke's image had now fallen from its pedestal in Vanbrugh's mind, and into what small fragments it was smashed his comment on the Duke's will may show. After remarking upon the enormous fortune he had left, Van continued . . ." and yet this man could neither pay his workmen their bills, nor his architect his salary. He has given his widow (may a Scotch ensign get her!) £10,000 a year for five years *to spoil Blenheim her own way*; £12,000 a year to keep herself clean and go to law. . . . She will have £40,000 a year in present." [3] And when the Duke was buried with all the pomp the

[1] 1st July 1719: *Gent. Mag.*, July 1836.
[2] *Hist. Comm.* xii, App. 6: 2nd Feb. 1721.
[3] D'Israeli, Ward, Thomson.

heralds could devise, it was noticed that ‘ Clarencieux was not there ’.[1]

The Duchess did not, however, spoil Blenheim her own way, for she employed Hawkesmoor to finish it according to Vanbrugh's design ; but go to law she did, for contention in the political sphere being now denied her, there was no other atmosphere in which she could thrive. The *Case* still dragged its weary length along, till finally, in 1724 Lord Macclesfield summed it up with perfect common sense and equity, thus pleasing nobody. It was clear, of course, that the Crown was to pay all debts incurred previous to the stoppage ; every one knew that had been Anne's intention. With regard to Vanbrugh it was also clear. It had been an honour to build Blenheim ; he was an official, and could claim no further salary. He could not make any claim for arrears of the four hundred a year he had once had, for that, on his own showing, had been a gratuity, and " a gratuity is quite another thing than a salary ". But if he could make no demand, it was not fair to expect him to reimburse what he had been given. (We can see her Grace had left no stone unturned.) Vanbrugh, the Lord Chancellor stated, had expected influence and place rather than pay.[2] True, Vanbrugh might have retorted, but in default of pay, where was the ‘ something lasting ’?

The architect of Blenheim, however, was not going to let the matter rest there ; the Lord Chancellor might say what he liked, for his part he would still look upon his ‘ gratuity ’ as a salary, and this had not been paid since the building had been taken over by the Duke. Moreover, at that period he had no longer been employed as a Crown servant, for the Crown had no more to do with Blenheim, but as a private architect. He considered some two

[1] Noble. [2] Ad. MSS. 9123 : June [1724 ?].

thousand pounds were owing him. At last Macclesfield, who was evidently wearying a little of the affair, suggested that an examination should be made as to what Vanbrugh deserved, and that what money he had laid out on the work should be repaid him out of the Duke's estate. In the meantime a perpetual injunction was to be made to stay Vanbrugh's proceedings.[1]

But if a legal armistice was thus declared, the Duchess did not dream of allowing personal hostilities to cease, and Vanbrugh was guilty of a tactical error, one might even say of an error in taste. In August 1725, a Castle Howard party, including Lady Carlisle, made up their minds to visit Blenheim, and to take its architect with them. Vanbrugh was delighted at the idea. Here was an opportunity to show his wife his great work, and also for himself to view it in its final state. The end crowns all, and he had not yet seen Thornhill's paintings, nor the statues of 'Marlborough's Misses' arranged in a row outside, nor yet the already crumbling monument Mrs. Freeman had erected to the memory of her poor unfortunate faithful Morley. But the Duchess was too quick for him, as he related in a letter to Tonson :

"We stayed two nights in Woodstock . . . but there was an order to the servants, *under her Grace's own hand, not to let me enter Blenheim* ! and lest that should not mortify me enough, she having somehow learned that my *wife* was of the company, *sent an express the night before we came there*, with orders that if *she* came with the Castle Howard ladies, the servants should not suffer her to see either house, gardens, or even to enter the park ; so she was forced to sit all day and keep me company at the inn ! "[2]

A doleful enough finale, with husband and wife facing

[1] Ibid., 7th Jan. 1725.
[2] 12th Aug. 1725 : *Gent. Mag.* 1837 ; D'Israeli.

each other over the table, or staring helplessly out of the window. One muses whether Vanbrugh's memory strayed back to the joyous revelry of twenty years ago when the foundation stone was laid. No doubt on that day he had blessed his lucky star, and in the glow of wine visioned his future glory. He did not then know that for all these years the great monument to the memory of Blenheim would bring him hardly intermitted trouble, public degradation, and, almost, financial ruin. He could not then foretell that after twelve years of heroic labour, after giving the best of himself in unceasing effort, he would be denied even entry to the place his genius had made. He had not imagined that the end of the work would be taken out of his hands, nor that he would come to execrate the loved, and perhaps too idolatrously honoured name of Marlborough. Instead of place and fortune he had incurred the ridicule of poets and the unjust revilings of a woman, to which now was added an insult his wife was forced to share.

A grim finale. But the curtain was not yet quite rung down. There was still one more speech to be made, in October, and it begins with a terrific rattle like that of a musketry *feu-de-joie*.

" I have been forced into chancery by that b- b- b- b- old b—— the Duchess of Marlborough ", Vanbrugh wrote to Tonson, " where she got an injunction upon me by her friend the late good chancellor, [late, and good, because in June Lord Macclesfield had been degraded for corrupt practices] who declared that I was never employed by the Duke of Marlborough, and therefore had no demand upon his estate for my services at Blenheim ; I say, since my hands were thus tied up from trying by law to recover my arrear, I have prevailed with Sir Robert Walpole [whom the bursting of the South Sea Bubble had made Prime Minister], to help me in a scheme which I proposed to him, by which I got my money in spite of the hussy's teeth, and, that out of a sum she expected to receive into her own hands towards the discharge of the Blenheim debt; and of which she resolved I should never have a farthing. My carrying this point enrages her much, and the more because it is of considerable weight in my small fortune, which she has heartily endeavoured to destroy as to throw me into an English bastile, there to finish my days, as I began them in a French one." [1]

And on that the curtain falls—even the epilogue is over; but in 1739 a faint echo of the comedy amused a world to which 'old Marlborough' was hardly more than a figure in the acid satires of Pope. For the executors of Travers brought a case against the Duchess for the cost of some lodges at Blenheim, and the law found her responsible; of which she complained with all her old raciness of groundless accusation, to her friend the Earl of Clancarty.[2]

But by now Vanbrugh felt the years gathering upon him, and that it was time to begin to close accounts. Already in 1723 he had been ill, had taken the waters at Scarborough, to "return thither with Lord Carlisle for a week's swigging more".[3] And in 1725 he thought he would have done with the gay intricacies of heraldry, so 'disposed in earnest of a place he got in jest, Clarencieux King of Arms', which he did in spite of "very great difficulties and very odd oppositions, from very odd folks". As he said, he 'sold it well', for he got two thousand pounds for a tabard which had cost him nothing.[4]

But before he did so he for the third time had his portrait painted, that he might once more appear to future

[1] 25th Oct. 1725: *Gent. Mag.* 1837.
[2] Marshall.
[3] Add. MSS. 33064: Aug. 1723.
[4] 25th Oct. 1725: *Gent. Mag.* 1837.

ages wearing about his neck the coroneted ornament of Clarenceux King. Richardson shows us him with a face grown fuller than it was in earlier years, almost fleshy indeed, and he wears the look of a man who has worked hard and lived well. Instead of a pair of compasses as in Kneller's picture, he holds in his still beautiful hand a plan of Blenheim, as though it were with that place above all others he would wish his name to be associated. His clothes are rich, and flow about his body as luxuriantly as his heavy wig flows about his head. He stands in a commanding attitude, not pompously, but as one who knows his worth. His eyes have lost their caressing look, and indeed one would say that not far behind them smoulder the dull fires of anger. Yet there is humour about his mouth, congruous with the fact that he was once the rival of Congreve, and has an unfinished comedy, *The Journey to London*, in his desk. A grand old brute, one would say, able yet to face a world he does not seem quite to understand.[1]

As far as posterity is concerned, the picture was done only just in time. For in March of the following year he was attacked by a quinsy, of which, on the 26th, he died.

And so, generous to the last, and still too simple-hearted for his time, John Vanbrugh, cheerful and unbowed, passed from the boisterous scene. Perhaps of all those who had known him well only 'old Marlborough', eaten up with rage and litigation, was glad. Even those who had had but small acquaintance with him regretted his going. Swift and Pope, when they published their miscellany confessed that "In regard to

[1] Portraits. Kneller Kit-Cat, reproduced in Mermaid edition. An engraving may be seen in the Print Room at the British Museum. The National Portrait Gallery portrait is reproduced in Palmer. This portrait is reproduced in Ward.

two persons only, we wish our raillery, though ever so tender, or resentment, though ever so just, had not been indulged. We speak of Sir John Vanbrugh, who was a man of wit and honour; and of Mr. Addison." But nothing could silence that 'poor dog' Dr. Abel Evans, whose spiteful words earn him a mean immortality for as long as Vanbrugh's name shall be remembered:

> Under this stone reader, survey
> Dead Sir John Vanbrugh's house of clay.
> Lie heavy on him earth, for he
> Laid many a heavy load on thee.

Indeed, ever since the 31st March 1726 the earth of St. Stephen's, Walbrook, crowned by a masterpiece of Wren, has lain upon him as heavily as need be; but ever and anon his name has arisen to receive the praises of a Reynolds or the plaudits of a Hazlitt, while in our day he holds an honoured place in architecture as well as in letters. If his spirit haunts the earth, it may have smiled in the last century at hearing the familiar voice of the puritan raised in protest against his 'licentiousness',[1] but I do not think it will have paid much heed. Rather, I believe, does his spirit wander about his homely Maze Hill at Greenwich, whence it will take a turn about the Hospital to see how the façade is wearing; or it will flit to see what is going on at His Majesty's Theatre in the Haymarket, on the site of his old, unfortunate venture. No doubt it will sometimes visit Blenheim, to which now no one can, nor would, deny it entry; but it will not linger about his old house in Whitehall. For heavier than the earth lies upon his clay, heavier maybe than the palace of Blenheim rests upon the earth of Woodstock, the ponderous mass of the War Office sprawls over the indifferent site of his cosy, comfortable, ridiculed 'goose-pie'.

[1] e.g. *Gent. Mag.*, Jan. 1836.

THE FIRST VICTORIAN

"To be negligent of what any one thinks of you, does not only show you arrogant, but abandoned."—*Spectator*, 104.

"There are many more shining qualities in the mind of man, but there is none so useful as discretion."—*Spectator*, 225.

To

F. H. Jeffery

Preliminary

The Victorian contribution to the art of social existence is in itself a remarkable achievement, and certain of its striking aspects are here to the point.

Englishmen living in full nineteenth century had a dangerous period of revolution to all appearance well behind, and still with them, a memory of military triumphs. They were filled with a sense of performance comparable to that felt by the Elizabethans, fortified by a complacence probably unique in the history of mankind. Their very recantations, their violent conversions, did not shake, but strengthened their certitude, for they believed that in them the soul of man had at length reached its continuing city. Preceding ages, such was their conviction, might have seen the blossom of humanity, but this, at any rate as far as concerned modernity, saw the fruit. Experience had come to ripeness in them, bestowing upon the world rich, delicious, and above all nourishing produce; and it behoved them to do justice to their good fortune.

Moreover, and here is the magnificence, if they felt bound to live up to this splendid conception, the universe in its turn had to live up to them. It was the old story, with a touch of transcendentalism to give a due tinge of awe to the age-weary thought: If the cosmos did not tally with their idea of it, so much the worse for the cosmos. Thus, knowingly or unknowingly, they seated themselves on the German mystic idealism that marched queerly enough with the harsh realities of the French Revolution. The comfortable cushion of this 'metaphysic pneumatic' offered conveniently, and they dumped heavily down upon it.

It is not easy to deduce their view from the most prominent figures, except where, as in Matthew Arnold's case, they are definitely in revolt against their time.[1] We must gather it rather from those who did not seem to realize that the view was there to be held, for it is the innocent who are the true recipient vessels of faith. Thus it need not surprise us if we find its most perfect expression in the casual remarks of one of the most accepting of men, one who did not look beyond the society of his time, or seek to question its assumptions. It is perhaps in the autobiography of Anthony Trollope that we can best perceive the exact social magnitude of the age, and we may take as the very marrow the passage where he compares the works of Annie Thackeray with those of Rhoda Broughton. By implication accusing the former of some insipidity, the latter directly of giving too much life to her figures, " making them speak as men and women do speak ", he goes on to say that Miss Broughton's novels " are not so sweet-savoured as are those by Miss Thackeray, and are, therefore, less true to nature ". In the mouth of a late eighteenth-century philosopher the remark would have been merely the expression of a sensitive optimism : here it reveals a sense of ' that ineradicable taint of sin ', of being, at bottom, something one abhorred, and to which one must as the most elementary basis of decent behaviour be blind.

" And are, therefore, less true to nature," It is staggering, it is monstrous if you will, but it is also sublime. The Victorians wished the world to wear certain features, and wear those features it did. They seemed to say with Spinoza " Per realitatem et perfectionem idem intelligo ", using the words as though they were plain English. It is the very matter of factness of

[1] See his scathing remarks in the preface to *Essays in Criticism*, 1865.

Trollope's phrase that reveals the extent to which our grandfathers definitely created the world. Such daring is now far beyond our wildest conceptions ; we should regard it as levity, as wanting in fundamental seriousness, as treating life too much like a game. We should be reminded of Belinda in *The Rape of the Lock* when " Let spades be trumps ! she said, and trumps they were ". But no taint of doubt crept into the really Victorian mind ; no heretical misgivings were allowed to tarnish the fair face of ' truth ' ; and to declare dubiety an honourable principle was well left to the naughty paradox-makers like Professor Huxley. To this extent the Victorian conception was a superb vindication of the liberty of the human spirit.

The medal, however, had its less pleasing reverse. The ideas involved an intolerable subjection of the individual ; the ideal was an idol that called for an unthinkable amount of spiritual blood. It could hardly have been otherwise, for it is probable that such an attitude of mind can maintain its validity only in the practice of the *qu'en dira-t-on*?—what will the neighbours say? philosophy, which was then, in fact, so remarkably developed, that acute thinkers reduced the sensation of conscience to the workings of the *qu'en dira-t-on* ? alone. But to us, it need hardly be said, the conception itself seems untrue to nature, harsh, rigid, stifling, extremely distasteful, apart from the hypocrisy the need for at least an apparent consistency involved. Hypocrisy, indeed, was itself ' virtue ', ' morality ' the subjugation of the old Adam. There was nothing insincere about it—it has even been held that such a struggle alone constitutes the personality—it was merely that the Victorians were impervious to their own paradox that to be moral one had perforce to be *un*true to nature, to do violence to one's instincts. They were startled to hear of the opposition of the 'ethical process' to the 'cosmic process'; it was what one might expect from a notorious atheist. And they stuck to their virtue. They would not see that although it may in individual cases be admirable for a man to force his emotions to conform to a conception of life, the general adoption of such a habit is bound to lead to lies. It is not surprising that under those conditions the honesty of a Newman should have been suspect, but what cannot fail to astound us is the rapidity with which the philosophy of the *qu'en dira-t-on?* came to be almost universally accepted. The days of "Publish and be damned!" seem centuries away, Palmerston an anachronism—as, indeed, the Queen only too acutely felt. How Mr. Creevey would have shuddered! How Shelley would have mocked and stormed! Each from opposing points might have asked, "How in the name of Heaven had society become permeated with this pernicious outlook?"

The frame of mind was, partly, the first-fruit of bourgeois power; the revolution had after all not been left behind. It was the effort of the middle classes to make good, to show that they too had a standard and so a right to leadership. Under those conditions it was obvious that what the neighbours said was of the first importance, for now society was organized on a broad bottom, that of the Reform Bill of '32. It did not matter if the individual did suffer so long as the community benefited. Individual sin as much as individual virtue became impossible, a contradiction in terms, for one could never be free from responsibility to one's neighbours, who—did they not themselves declare it?—walked hand in hand with God. *Vox populi, vox Dei.* There were, possibly, facts that seemed to contradict the theory that everybody acted for his neighbours' good in the full glow of the middle-class virtues; but these were best ignored, at any rate not talked about. The great sin was to let one's sin be seen, because then the appearance was ruined, confidence shaken. Such facts were not really true to nature, taken in its totality, so they could be set aside when it was not possible to hide them. By such sentimental discipline the richer bourgeoisie held firm in perplexity—a not unnatural bewilderment in a difficult medium, for times were changing with distressing speed, a change known as the Industrial Revolution.

And—it is here our subject intrudes—it is significant that the great example the Victorians fetched from the past world to serve as a model of conduct and the ideal of character, was Joseph Addison. His first extensive biography, by Miss Aikin, appeared in the early 'forties, to be reviewed by Macaulay in an almost lachrymose appreciation of the man. To his own age, the historian declared with a pride that overwhelmed regret, had been left the honour of erecting in the Poets' Corner a statue to the author of *The Loves of Hilpa and Shalum*. At last Addison had come into his heritage; at last, in the Victorian age, his soul could move among its peers. To them the voice of the present seemed to speak out of the past. Here, amazingly before his time, was a man who believed firmly in their own social philosophy, whose behaviour was regulated by what he would like his neighbours to think of him. Here, that is, was a man truly moral, and enough of an idealist to be blind to the things he did not wish to see.

It is true that Addison's mask was not so intact as that of the Victorians: having less sense of sin, he could allow a few cracks, such as are evidenced by many passages in the Vision of Justice[1] and other essays, where he makes statements as to the violations of the marriage tie that belong at farthest date to the era of Lamb and the *Chapter upon Horns*. The later admirers of Addison did their best to ignore such passages, they passed them by with expressions of regret, they were not true to Addison's nature, they were probably interpolations by Steele; for they contained admissions such as no true Victorian could possibly make: for though Victorianism was largely due to the earlier effects of the Industrial Revolution, it was also a little the fault of the Romantic Revival.

If the fructifying influence of the nineteenth century ripened society into clusters of edifying grape, it is only fitting that the age of Anne should have produced at least one Addison. For that age too had a period of revolution behind it, if not so securely behind; that age too, thanks to the defeat of Louis XIV, its sense of power; finally, in the last Stuart reign the middle classes were beginning to come into their own, and were in consequence trying to settle their values—for times were changing with distressing speed, a change known as the growth of the party system. Addison was the priest, and would-be prophet of these classes, and as such his philosophy unavoidably contained many elements in common with that of the Victorians.

It was a philosophy peculiarly suitable, for under Anne ideas of civic duty were gaining strength. After a tumultuous period security was coming to seem more desirable than freedom; and in consequence, passion, with capacity for enjoyment and success in obtaining it, was no longer given its proper, Renaissance, value, or being admired. The cynicism of a Wharton was not

[1] *Tatlers*, 100, 102.

regarded as an ornament to ability as it had been in the case of Shaftesbury or the Marquis of Halifax, and a typical social figure of the time would be not Etherege, but Dr. Garth. Public opinion was becoming operative, set in its course by such men as Jeremy Collier, and of all the distinguished figures of that age, it is Addison who was the most markedly sensitive to it. It was indeed to this very sensitiveness that he owed his distinction.

How far Addison was before his time may be judged by the attitude towards him of the eighteenth century, on the whole one of admiration, yet shot with doubt, tinged with a curious uneasiness amounting almost to dislike. It is as though in face of so astonishing a reputation no one quite dared tell the truth. Fielding, it is true, is frank enough in his poor opinion,[1] but Horace Walpole's derogatory utterances appeared only in his private letters,[2] and even Johnson seemed afraid to express his real view, though in the *Life* he did not overmuch mince certain incidents. In conversation the sturdy Doctor fought against the middle-class worship of a character he could not altogether like. One day when discussing Addison's behaviour to Steele in the matter of his debt, Boswell "mentioned to him that some people thought Mr. Addison's character was so pure that the fact, *though true*, ought to have been suppressed. He saw no reason for this. 'If nothing but the bright side of characters should be shewn, we should sit down in despondency, and think it utterly impossible to imitate them in *any thing*.'"[3]

The Victorians felt none of this despondency; they

[1] *A Journey from this World to the Next*, viii.

[2] e. g.: To Mr. West, 2nd Oct. 1740.
To Sir H. Mann, 14th May 1759.
To Rev. W. Cole, 12th July 1778.

[3] Boswell's *Life*, iv. 50, 1781.

were, so to speak, *à la hauteur*. For Miss Aikin, Addison was a hero who could do no wrong, make no mistake. She rejected the story about Steele; it was not true to nature. Macaulay went a step farther. With his schoolboy enthusiasm and lack of subtlety, with his black is black and Whig is probably white, he justified, even praised the action Dr. Johnson could not condone and Miss Aikin would not accept. For he worshipped Addison barely this side idolatry. Indeed, what else could he do? Addison's whole theory of life, his sense of 'the good, the beautiful, the true', his air of condescending superiority towards women, insufferable to us, fitted so exactly into the Victorian's conception of what things should be. His very method was identical with theirs; like them he believed hypocrisy was "to be preferred to open impiety".[1] Thackeray, to be sure, seems to have been a little uncomfortable, if we have read correctly between the lines of *Esmond*—but for him also the current philosophy proved too strong; he was forced to *come* to bless, even if he stayed to wriggle.

But to arrive at a clear view of Addison is no easy matter; there remains always something puzzling, even baffling about him. In his life there are such a number of little points, trifling events, each in themselves of small significance, that adding up to a body of unexplained material make it seem as though somewhere there had been deliberate and consistent distortion of facts, or at least burking of issues. He has always been a trial to biographers. Tyers, prefacing his essay, remarked sadly:

"If Mr. Addison . . . had been the Plutarch of his own life (for Plutarch enters into a thousand interesting particulars, and brings his hero into the closet) it must

[1] *Spectator*, 458.

have made an entertaining volume ; though the modesty and diffidence that accompanied him through every scene of life would have prevented him from enlarging on a multitude of things to his own glory and the disadvantage of others. For on many occasions he chose rather to hide himself than to be seen." [1]

It is, indeed, his extraordinary gift for secrecy, almost amounting to a craze for mystification, that makes him so inviting a study. In truth he was no Rousseau—he never gave himself away. Montaigne, he shrewdly observed, would have passed for a much better man 'had he kept his own counsel '.[2] He would profit by the example : there was no quality in the mind of man more useful than discretion, and his history, his reputation after death, are triumphs of a life regulated on this precept, and on those others which typical Victorians did their best worthily to inherit.

[1] Tyers. [2] *Spectator*, 562.

I

EDUCATION

I

School and University

ONE day in or about the year 1682 a ten-year-old boy, his tear-stained face white and anxious, slipped into the woods about Amesbury. He had been naughty at school; and, in dread of punishment, his whole being shrinking in agony at the thought of degradation before his schoolfellows, he was running away to hide. He felt prepared to face anything rather than the mortification of mockery, of being publicly humbled, and for two or three days fed on nuts and berries, sleeping in a hollow tree. At last he was found and brought home to his father, the Reverend Lancelot Addison, rector of Milston near Salisbury.

A year or so later the school at Lichfield was about to break up, and the boys, in a state of ebullience proper to the occasion, conceived the idea of barring the master out of his own house—a school prank in those days not uncommon. And the very same boy who had been so timid at Amesbury was the leader of this bold sally, having been entered at the school when his father transferred to Lichfield as Dean of the Cathedral.

" If these stories be true," Macaulay wrote, " it would be curious to know by what moral discipline so mutinous and enterprising a lad was transformed into the gentlest and most modest of men." These stories are apocryphal, and they seem to reveal an ambition far from modest, a desire indeed to lead, to count for something among his fellows, coupled with an almost morbid fear of failure and a horror of being made to look ridiculous. But rather than invoke the dubious effects of moral discipline, would it not be just as curious to know whether the child were not after all father to the man? We might even find his days bound to each other by the most natural unity.

After a short period at the Charterhouse he went at the age of fifteen to Queen's College, Oxford, a studious, timid boy, ignorant of the world but conversant with the classics. And the change from the quiet cloisters of his school to the Oxford of 1687 may well have been disturbing, for one college of the University was actually in dogged rebellion against its King, that divinely appointed monarch to whom only two years before the ancient foundations had vowed enthusiastic, not to say abject, submission.

At this time James, riding ever more recklessly the prancing horse of Popery, flushed with his success in Ireland—where Tyrconnel was serving majesty's religious purposes with as much zeal as he had in earlier days ministered to its amours [1]—thought he could now stretch his converting hand towards the centres of learning. Baffled at Cambridge, where a trembling Vice-Chancellor, John Pechell, had from behind a Bardolphian nose, and in the face of the terrific Jeffreys himself, maintained it was more fitting to grant honours to Moslems than to Papish priests,[2] he turned his eyes towards the sister University. Oxford, with its tradition of being "farther behind the age than any other portion of the British people", seemed to offer a fair field. But

[1] Grammont, ix.
[2] Burnet, 1686; Macaulay, *Hist.* II. viii; Pepys, 5th April 1667.

such a tradition, although it has its drawbacks, carries with it the often useful virtue of extreme jealousy of privilege, and the King met with an opposition that did much to rally against him the tempers of his people.

The occasion arose on the death in 1686 of the President of Magdalen College. The King arbitrarily ordered the Fellows to elect in his stead a certain Dr. Farmer, which gross infraction of right was made the more intolerable by Farmer being a convert to the Romish persuasion; and the Fellows, not having received a reply to their contrary petition, ignored James's order, and proceeded to elect one of themselves, Dr. Hough, a man of learning, and of solid Anglican principles. The King was furious, but in view of the exposure the college made of Farmer's character, which was vilely disgraceful, even the court party had not the face to insist upon the choice. All that could be done was to order the college to annul their election; but that body maintained it could not adopt this procedure, as it was contrary to oath. The illegally revived Court of High Commission was instructed to give judgement on the matter; and its members, evidently thinking with Dryden that

> Colleges on bounteous Kings depend
> And never Rebel was to Arts a Friend,

took on their own shoulders the responsibility of abrogating the oath. They declared the election void and the Fellows in suspension; whereupon the King nominated Parker, Bishop of Oxford, to the vacancy. Parker was an excellent man, who not only was so far a Papist as to think it idle to attend Protestant worship, but held stimulating views on the position of royalty. He contended that "the ordinary form of saying the King was under God and Christ was a crude and profane expression; . . that though the King was under God, yet he was not under Christ but above him ".[1] The Fellows of Magdalen, however, were not to be seduced even by this ingenious prelate ; they declared it was not in their power to elect Parker, and remained in suspension.

When the King visited Oxford in 1687 he summoned the Fellows before him, rated them in ' foul and angry ' terms, and swore that if they did not incontinently elect his good bishop, " they should feel how heavy a hand the King had ".[2] The body of electors, though professing humility, remained gloriously stubborn : Hough they had chosen and Hough they would have. Thereupon a minor ecclesiastical commission, armed with full powers, was sent to deal with the question—and with the Fellows. It declared Parker President, and since Hough refused to deliver the keys of his house, the doors were burst open, and lawn sleeves forcibly installed in the place of the scarlet hood. All the Fellows but two flocked away, leaving their posts comfortably open to Papists, twelve of whom were admitted in one day.[3]

And, except that Parker died and was replaced by a Roman bishop called Giffard, there the matter rested until the next year, while the vessel of Popery and prerogative, helmed by Father Petre, sailed ever closer to the rising wind of protest. The new occupants of Magdalen felt comfortable enough ; but all at once, at the beginning of October, the King relented, and sent an order for the reinstatement of Hough and the original Fellows.[4] News had been brought him that William of Orange was about to set sail. But a north-west gale drove back the Dutch fleet, with the loss, it was declared, of " nine men of war, a thousand horses, and Dr. Burnet ",[5] so the concession was recalled, and Giffard stayed.

[1] Burnet, 1686. [2] Reresby, 1687. [3] Green, ii. 632.
[4] Tindall, 1st Oct. 1688. [5] Traill, p. 29, footnote.

However, Dr. Burnet was not lost, nor was the Revolutionary cause ; and when the King's nephew landed on the 5th November, Hough and his electors made ready to return and settle down once more to their splendid, if somewhat unjustified, tradition of high Toryism.

The game of history thus played is alone an education, an education that forced itself upon the notice of the young, plastic-minded student. However distant the secluded places of learning might seem from the bubbling centre of affairs, however much the boy might be intent upon writing an impeccable copy of Latin verses, he could not ignore the struggle that had taken place on his doorstep. The case of the seven bishops might seem a long way off, as far as it did to Etherege in Ratisbon, but that of Dr. Hough was fought under his nose. Moreover, he was involved in its results ; for in 1689, the previous year's elections having lapsed, the Fellows of Magdalen proceeded to a 'golden election' of double the usual number of honours, and Addison became a demy.

We learn only what we are prepared to digest, and by these events young Addison was taught, not what the righteous courage of revolutionaries may accomplish—for the Fellows of Magdalen were far from earning that title—but the folly of ever putting oneself in a false position, as James had done. Here, on a magnificent scale, was his own childish Amesbury scrape repeated by no less a person than the King of England. The lesson was too palpable to be ignored. Never, Addison silently vowed, would he put himself in the wrong ; never by a rash word or an imprudent action take the risk of incurring the blame, or above all the ridicule, of his fellow men. And never would he allow passion to run away with him or direct one of his actions. He must find some other principle to direct his life.

What was it to be? It was difficult to find guidance. The classics, the Latin poets especially, were full of sound moral; but they were apt to be contradictory. The lesson must be sought in life itself, and as it happened his own father's case came very pat. Lancelot Addison was a mild, generous man, withal of somewhat adventurous temper, who had spent many years in Tangier. He had received royal favours, he had been made Dean of Lichfield, his reputation as a sound churchman and a good man seemed to make a bishopric certain: his chances were even now canvassed. But his impulsiveness provided the element lacking in Joseph's education, for he lost all hope of the chimere by too openly declaring in the Convocation of 1690 that he disapproved of the Revolution. Discretion—there was the moral. It was clear that one should never set oneself up against the general temper of the majority. There was a deal of sound sense in the familiar tag, *vox populi, vox Dei.*

With regard, however, to his own career, it was not easy straightway to discover what either of these voices might be saying. The easy course was open, a demyship being a normal preliminary to a Fellow's stall. But merely to be a Fellow of Magdalen was not a prospect which seemed to give scope to a man whose brilliance in writing Latin verse marked him out for more extended activities. Nor did the idea of passing his life in such company seem the most agreeable Addison could conceive; for though gallant preservers of their ancient liberties, the Fellows were, after all, close predecessors of those whose deep and dull potations excused the brisk intemperance of Gibbon's youth. Thus during the long night hours, when a light could be observed burning in his room; or in those meditative strolls by the river walk which has ever since borne his name, Addison's mind often turned from the consideration of his favourite Latin poets to muse upon his destinies. And since the only alternative to ordination and the academic life seemed to be poetry, he decided that he would, for a time at any rate, dally with the delights of song.

In those days a formal introduction to the muse was necessary, and Addison set himself to procure one. Thus his first English poem was an address to the venerable person of Dryden, who, however faulty his religious or political views might appear to the young Oxford graduate, was undoubtedly the king of English letters, holding undisputed sway at Wills's. The poem, written in 1693, when the young aspirant was twenty-one, might nowadays be considered fulsome ; but it was merely in the best adulatory style of the time, a vein in which Dryden himself excelled. It is, however, curiously revealing. In it the old displaced laureate is treated, not as the writer of masterly plays, as the poet of the most brilliant satires our literature had produced, nor as the critic who ' found our language brick and left it marble ', but as a translator whose lines had heightened Virgil's majesty, Addison proclaimed, to continue,

> And Horace wonders at himself in thee.
> Thou teachest Persius to inform our isle
> In smoother numbers, and a clearer style ;
> And Juvenal, instructed in thy page,
> Edges his satire, and improves his rage . . .

and since Dryden's copies ' outshone the bright originals ', Ovid, on whom he was now engaged, would ' boast the advantage of his song '.

We may doubt if Dryden was altogether pleased at the form the compliment took ; in any case it is not likely he was dazzled by such praise : but the verses showed skill, together with an appreciation of poetry, and whatever

Dryden's character may have been, his main characteristic was a passionate love of literature. He therefore answered Addison's effusion with a complimentary letter, and opened the door to further introductions.

Yet doubts crossed Addison's mind. It was evident from Dryden's case that poetry was not a lucrative trade—and perhaps his own talents were not very great: he was not conscious of any poetic fury, of being of imagination all compact. Poesy might be gum which oozed from whence 'twas nourished, but, like gum, it did not seem to ooze very fast. Under these circumstances it might be imprudent completely to embrace a literary career. It might put him irrevocably in the wrong, and in no career is failure more subject to ridicule than in this. On maturer consideration he thought he would, after all, go into the Church; it was at any rate safe. So the next year, after one or two exercises, such as verses on 'the great Nassau'; he concluded a poem to his friend Sacheverell by saying:

> I've done at length; and now dear friend receive
> The last poor present that my muse can give.
> I leave the art of poetry and verse
> To those that practise them with more success.
> Of greater truths I'll now prepare to tell,
> And so at once, dear friend and muse, farewell.

But the priestly life was not so safe as he had thought. Even there, a little study showed him, it was but too easy to make mistakes. In the very folds of the Church's lap it was not impossible to be put most humiliatingly in the wrong. 'Let your light so shine before men . . .' that was his ambition; but suppose it shone on a false track, suppose he fell *out* of the hands of the living God? He would like to lead, but a leader to gain the applause of the led must go in the right direction. What was the right direction? Unfortunately, the deeper he plunged, the more inspissated the gloom of theological controversy became. Dr. Burnet, now Bishop of Sarum, a leading authority on Church matters, let slip his opinion that some of the Thirty-nine Articles were, to say the least of it, 'injudiciously phrased'; while, it was rumoured, Tillotson, no less a person than the late Archbishop of Canterbury, had remarked of the Athanasian creed, "I wish we were well rid of it"![1] These were whispered scandals, but indeed mother Church exposed her rent garments. Contending divines published strenuous tracts upon the Trinity, some of which seemed so completely to miss grace as to be "looked on as plain Tritheism"; while not only were the words Socinian and Arian freely used as polemical missiles, but the horrid word Sabellian was viciously hurled about.[2] Thus, perhaps to the high entertainment of the angels, but to the obfuscation of Addison, the leaders of the blind pelted one another with heresiarchs as William and Louis defied one another with dynasties.

And if dogma was difficult, natural piety itself might be heretical. Goodness of soul, it appeared, was not inconsistent with vile doctrine. The pious Thomas Firmin, who made London resound with the fame of his charities, was notoriously a Socinian, suspected even of Arianism![2] What was a young man to do? It is possible that within himself he came to the conclusion Bolingbroke was later to state, that "In natural religion the clergy are unnecessary, in revealed they are dangerous guides".

In any case Addison put the matter by for a while, and engaged, at the suggestion of left-legged Jacob Tonson,

[1] Burnet, vi. 1417. [2] Ibid., 1698.

in translations from the Latin poets and from Herodotus. His version of the fourth Georgic brought forth Dryden's customary self-depreciating phrase. " After such a swarm as Addison's, my bees are scarce worth the hiving ", he declared. Moreover, he persuaded his young friend to write an introduction to his Virgil, a task Addison performed gracefully, and—anonymously. " To write a preface for Dryden . . . was an undertaking too hazardous to be avowed by any literary novice " his biographer explained.[1] We might suppose a novice could want nothing better than to appear in the arena armed with so crested and prevailing a name, but Addison thought a man a fool who did not give his works a trial in the world before owning them, and was convinced that " few works of genius come out at first with the author's name ".[2] Openly to publish a work that might prove a failure was imprudently to run the risk of ridicule, whereas one of the objects of writing was to gain the esteem of the world. For him the last infirmity of noble mind was actually its first duty: for if your worth does not shine before men, it is no benefit to them as an example.

It might be doubted whether translations from the Latin poets would bring light to a young man struggling to decide upon his profession; but Ovid was destined to be of quite singular assistance. Although, as he told Tonson, he found many of the stories in the *Metamorphoses* silly, there was one which seemed to have been written especially for him. It was that of Phaëton, the young man who dared too much. There is in Addison's version a fervour, a conviction about Phoebus's admonitions to his son lacking in the rest of the piece:

But neither mount too high nor sink too low . . .

[1] Aikin, i. 30. [2] *Spectator*, 451.

the rendering goes :

> Keep the mid-way, the middle way is best.
> Nor, where in radiant folds the Serpent twines,
> Direct your course, nor where the altar shines.
> Shun both extremes ; the rest let fortune guide,
> And better for thee than thyself provide.

Fortune, it seemed, had chosen this way to guide him, distilling wisdom from a silly story. " Nor where the altar shines." He could not neglect this warning, especially as, according to his first editor, Tickell, who so much roused Steele's ire by the suggestion, he felt his capacities unequal to so high a calling.[1] Where indeed was the mystic ardour that could embrace a dogma? where the dialectical enthusiasm for tracking down the subtleties inherent in any doctrine of the Trisagion? If the whole world had been plunged into discord for the sake of a diphthong, how easy would it be for a slip to draw upon him the hard stones of theological ridicule !

> The masters of the subtle schools
> Are—controversial, polymath,

while he hated controversy, and could never master the intricacies of his own homoousian faith. Only in the obscurity of a country parsonage would he have felt shielded ; but his mind, anxious to do all the good of which it was capable, rebelled at the limitation. On the other hand, if the lines to Sacheverell must be forgotten, what else was there? Let fortune guide ! That was all very well, but it was not in Addison's nature carelessly to throw her the reins. He preferred to be tolerably certain that she showed some disposition also to provide.

[1] Tickell, and Preface to *The Drummer*.

2

Travels

LUCKILY, Addison's literary ventures had made him acquainted with Congreve, and Congreve introduced him to Charles Montague,[1] just appointed Chancellor of the Exchequer, who in turn made him known to Sir John Somers, Lord Keeper. The Address to King William, with a prologue for Somers, already declared the poet a supporter of the Revolution, as one might expect from a *young* member of the society of Magdalen; and 'Mouse' Montague, who had launched Prior, his collaborator in the work that earned him his nickname, was ready to meet another young author. He got his reward soon enough in the dedication of a set of Latin verses on the Peace of Ryswick—for Addison had quickly seen the way into the Chancellor's good graces.

Montague, though vain, was by no means the God Almighty's ass of Pope's Bufo. Not only was he an extremely able financier, largely responsible for the foundation of the Bank of England and the funding of the national debt, but he could spot good men, and it was he who at the issue of the new coinage had made Newton Master of the Mint. Together with Somers he liked to encourage literary talent, largely for its own sake, but partly also because able pens might on occasion help the party. The pamphlets and satirical verses of the past years, especially in the Popish Plot days, had shown the force of trenchant quills; and now that power was really to some degree pliant to the general voice, it

[1] Steele.

was only natural that power should try to influence opinion.

It seemed to these leaders that Addison would be the very man for the work. He had literary skill, professed himself in the Whig interest, was no advocate of high-falutin-church notions, and, what was more to the point, appeared to be prudent, malleable, and not too eager to thrust himself forward. Moreover a very considerable charm emanated from the even features, radiated from the shining pale blue eyes of the young poet ; and charm was at that time as good a recommendation to lesser political posts as it yet is to junior appointments on the military staff. It helps to make things run smoothly, is indeed invaluable in intermediaries, besides being agreeable to those in high places. Thus Addison was approached with a view to engaging in a political career.

He was not averse from the suggestion. His last literary attempt, a play, had met with Dryden's usual compliment, but at the same time it had been made clear that success on the stage could not be hoped for. Only Congreve, it seemed, was lineal to Dryden's throne. If literature then, equally with the Church, was unsafe ; and if ' the middle way was best ', politics appeared to guide very nicely between the barren cliff of poetry and the quicksand of devotion. Besides, with such backing, the prospects seemed good, now that William had survived the assassination plot, and his régime had overcome the obstructions of a capricious House of Commons as triumphantly as the intrigues of a jealous House of Lords. Addison was neither too lazy nor too careless to be ambitious, nor too proud : and as Whiggism seemed firmly glued in the saddle of affairs, he was inclined to take the leap.

There was, however, a difficulty. After four years of

doubt Addison had in 1698 accepted a Fellowship, a step which involved the taking of orders. This might not hinder him from using his pen, but it would be fatal to his political advancement. So a courteous struggle took place over Addison's body between Montague and Dr. Hough, the former imploring the President to grant the young aspirant after political fame a dispensation from the holy life. Hough at first resiled, being unwilling to lose so promising a churchman: but the Chancellor's 'warm instances', his plea that "the general pravity and corruption of men of business, who wanted liberal education", made urgent the infusion of purer blood, proved too potent. Enemy to the Church as he might be represented, Montague vowed, "he would never do it any other injury than keeping Mr. Addison out of it".[1] The Church accordingly sacrificed the Fellow of Magdalen to the good of the State, as it had previously relinquished the genius of Montague himself, while Addison retained his academic emoluments.

All that was now to do was to complete the recruit's education by sending him abroad to learn French and to enlarge his mind. Somers, now a peer, obtained for him a pension of three hundred pounds from the King; and in 1699, having previously published his Latin poems, Addison left England for over four years, definitely launched upon a public career in which it would be more important than ever not to make any mistake.

Though received in Paris with the utmost kindness by the English representative, the Earl of Manchester, a cousin of Montague, he stayed there only long enough to visit the famous sights before proceeding to Blois to learn the language, of which he must have been sorely ignorant, to judge by the incomplete impression he

[1] Preface to *The Drummer*, and Steele.

received of the literature of his day. Writing to Montague[1] he remarked : " There is no Book comes out at present that has not something in it of an Air of Devotion . . . nay the Humour is grown so universal that it is got among the poets who are every day publishing Lives of Saints and Legends in Rhime ", a result he ascribed to the King's pietistic phase. It is as though a foreigner visiting England in 1700 should have based his opinion of literature on Collier and Toland, ignoring the *Essay on Human Understanding* as well as *The Way of the World*. For there was something in French literature besides cant. There might be an *air* of devotion about Fontenelle's Oracles and Dialogues, his discussions of fables and astronomy, but a very different spirit underlay them—the spirit indeed at that very moment being breathed in by the young Montesquieu. Nor could the Christian metaphysic of Père Malebranche be ascribed as sycophancy towards a God-aspiring monarch who would certainly not understand the arguments. And though no doubt there were many devotional verses being written—England too had her Dr. Watts—Paris flocked to see the frothy, amusing, and not always decorous farces of Dancourt, Baron, and Dufresny, or those amazing torrents of inspired and witty buffoonery that constitute the comedies of Regnard.

For some young men to go alone into the heart of a strange country would be an adventure full of moral dangers ; but Addison was safe. He was not a victim of that reaction so often suffered by those who have led secluded lives, and to which the sons of parsons seem peculiarly liable. " The only return I can make your L^d^ship ", he wrote Somers from Paris, " will be to apply

[1] Aug. 1699. The letters, except where otherwise stated, are quoted from Aikin.

myself entirely to my Business, and to take such a care of my Conversation that your favours may not seem misplaced." He never lapsed from his resolve. During the whole of his year at Blois he used to work so hard as to think himself into a muse. One can only wonder what, in view of so stainless a life, he can have meant by writing in later years:

> When in the slippery paths of youth
> With heedless steps I ran.

But it was not only to learn French that he had been sent abroad; it was also to enlarge his mind by the observation of foreign things and continental manners, of which he wrote home with much of that humour, and traces of that mild censure, that were afterwards to make his writings so popular. It was not to be supposed that queer customs could affect his settled convictions any more than the genial air of Touraine could shake his virtue, especially as these customs, these different habits of thought and behaviour, suffered sadly by comparison with the better inspired modes of academic life. "Modesty is so extremely scarce", he told Montague, "that I think I have not seen a blush since my first landing at Callice"; and the Sorbonne Latin was such as you might expect from a nation where the physicians "are as cheap as our English Farriers and generally as Ignorant". It was evident they had no Garth, or Blackmore, or Arbuthnot. Nor was their art in better case, and of Le Brun's paintings at Versailles he wrote to Congreve, "The painter has represented His most Xtian Majesty under ye figure of Jupiter throwing thunderbolts all about the cieling and striking terror into ye Danube and Rhine that lie astonished and blasted wth Lightning a little above the Cornice". In all this there was nothing of the nice decorum of a Kneller.

Indeed the French were an incomprehensible people, their manners and temper fantastically topsy-turvy. Montague was finally enlightened as to the sinister nature of these enemies to the peace of Europe.

"They are the happiest people in the world. 'Tis not in the pow'r of Want or Slavery to make 'em miserable. There is nothing to be met with in the Country but Mirth and Poverty. Everyone sings, laughs and starves. Their Conversation is generally Agreeable; for if they have any Wit or Sense, they are sure to show it. They never mend upon a Second meeting, but use all the freedom and familiarity at first sight that a Long Intimacy or Abundance of wine can scarce draw from an Englishman."

It was clear that besides exhibiting astonishing contradictions in nature, they lacked the useful quality of discretion. And as for their women, their beauty was but a *painted* hell, and they lacked everything except a meretricious quality of artifice. They

"are perfect Mistresses in the Art of showing themselves to the best Advantage. They are always gay and sprightly and set off ye very worst faces in Europe with ye best airs. Ev'ry one knows how to give herself as charming a Look and posture as Sr Godfrey Kneller c^d^ draw her in."

No wonder that throughout his stay in France he showed no vestige of an amour.[1]

In March 1700, having mastered the language, he returned to Paris, where Boileau, impressed by his Latin verses, received him graciously. But he did not stay long in the capital; for the French, all cock-a-whoop at the turn the Spanish succession had taken by the death of that prince who alone seemed to guarantee the existence of the Pyrenees, felt that God and the diplomacy

[1] Spence.

of Louis had outwitted the brilliant intelligence of William and rendered his painful efforts null. As is their way, they did not scruple to show their elation, thus making Paris decidedly uncomfortable for an Englishman. So in December, Addison, still in pursuit of education, embarked on a journey to Italy with his friend Edward Wortley, who besides being a fitting companion in erudition and intelligence, could pass the highest tests as a model of worldly prudence, knowing even how best to dispose of superfluous gifts.

Here again Addison was perfectly safe from subversive influence, for he travelled not through Italy, but through the Latin poets, to use Horace Walpole's phrase [1] rather than Sterne's racier idiom,[2] which would have amused Swift, but which remained unnoticed by Miss Aikin. Intent upon those spots that would afford him opportunity for a quotation from Virgil, Lucan, or Silius Italicus, searching for 'celebrated floods', for 'streams immortalized in song', delighting to tread only 'classic ground', his vision soared above the actualities around him. He darted but a contemptuous look at the monuments of over-zealous faith, and when forced to admit the magnificence of certain edifices, qualified his praise with the words 'but of a Gothic structure'. It was natural to the age to prefer the simple classic grandeur of Rome to the more unruly imagination of medieval workmen, and it is in keeping that Addison should have found the 'artificial wildness' of Fontainebleau more satisfactory than the terrifying savagery of the Alps. And if these held no beauty for him, we need not be astonished that in the intensely serious carvings of the Gothic decorators, symbolic of the immanence of things

[1] Letter to Mr. West, 2nd October 1740.
[2] *Tristram Shandy*, Book VII, chap. iv.

unfelt, unseen, he could distinguish nothing save frivolous 'affectation'.[1]

Frankly, there is something in the spirit of Addison's remarks that makes one think of a very little schoolboy visiting another school, determined to find nothing but material for scorn; one cannot help wondering if Somers and Montague were satisfied with the education their protégé was imbibing. Did it not seem to them that the skin of provincialism proper to a man of Addison's upbringing was being not sloughed, but wrapped ever more closely round him as a cloak? He seemed impervious to new ideas, distasteful of manners different from those prevalent in England; still naïvely astonished by modes of living, reactions to the events of life unfamiliar to him. Such comments as he made were eminently safe; they showed no tendency to dangerous aberrations: but they were of the sententious kind, implying some miscomprehension. Might it not be that this young man was even a little stupid, endowed merely with a talent for committing to paper what oft was thought, no doubt, but was scarcely worth the labour of expressing? Perhaps it merely was that he was too eager to find the laughable and ridiculous when he should have been trying to understand. Yet a more supple-minded man—and of what use was a politician whose mind was not supple?—would have thought that the flamboyance of the Versailles decorations *might* have its appropriateness, as had the equally rhetorical Rubens ceiling in Whitehall. As far as education went, the pension obtained from William must have seemed money wasted.

But not to Addison, who from his travels obtained much of that material he used so exhaustively, and exhaustlessly, later in his essayist's life. When gravelled

[1] *Travels*, and the poem entitled 'Letter to Lord Halifax'.

for want of matter he could always refer to the shocking levity of the French, the poverty of their literature, or the distressing cosmetic habits of their women. For Addison's mind was so just, his judgement so sure, that never throughout his career did he find it necessary to change his opinion ; and even the letters he wrote home as a young student of Europe served with scarcely any change to make up some of those papers he contributed to the *Guardian* when he was a mature man of the world, an arbiter of moral elegance, and a political figure of distinction.

In the meantime, while he was abroad, Addison's prospects underwent alarming fluctuations. Somers had been attacked for encouraging the buccaneering Captain Kidd, and twice again on other grounds. In 1701 the Tories came into power, and though Montague had earned, besides the damning nickname of Filcher, the Barony of Halifax, his elevation to the peerage was something in the nature of being kicked upstairs. Both he and Somers were impeached, but though the House of Lords dismissed the impeachments, their patronage could no longer be of any great value. At last, however, Louis played into William's hands by acknowledging the Pretender, and on war being declared by the disgusted Tories, Addison was offered the post of Secretary to Prince Eugène. But unfortunately, at that moment, in March 1702, William died, and the appointment vanished into thin air with his pension and the immediate prospects of the traveller. For owing to Anne's dislike of the principles which had made her Queen, the Tories maintained their ascendancy, Halifax was struck off the roll of Privy Councillors, and Somers was obliged to content himself with the Presidency of the Royal Society.

Addison, however, continued his journey at his own

expense, wandering through Austria and Germany, perhaps taking a pupil. In Vienna, in Hamburg, as elsewhere, he took care always to consort with his own countrymen, and there is scarcely an indication, save in one frustrated visit to Bayle,[1] that he ever sought the company of an enlightened foreigner, preferring men with whom he could drink Halifax's health. Perhaps he had found Boileau's flattery too overwhelming. Finally, in the summer of 1703 he found himself at Rotterdam; and there he made a slight mistake.

The Duke of Somerset, wishing to find a tutor to take his son, Lord Hartford, on the foreign tour, was recommended Addison by Jacob Tonson. The Duke offered all expenses and a hundred guineas at the end of a year, when, if the arrangement proved satisfactory, the tour would be extended another two years. Addison wrote to accept; but whether he meant to be polite and was over-polite, or whether he asked too obviously for patronage, the phrasing of his letter, like that of the Thirty-nine Articles, was injudicious. The Duke took offence at the words, "As for the recompense that is proposed to me, I must take the liberty to assure your Grace that I should not see my account in it, but in the hopes I have to recommend myself to your Grace's favour and approbation". Either this was too honest, or the Duke, who was vengeance proud, thought it a reflection upon his generosity; and regarding the rest of Addison's letter as mere formal compliment—though indeed the desire to accept is obvious enough—cancelled the proposal. All contrition, Addison wrote regretting he "had not made use of such expressions as were proper to represent him the sense he had of the honour his Grace designed him", protested his willingness to obey

[1] Add. MSS. 22908, to Colbatch, date uncertain.

any commands, and to be 'any-ways serviceable to my Lord Hartford' during his stay abroad. His offer, however, was ignored; and the episode reinforced a lesson ill-learned—for it was but a variant on the theme of discretion. It was clear that in matters of this kind one should never say quite what one thought.

Addison did not stay abroad long after this disappointment, for hearing at the end of the summer that his father had died, he made his way home prospectless. But at least he was still a Fellow of his College.

3

The World

THE world to which Addison came back differed terribly from the happy Whig hunting-ground he had left. Although it was Whig policy that kept the Queen on the throne, although it was chiefly in defence of the Revolution Settlement that bitter war was being waged against France, not one of the leaders of the party was in office, and some were even in disgrace. The gentle Somers and the lettered Halifax were replaced by the honest but insensitive Godolphin and the furiously reactionary Rochester, the Queen's uncle. So violent indeed was the atmosphere against freedom of thought in any sphere, that the divines of the University of Oxford had banished the *Essay on Human Understanding* from the republic of letters. Somers, then, could do nothing for Addison, who was for the moment condemned to a garret up three pairs of stairs over a mean shop in the Haymarket.[1] But Halifax was still Bufo, and 'rich as fifty Jews', could provide him with wine; and still 'tripping hand in hand with song' could introduce him into the Kit-Cat. Addison was probably more grateful for the first than for the second favour, for he always found company damping, and in this case it was combined with the chance of meeting the 'proud' Duke of Somerset, who was one of the famous thirty-nine, and to whose son he had not become tutor. But he did, in accordance with rule, inscribe his toast on a glass, choosing for the honour the Countess of Manchester, whom he had known

[1] *Curiosities*, 2nd Series, 246.

in Paris. The verses were pretty, patriotic, and deftly pointed a moral, stating:

> While haughty Gallia's dames, that spread
> O'er their pale cheeks an artful red,
> Beheld this beauteous stranger there,
> In native charms divinely fair,
> Confusion in their looks they showed,
> And with unborrowed blushes glowed.

Thus Addison did his duty by the club; but to be a member of this brilliant gathering, though a signal honour, was a trying one. What attitude could he adopt but one of diffidence amid the bluff jovialities of a Carlisle or a Wharton, the sneers of a Mohun, the genial scepticism of a Garth, or the polished, kindly wit of a Congreve? Halifax might support him, but he had no chance against the irrepressible Rowe, especially under the faintly disapproving eye that peered from under Tonson's rufous brows. One can imagine him sitting stolid and silent, nursing his regular features into a slight smile to hide his discomfort, amid the hard-headed, high-spirited, and very realistic society where not even generous draughts of wine could loosen his tongue.

At any rate the experience taught him that if one wishes to shine, and cannot impose oneself on a certain *milieu*, the only thing to do is to create one's own; but this takes time, and for the moment Addison preferred a retired life, with occasional outings to the theatre, and rare visits from Steele, who for the more part was drilling his company at Landguard Fort in Essex.

Theirs was a curious, almost an inexplicable union. Born in the same year, they had been at Charterhouse together; and perhaps because the volatile Dicky had been drawn to the prudent stability Addison had in so high a degree, certainly because Addison could not resist

Steele's frankness, his naïve weakness, his absurd repentances and his admiration, they had become firm friends. Addison had even carried the orphan home for the holidays, where he had been much liked by the sympathetic Dean and his family.

Steele had followed Addison to Oxford only when the latter was already a demy of Magdalen, and, leaving without taking a degree, had early embarked on his strangely dynamic life. While Addison was yet in silent meditation at Oxford, or on his travels abroad, only preparing for his career, Steele was plunging with almost fanatical ardour into every variety of religious and irreligious experience. He even dabbled in alchemy. In the exciting reign of King William, amid the helter-skelter of intrigue, of early Jacobite plots and foreign wars, he enlisted as a trooper, thereby, characteristically, sacrificing the legacy of an estate in Ireland. But a poem dedicated to Captain, afterwards Lord Cutts, whose bravery earned him the title of Salamander, procured Steele the rank of ensign, and for a while his life was not unlike Vanbrugh's at the same period, half literary, half warlike. But a feather for every wind that blew, provided it was not a Tory one, incorrigibly careless, he was always fighting duels, sustaining actions for debt, or involving himself in the debts of others with a generosity he was unable to substantiate; and he was much too often drunk. Then, intimacy with Jacob Tonson's daughter having made him a father, he was rendered temporarily conscious of his shortcomings, to control which he composed a manual of piety called *The Christian Hero*, also dedicated to the astonished Cutts. Such an effusion, of which, however, more than one edition was called for, made him, as he complained, unpopular with his mess-mates, and to retrieve his position he wrote an amusing semi-satirical trifle, *The Funeral, or Grief à la Mode*, set by Rich on the Drury Lane stage. A second play, *The Lying Lover*, largely from Corneille's *Le Menteur*, written, as he said, in the severity required by Collier, was acted in December 1703, shortly after Addison's return from the Continent.[1]

Tossed up and down though he was on the waves of his impulse, he had, however, one point in common with Addison, he was a believer in Whig principles, and so at this time could hope for no one of those congenial little employments with which the great patrons rewarded the loyalty of the smaller fry. The astounding victory of Blenheim, however, changed the whole face of affairs, and in the blaze of popularity consequent upon it, Marlborough and Godolphin no longer thought it necessary to conciliate their Tory friends. In the elections of 1705 the Whigs were returned in a majority, Halifax and Somers were sworn of the Council, Cowper given the Privy Seal, and the wheels of the political world seemed well oiled for supporters of the Hanoverian succession.

But even before this happy consummation of true blue Protestant hopes Addison was given his chance. The appalling quality of the poetic lucubrations called forth by the battle of Blenheim shocked even Godolphin, who could not with any delight

> Think of ten thousand gentlemen at least,
> And each man mounted on his capering beast

into the Danube being pushed in shoals, as he was asked to do; nor could he revel in the vision of his friend Marlborough as a man of prodigious muscular development 'urging his way o'er hills of gasping heroes', and 'dyeing his reeking sword in Gallic blood'. Nothing could be more calculated to bring the whole magnificent

[1] Aitken.

exploit into ridicule, and he consulted Halifax, notoriously Maecenas, as to a suitable quill for its celebration. Halifax, deep in the knowledge of court promises, was sagacious enough to say that he knew the very man for the purpose, but that he certainly would not ask him to write the poem for a ministry that allowed men of genius shamefully to languish in obscurity while it rewarded fools and blockheads. Godolphin imperturbably replied that Halifax's criticism might very well be just, but that at all events on this occasion the poet would not have cause to regret his labours. Halifax further insisted that Godolphin should send to the poet in person, and this being agreed to, Addison was named ; thus a short time later no less a figure than Boyle, the Chancellor of the Exchequer, clambered up all the stairs to the little room in the Haymarket, and prayed Mr. Addison to celebrate the great general and the king-making victory.[1]

Nothing loath, the poet set to work, and carefully avoiding rhetorical nonsense, produced a creditable *poème d'occasion*, which, though hardly an adornment to the muse, need never have caused her to blush. But to Addison's contemporaries *The Campaign* appeared little short of a great masterpiece ; his friends were wild with joy. The simile—*pace* Dr. Johnson—of the angel seemed to them finer than 'anything to be found in Homer or Virgil', and it was left to the perverse ingenuity of Pope to use its culminating line, 'Rides in the whirlwind and directs the storm' to describe the gleeful activities of Rich behind the scenes in Drury Lane. Godolphin was charmed, and almost at once presented Addison with a Commissionership of Appeals worth three hundred pounds a year, a post made vacant by the death of John Locke. Steele's reward came in 1706 with

[1] Budgell.

the position of Gentleman Waiter to the Prince of Denmark, the Queen's husband, and 'the lowest place in the ministry', namely that of Gazetteer.

Although now a civil servant, cleared of his university debts by the profits of *The Campaign*, and still drawing the emoluments of his Fellowship, Addison did not neglect other means of increasing his fortune; it was a moral principle with him.[1] A Government employment, he was only too aware, depended upon party fluctuations. Thus besides being educational adviser to the Countess of Warwick, who had a young son to bring up, he used his pen, not in the service of faction, but in the realms of pure literature. In 1704 he published his *Travels in Italy*, with a dedication to Somers, without, however, much immediate profit, for the book was slow to reach its eventual popularity, most readers agreeing with Hearne that it was "a book very trite, being made up of scraps of verses, and things which have been observed over and over . . ."[2] The antiquary was of the opinion that it would please superficial readers; but that is precisely the sort of reader the book will never please, simply because it does indeed contain nothing new. Its undeniable charm, faint though it is, depends just upon its simple sincerity, its very lack of arresting quality, its clear prose, and, added to its prolixity of Latin verse quotations, a quite unaffected contentment with the insignificant.

But Addison was engaged upon a more original work. Dissatisfied with the Italian opera then so much in vogue, which, like Dr. Johnson, he regarded as "an exotic and irrational entertainment", he was worried by the incongruity of word with music so evident in translations from the Italian; particularly on one occasion where,

[1] *Spectator*. [2] Hearne, 28th Nov. 1705.

under the exigencies of the verse, " the soft notes that were adapted to pity in the Italian fell upon the word ' rage ' in English, and the angry sounds that were tuned to rage in the original were made to express pity in the translation ". Music, for him, was meant to illustrate literature, and he found it absurd to be " entertained with many a melodious ' the ' ". " I have heard ", he wrote, " the most beautiful graces, quavers, and divisions bestowed upon ' then ', ' for ', and ' from ', to the eternal honour of our English particles."

About music, it is true, he knew nothing, to judge not only from Dr. Burney's somewhat belated authority, but on the evidence of such passages as the one wherein he assured the young Earl of Warwick that at a concert of birds ' he would entertain him with much better music than ever he met with at the opera ', for the roulades of a Tofts were clearly less true to nature than were those of a throstle. Music, indeed, was an inferior activity, since other arts had " a much greater tendency to the refinement of human nature ".[1] At the same time, if there had to be opera, it might as well be sensible stuff, and in English ; and since a librettist need not know much about music, Addison made up his mind to try his hand at this dramatic form.

The moment seemed ripe. At the end of 1705 an altogether home-made article, *Arsinoe*, by Thomas Clayton, had some success even in Vanbrugh's ill-starred Haymarket theatre : public taste was evidently prepared, and with the aid of the same composer the possibilities of failure would be small. Addison felt sure he could write just the thing, and produced the libretto of *Rosamond*, the theme having been made familiar to the public in a play by John Bancroft printed some dozen years before.

[1] *Spectator*, 18.

But alas! the opera failed when played in 1706, contemporaries agreeing with later critics that Clayton was a bungler, who on this occasion produced " a confused chaos of music, the only merit of which was its shortness ". The play itself is a performance incredible to one acquainted only with Addison's later work, a *jeu d'esprit* that deserved better fortune. Mr. Courthope suggests that it would have failed with a better composer because it is " neither a tragedy, a comedy, nor a melodrama "—what, it might be asked, is *The Magic Flute*?—but the real reason of its failure is that it was two hundred years ahead of its time, for it is nothing less than a musical comedy, a burlesque that may have suggested much to Gay. Dr. Johnson was right in supposing that had Addison developed this vein he might have excelled in the lighter forms of verse. There is, for instance, the passage where King Henry returns from the wars eager for a sight of his fair mistress who has been confided to the care of old Sir Trusty:

> *King*. Where is my love! my Rosamond!
> *Sir T*. First, as in strictest duty bound,
> I kiss your royal hand.
> *King*. Where is my life! my Rosamond!
> *Sir T*. Next with submission most profound
> I welcome you to land.
> *King*. Where is the tender charming fair!
> *Sir T*. Let me appear, great Sir, I pray,
> Methodical in what I say . . .

Imagine the passage appropriately set by a competent musician, a Sullivan or a Richard Strauss, what a deal could be made of this comic foolery! and indeed, the play did achieve a certain success when rehandled years later by Dr. Arne.

But it is an amazing performance from other points of view. Whether it was the comparatively unrefined nature of music, or the notoriously dangerous atmosphere of the stage that ran away with Addison, there is in some of the verse a flippancy, a disregard of moral proportion to be met with nowhere else in his writings; it really does seem as though he were treading in slippery paths when he wrote

> Since conjugal passion
> Is come into fashion
> And marriage so blest on the throne is,
> Like a Venus I'll shine
> Be fond and be fine
> And Sir Trusty shall be my Adonis.

The lines have almost a Restoration ring, and come strangely from the sometime aspirant to Holy Orders, the soon to be famous *censor morum*, or the future compiler of *Evidences of the Christian Religion.*

The locality of the play being Woodstock, the work was not unnaturally dedicated to the Duchess of Marlborough; and since Blenheim House was about to be built, Vanbrugh, whom Addison was in June to accompany to Hanover under Halifax's aegis to present the Garter to the Electoral Prince, came in for a compliment:

> Behold the glorious pile ascending,
> Columns swelling, arches bending,
> Domes in awful pomp arising,
> Art in curious strokes surprising,
> Foes in figured fights contending,
> Behold the glorious pile ascending.

Alas! the glorious pile was still ascending on the day that Addison died.

But though failure of the opera was an uncomfortable lesson, a severe illustration of the virtues of anonymity, it had its compensation in procuring for Addison the admiring friendship of a young 'pretender to poetry', a member of Addison's original college, Queen's. Thomas Tickell, then some twenty years of age, adorned with those intellectual graces he declared inseparable from a classical education, addressed a poem "To Mr. Addison on his Opera of *Rosamond*". His 'artful song', he proclaimed, was "soft as Corelli and as Virgil strong", and thus he set the fashion of bracketing Addison's name with the Mantuan's, a precedent so universally followed that even Pope had in the end to conform. Tickell himself could hardly write a poem on any subject without dragging in the comparison. Equally admiring in *Rosamond* the manner and the matter, he said of the verses,

> Their cadence in such easy sound conveyed
> The height of thought may seem superfluous aid :
> Yet in such charms the noble thoughts abound
> That needless seem the sweets of easy sound.

Who could resist such an approach from a young votary, who, moreover, proved on acquaintance to be not only intellectually agreeable, but personable? He soon became one of Addison's intimates.

One of several; for at this period Addison had leisure to increase his acquaintance, and began to gather about him that group of young minor authors afterwards to form so close and renowned a coterie. Most important among these were Eustace Budgell and Ambrose Philips. The first was a not very distant relation of Addison, only twenty years old in 1706, and at that time a Templar. He was young, he had literary leanings, he admired beyond his poor stock of words the author of *The Campaign*. It was enough to arouse the affection of Addison; he took 'the man who calls me cousin' under his wing, and kept him there for ten years, deriving much gratification from his company. Yet not so much as he derived from that of Ambrose Philips, who, after all, was more of his own age, being only three years younger than Addison. He too wished to scale Parnassus, and had written some pastorals, agreeable enough nothings ; but his character was mixed. It was not fair to say

'Twas all the ambition his poor soul could feel
To wear red stockings, and to dine with Steele,

yet he had much of the fop in his nature, and his dapper little person was always neatly dressed. He was a skilled swordsman, while an unduly long, yet elegantly curvilinear nose shrunk still further a mouth already set in the contracted Antinous folds fancied by fashionable painters. Although he had a genuine love of the country and felt lonely in the town, he had allowed himself to be dragged into the political arena, having been employed in diplomatic affairs at Utrecht in 1703, while still a Fellow of St. John's, Cambridge. His personality, ruled by a certain childish and engaging weakness—for he had none of Steele's rather uncomfortable independence—appealed very strongly to Addison, who became " more than he was able to express, his most affectionate and most faithful servant " : the words do not read as empty formality. Addison did all he could to obtain his friend government posts, to aid his literary ventures, and ' Pastoral Philips ' became so closely attached to him that at one time the two seem never to have been apart. Swift could not meet Addison in the park or the Mall without finding Ambrose—" more of a puppy than ever "—walking with him : and when the younger man had to go to Bath for eye treatment, his protector went too.[1]

But the person of most note who now appeared in Addison's life was Swift himself, not so much in the Whig interest as ready to court any party that would

[1] *Stella*, several entries, the Bath one, 24th Aug. 1711.

obtain the extension of Queen Anne's Bounty to Ireland. Something uncouth in appearance, with an odd abruptness in his manner, and an eccentricity of behaviour that might have earned him the epithet ' mad ' had there not lurked some mysterious sense of savage power behind the already gnarled forehead, he moved like an ominous vulture among the swan-like wits of the coffee-houses. Since it was an open secret that he was the author of that deadly, pungent satire, *The Tale of a Tub*, which not only seemed to many to strike formidably at the roots of revealed religion but also at the delicate framework of human self-love, he was able to inspire fear. But his emotions were deep, and if endurance is the test of passion, his friendships were passionate as his hatreds were overwhelming. He took to Addison, whose character, with its gentle diffidence, showed such striking contrasts with his own, and perhaps even forced himself into his company :[1] the tempestuous parson of Laracor was not one who could ever have said " Par délicatesse j'ai perdu ma vie ". Addison, who could never reject advances, responded, and was so impressed by the not yet famous satirist that he presented him with a copy of his *Travels* inscribed to " Dr. Jonathan Swift, the most agreeable companion, the truest friend, and the greatest genius of his age ". In Swift's own words, " Addison, Steele and me " formed a veritable triumvirate.

But Addison did not long have so much leisure, for he was now definitely launched on his political career, and in 1706 was made Under-Secretary of State to Sir Charles Hedges, who had been the legal member of that very commission which had ousted Hough from the courts of Magdalen. But Hedges, being a Tory, did not long

[1] Scott, footnote, 70, 71.

survive the ministerial turnover, and Addison soon found himself serving under the Earl of Sunderland, the son of Etherege's correspondent, a vehement and intriguing Whig, whose austere demeanour consciously masked an almost uncontrollable violence. No doubt Addison found points of contact with him, for though not so brilliant or so wide a thinker as his father, Sunderland was an eager collector of ancient books, his stock ultimately becoming the famous Blenheim library.

However, this relation too was shortlived. In 1707, during a debate in the House of Lords, the Earl of Wharton, though one of the Whig junto, pronounced an upsetting harangue upon the decay of trade and agriculture brought about by the war. Meeting him afterwards on the staircase, the Duke of Marlborough buttonholed and gently remonstrated with him. The conversation, begun in a whisper, gradually grew louder; and the Duke, fearful lest some of the damaging reminiscences in which the Earl was beginning to indulge should come to the ears of some idle stander-by, hastily closed the colloquy by promising Wharton the viceroyalty of Ireland, in which he had shown such interest during the Tyrconnel administration.[1] He knew that friends are often dangerous when out of office. When appointed in December 1708,[2] Wharton chose Addison as his secretary, and thus the latter had as his commander a man whose character was more strikingly in contrast with his own than even Sunderland's.

Lord Wharton's was of that type of realistic, even sceptical, mind, of which the Revolutionary period can show so many examples, Shaftesbury, Savile, and lastly St. John, all of whom were able to add to the subtle clarity of Macchiavelli the useful principles of Cartesian

[1] *D. N. B.*, Wharton. [2] Luttrell.

doubt. Wharton, though no great philosopher, was enough of one to think that, politically at least, " a lie well believed was as good as if it were true " ; and though it may be that his moral credit has suffered by confusion with his son's, it is certain he was indifferent to a personal reputation he had no impulse to preserve falsely pure. A man of great natural ability, vigour, and versatility, he was a firm disciple of the great Trimmer, whose experience as well as his precepts convinced him that salvation, personal and national, lay in the unshrinking prosecution of party. Thus it was his proud boast that as author of *Lilli-Burlero* he had sung a deluded prince out of three kingdoms, though some credit must surely be given to that tripping tune of Purcell's which, at about this time, Captain Toby Shandy was so fond of whistling.[1] And certainly he showed judgement in choosing as his subordinate a man so eminently safe and honest as Addison.

The appointment caused tattle in politico-social circles, Peter Wentworth suggesting to Addison that he might have been generous enough to procure the post for his second brother Lancelot, a Fellow of Magdalen : but Peter's only reason seems to have been that Lancelot was a friend of his own brother, Lord Raby. Rumour also ran that Steele would get the reversion of his friend's last job ; [2] but the mercurial author of *The Tender Husband*—in which Addison had helped him—was obviously not the person for a comparatively high political post where stability was the first desideratum, and he was fobbed off with a promise of the next vacant post should it prove consistent with his retaining the office of

[1] The words (1st Part) may be found in Percy's *Reliques* ; the tune in Messrs. Novello's *Ten Purcell Melodies*, ' A new Irish Tune '.

[2] Wentworth, 68, and Luttrell, 23rd Dec. 1708.

Gazetteer: and in fact he was shortly given a lucrative appointment at the head of the Stamp Office.

But if Addison did nothing for Lancelot—perhaps Lancelot wanted nothing—he did a great deal for his first brother Gulston, and Peter Wentworth had occasion to be more than ever amazed.

"Since I writ this", Lord Raby read in January 1709,[1] "I am told a great Peice of News that Mr. Addison is really a very great man with the juncto, and that he has got his elder brother, who has been a factor abroad in those parts to be Governor of Fort St. George, and the Great Pits [2] is turn out, his son here has a great while constantly votes with the Torys which has been a great help to Mr. Addison. It seems Mr. Addison's friends can do what they please with the cheif of the East India Company, who I think have the liberty of naming their Governor, and by management with them this place is got which they say some years are worth 20,000 pound."

It was clear that the Whig side was the right one, for after Anne's abortive attempt in 1708 to shed her faithful Mr. Montgomery and the too magnificent Mr. Freeman, the Whigs were so firmly in possession of keys, wands, seals, that Sunderland could parade his highly Spartan republicanism, and entertain the Sovereign with pithy remarks on the habitual failings of ruling princes. It was not Godolphin and Marlborough who had disappeared from the council table, but Mrs. Masham's cousin Harley, and his ambitious young friend Henry St. John.

Accordingly, in April 1709, Addison travelled to Ireland in a train that included for the Earl's pleasure Thomas Clayton the composer, and for his own, Eustace Budgell, whom he made his clerk. Mr. Secretary's place was worth two thousand a year; besides this he earned four hundred as keeper of the Records in Birming-

[1] Wentworth, 75, 76. [2] Grandfather of the great commoner.

ham's Tower, and since he still retained his Fellowship, he was more than comfortably off, removed from the temptation of "gratifications, tokens of thankfulness, despatch money, and the like specious"[1] gifts. But in any case there is no doubt Addison was filled with a profound sense of the desirability of honourable dealing: without certainties of an elementary kind the world is an uncomfortable place to live in, 'nasty and brutish'. His justice was impartial, and he would never remit his friends any of their fees, remarking with sanguine sense that he might have forty friends, and whereas they would each gain only two guineas, he would lose eighty. Swift need not have been afraid that going to Ireland would spoil the 'best *honnête homme* in the world'.

Wharton was not the kind of man to whom Addison could give whole-hearted approval, but luckily he was able to praise the official. Writing to Halifax in May, he expressed pleasure at the progress the Lord-Lieutenant was making. The addresses from the House of Commons showed that "all parties set out in good humour, which is entirely owing to his Ex^ly's conduct who has addressed himself to all sorts of men since his arrival here with unspeakable application". He wisely refrained from repealing the Test Act, otherwise "all things would have been thrown into the utmost confusion and a stop put to all publick Business. His Ex^ly however gains ground daily . . .

"I have the Happinesse every day to drink your Lordship's Health in very good wine, and with very Honest Gentlemen . . ."[2]

But such a rosy state of mind did not last very long. Genial and tolerant as the Earl appeared to be, it was noticeable that only Protestants were admitted to those almost bourgeois routs at the Castle; and if the ease of

[1] *Spectator*, 469. [2] Add. MSS. 7121, f. 9: 7th May 1709.

her Ladyship's manners were at first sight commendable, easiness may go too far ; it may lapse into latitude. It was rumoured that the coffers of their Excellencies were enriched beyond their rightful due. And as, little by little, Wharton found his feet, firmly straddled as they were upon a Parliament composed of, and elected by, Protestants alone, he passed acts equalling in savagery the anti-Protestant measures of Tyrconnel himself. For instance, to the abominable Act of 1703, forcing Catholics to leave their property to Anglicans, was added that compelling priests to take the Oath of Abjuration on pain of banishment or death, in gross contravention of the Treaty of Limerick.[1] The party in power, Addison came to think, " seemed to suppose that the principles of a Whig consisted in nothing else but damning the Church, abetting the dissenters, and spreading contempt of revealed religion ". But the phrase is Swift's, and it is doubtful if Addison shared the clergyman's loathing of non-churchmen.

It is certain he did what he could to soften the rigour of the Protestant rule. He became Parliament-man for Cavan, and sufficiently overcame his bashfulness to speak in the Irish gathering, where, since all men were of one party, though there might be sects, opposition would not be fierce or acid. Indeed, he made himself so beloved that when he left Swift wrote to say that if only he would come back they would raise an army and make him King of Ireland. Nor did he by undue opposition to Castle politics forfeit the esteem of the viceroy, who gave him the borough of Lostwithiel ; and when he was displaced on appeal,[2] presented him with Malmesbury, for which he sat at Westminster for the remainder of his life.

[1] Lecky, *Ireland*. [2] Luttrell, December 1709.

Wharton, however, was not long in Ireland. On the 5th November 1709, Sacheverell, believing in the pulpit as a 'safe and sacred organ of sedition', preached the famous sermon that set all London in an uproar. Cleverly mingling the Tory doctrine of non-resistance with scarcely concealed libels on the ministry, he welded his themes together with the stirring cry "The Church in danger!" The Church, which together with the Crown, the corner-stone of the realm, was the great bulwark against Papal tyranny! It was a plain issue; yet the sermon was full of difficult points, for it might be taken as an offence to Anne, who was, after all, a usurper. And so at first she took it. In spite of the popular applause that hailed this statement of her cherished Tory doctrines, she was annoyed: it was, she said, a disgraceful sermon. But as the Whig leaders became ever more violent in their clamour for prosecuting the preacher, and the people ever more turbulent in upholding him, she began to think that it might after all be a very useful sermon; it might even rid her of a tyranny far more galling to her than any conceivable imposition of a far-away Pope—namely that of her dear friends Mr. and Mrs. Freeman. More and more often did the tactful Mrs. Masham open the backstairs door of the royal apartments to Mr. Harley; more and more despairingly did the good bishop Burnet, to ease his conscience, do his level best to argue the Queen out of her almost traitorous Jacobitism: he could make no impression. The once vacillating but now obdurate old lady saw her opportunity, and, backed by the London rabble, was going to take it.

The junto summoned Wharton to manipulate the prosecution, and the 'scavenger of his party', as Bolingbroke called him, rushed over in eager haste to do a piece of work so much to his liking. He did it heartily, too heartily; for the more vigorous his procedure, the worse it was for his friends: his sparks only served to inflame the mob. But in any case the Whigs were doomed. "The intrigue of the Earl of Oxford might facilitate the means, the violent prosecution of Sacheverell . . . might create the occasion . . . but the original cause was the personal ill-usage"[1] the Queen had received in her private life from Atossa. Once aroused, there was no wearing down the stubborn resolution of a Stuart. Supported by a country frightened by such Pyrrhic victories as that of Malplaquet, by a people weary of a war for the monstrous continuance of which they rightly saw no reason but only too keenly felt the burden, Anne took her course. The bonfires which celebrated the nominal sentence passed on Sacheverell expressed her own jubilation and assured her of her power. Gradually she made her changes. Shrewsbury became Lord Chamberlain; Sunderland was dismissed, shortly to be followed by his mother-in-law, Sarah Marlborough, and, to his literally crying mortification, Godolphin. Rochester became Lord President of the Council. And when at the close of the year Wharton resigned, narrowly escaping impeachment for malpractices,[2] Addison, who occupied too high a position to be left unmolested, was condemned to the obscurity of a subordinate whose party is out of power. But he had served his apprenticeship; and what better education than his, in theory and practice, could an ambitious man desire?

[1] Letter to Windham. [2] Wentworth, 161.

II

THE FRUITS OF EDUCATION

I

Friendships

THE blow of being out, though not unexpected, was none the less severe, coming as it did in a downward turn in Addison's other affairs. " I have within this twelvemonth ", he wrote to Wortley, " lost a place worth £2,000 per ann.; an estate in the Indies worth £14,000, and what is worse than all the rest, my mistress . . . I find they are going to take away my Irish place from me too; to which I must add that I have just resigned my fellowship, and that stocks sink every day." The Indian estate was a legacy from his brother Gulston, who had died in the previous year, and which proved mainly irrealizable;[1] the Irish place was the keepership of the records, which he was allowed for some time to retain; but since discretion has blotted out any further vestige of the mistress, we must confine ourselves to sympathy with a man apparently faced with penury. " Wonder at my philosophy! " he bade Wortley. But Wortley need not have wondered much at the fortitude which could bear this indigence. For at the end of the year Addison was able to spend ten thousand pounds in buying the charming country house of Bilton, near Rugby.

Yet he could well have felt some dismay, and it was

[1] Egerton MSS.

perhaps at this crisis he exacted from Steele the repayment of the famous debt. Steele, it appears,[1] had borrowed some money from him—whether a hundred or a thousand pounds is uncertain—on the security of his new house at Hampton Wick, the term of the loan being one year. Of course the money was not forthcoming at the right time; any one who knew Steele would have foretold this, as they must have known he believed that

> An ounce of debt was nere seene yet
> Paid by a pound of sorrowe,

and that regard for his 'dear Prue' would make any reduction in the family style of living out of the question. But Addison seems to have been much disturbed at the sight of a man, his friend to boot, frivolous enough to enjoy himself when he ought to have been weighed down by a sense of obligation unfulfilled. But could even Steele, knowing Addison so well, aware of his rectitude, have imagined that Addison would instruct his attorney to enter up an execution, sell the house and furniture over his head, and send him the surplus money? It hardly seems the behaviour of a friend; yet Addison was sure he was acting from something even higher than the purest motives of disinterested love. One can almost hear a voice saying, "My boy, it hurts me more than it hurts you". For, with the money over from the sale, he sent Steele "a genteel letter to assign his friendly reason for taking so extraordinary a step, viz. to try (if possible) to awake him from that lethargy, which must end in his inevitable ruin".[2]

One would think such a step must end in the inevitable ruin of a long and close friendship; it was certainly taking an enormous risk. But Steele, with his marvellous

[1] Aitken, i. 342-4.   [2] Victor to Garrick, Sept. 1762.

generosity, his wide acceptance of human nature, his real superiority of mind which in spite of his journalistic moralizings could be so splendidly heedless of opinion, took Addison's behaviour, genteel letter and all, as being merely another of those tiresome events of which life was full. He " met his friend with the same gaiety of temper that he had always done ". Here in truth is a philosophy to wonder at. Yet could he quite forget? Did the memory never, just a touch, rankle?

Addison, indeed, was a little too exacting in his friendships; in the end even Steele, in spite of a life of devotion, could not quite stomach the methods of the master. 'The master', the word seems unavoidable: Steele was Dicky to Addison, but it is nowhere recorded that Steele ever called Addison 'Joe'. For, for a man to be a friend of Addison, he had to see behind the rather expressionless features a king, a supreme law-giver, one who could indeed give, but to whom nothing could conceivably be given. Addison—it is a very human failing—liked to be the only fount of blessings; but he also—and this failing is less human—wished to be the final justiciar.

It is, we know, much pleasanter to give than to receive; but it is sometimes more blessed to receive than to be the patron, and this Addison could never do on the level of friendship, however easy he found it on the circus-floor of political favour. Swift was to discover it.

That tremendous personality, even when chaplain to Lord Wharton, was in no position to patronize either the author of *The Campaign* or the Secretary to the Lord-Lieutenant; nor did he wish to do so. Addison was one of the few men he genuinely liked and admired, and, as we have seen, Addison returned the admiration. But during the Tory ascendancy of the last four years of

Queen Anne's reign, when Swift was, or at least appeared to be, the greatest unofficial political power in the country, something came between the friends, something Swift could not destroy, and which caused him a chagrin even the carefully unemotional pages of the *Journal to Stella* cannot conceal.

Swift's most pleasurable anticipation on coming back to London in the autumn of 1710 was that of once more meeting the other two members of the triumvirate ; his earliest journal mentions Steele, to whose office his letters were to be addressed under cover. At first he saw Addison nearly every day, dined in his company three or four times a week ; and when Steele was turned out of his office, Swift's letters were sent to Addison. But then, heedlessly, Swift, who despised party and loved the warmth of friendship, was ill-advised enough to try to use his influence to keep Steele in his other place, that of Stamp Commissioner. He " went to sit with Mr. Addison and offer the matter at a distance to him, as the discreeter person ; but found party had so possessed him, that he talked as if he suspected me, and would not fall in with anything I said. . . . Is not this vexatious? and is there so much in the proverb of proffered service? When shall I grow wise?. . . . What must a man expect from his enemies? " The next evening he behaved himself " coldly enough to Mr. Addison ".[1]

There was, however, no rupture, and the triumvirate continued to dine together ;[2] but in less than a month we read, " Mr. Addison and I meet a little seldomer than formerly, although we are still at bottom as good friends as ever ; but differ a little about party " ;[3] and after a similar interval, " Mr. Addison and I hardly meet

[1] *Stella*, 22nd and 23rd Oct. 1710.
[2] e.g. 25th Oct. and 4th Nov. [3] 16th Nov.

once a fortnight; his parliament and my different friendships keep us asunder".[1] Addison, however, made one or two efforts to avoid the appearance of estrangement, and once hauled Swift out to supper. Yet in the very same letter where this is recorded Swift wrote, "Mr. Addison and I are different as black and white, and I believe our friendship will go off, by this damned business of party . . . but I love him still as well as ever".[2]

Swift then, till this point, ascribed the cooling off to party feeling, but the next day, Steele having failed to take advantage of an offer, he wrote with a flash of insight, "I believe Addison hindered him out of mere spite, being grated to the soul to think he should ever want my help to save his friend". There was the rub. It did indeed grate Addison to the soul to think that others should invade his right to give. It was more than he could bear. He tried, but he could not battle against this insidious jealousy: he wanted too much to possess his friends as God possesses his creatures. Another meeting occurred, uncommented, but at the next Swift records he "talked coldly awhile with Mr. Addison; all our friendship and dearness are off: we are civil acquaintance".[3] Civil! that meant as cold as charity. Party was no longer dragged in to provide an explanation and a salve, and at last we read, uncommented, "all our friendship is over".[4]

This was in March 1711, and a few rather bitter references at the way he has been treated for trying to help Whig poets and Steele and Addison is all that we hear, except that Swift sees neither of the last. But in July the old three met again at young Jacob Tonson's dinner-table, where Swift and Addison "talked as

[1] 12th Dec. [2] 14th Dec. [3] 14th Jan. 1711.
[4] 6th March.

usual ".[1] But meetings were rare, through no fault of Swift's, and they appear also to have been casual, though once or twice they ended in their supping together, to the parson's delight, for " I yet know no man half so agreeable as he is ".[2] But Addison was always frigid, and Swift once said, " the Secretary [St. John] is as easy with me as Mr. Addison *was* ".[3] For a year the erstwhile friends do not seem to have met—Swift's letters are now sent elsewhere–and when they did encounter in the park, Addison " looked terrible dry and cold ".[4] And though the late Irish Secretary was present at the funeral of their mutual protégé Harrison, and perhaps drove in the same coach as the intimate of Harley, Swift does not mention the fact.[5] He is silent also as to the breakfast where he invited Addison and Berkeley to meet each other.[6] Was he too sick at heart to talk about his friend, to refer to meetings that were hideous, and attempts that were failures? Jonathan was loyal—but what had happened to David?

The future author of the most terrible satires since Juvenal's behaved, however, with a magnanimity equal to Steele's; or else it was that Addison had some quality, maybe some weakness, that made his friends forgive him anything. When he thought Addison would need all possible support for a play he was going to have acted—was it to tell him so Addison came so surprisingly to his levee? [7]—Swift prevailed upon Bolingbroke to invite him to dinner. Did it help to soothe the already tingling lacerations of the great heart that his friend immediately accepted *that* invitation? As he wrote of it to Stella, all his warmth, all his bitterness, seem gathered in the

[1] 26th July. [2] 14th Sept. [3] 3rd Nov.
[4] 27th Dec. 1712. [5] 15th Feb. 1713; and Wentworth, 319.
[6] Berkeley's *Letters*, 1713. [7] 28th March 1713.

single stabbing phrase, " I suppose we shall be mighty mannerly ".[1]

Truly, a friendship on equal terms, necessarily involving some of the rougher edges of human relationship, was impossible to Addison. Intimacies of that kind are never quite safe; they may even be imprudent. " Take heed of thy friends ", Addison quoted,[2] just as Tupper, so dear to the Victorians, in his poem on friendship advised, " Be shy of too much openness with any ". With the timidity that lay at the root of his nature Addison needed to feel safe, indeed superior. He could not bear to be in any way *froissé*; a hurt to his dignity was intolerable. He had what a modern psychologist would call an ' inferiority complex ', which, combined with his ambition, made any exposure of weakness an appalling contingency. Order, formality, in fact the protective frame of social use and wont was what he chiefly craved; a realm where discretion was the better part of philosophy, and method rather than unaccountable man, the natural measure of things.

It is perhaps this which can most readily explain his dislike of women—less accountable even than men—for that marked aversion from the ' fair-sex ' which yet engaged so much of his thought. For women will not, as the generality of men are apt to do, accept a man on his supposed merits: they often have a disconcerting realism in their make-up, a knack of seeing through male pretensions. And Addison, without attaching any opprobrium to the word, was pretentious; he deliberately tried to model his life on a formula, on a preconceived idea. However laudable this may be in the outer commerce of the world, it will not do where closer relationships are concerned; it easily becomes

[1] 1st April. [2] *Spectator*, 68.

dishonesty, a pose. In intimacy with a woman, it is not the moral value, but the emotional reality that counts, and here there must be equality. Addison knew that in conjugal life, though to the world the man may, to use the vulgar idiom, wear the breeches, there is a complete equality of the bedchamber, where breeches are not worn. Thus his intuition warned him against commerce with the fair sex, which, however, he never ceased to ridicule or try to improve. For although he knew their nature was antipathetic to his, it was not altogether foreign; some effeminacy in his own nature made them strangely fascinating to him; he could not leave them alone in his essays. When Steele invented Mrs. Distaff, he eagerly seized the pen and threw himself into feminine guise, in a glow one is tempted to think, of mental transvestitism, for as many papers as he thought his readers could bear.[1] Indeed his absorption in the subject became a byword. "I will not meddle with the *Spectator*", Swift wrote of the journal he seldom read, "let him fair-sex it to the world's end."[2] Addison, however, preferred to fair-sex it on foolscap rather than in drawing-rooms. Women might be "the most beautiful part of the creation, entirely amiable",[3] but their amiability was rather too theoretic for his taste, their 'blemishes' too many.

But telling most heavily against his forming any friendship on terms of parity was his need of self-reclusion. It was not only the fear of failure or retaliation that caused him to publish anonymously, it was also delight in the masquerade. If he preferred to write 'behind a curtain', as Gay said, he loved to live behind a veil; he sought cover with a profound, irrational instinct. It was as though he wished to keep in his soul something

[1] *Tatlers.* [2] *Stella*, 8th Jan. 1712. [3] *Spectator*, 57.

inviolable that even the dearest friend should not touch, a trait that comes out curiously time and again in his use of the adjective 'secret'. In a certain *Spectator* it occurs no less than three times in one paragraph,[1] and his mania for the word went so far as sometimes to endanger the sense of a phrase. Why, for instance, should Public Credit in the allegory, 'smile with a *secret* pleasure' as she gazed at the Act of Settlement and the tablets that embodied beneficent funding measures? [2]

It is really not always easy to discover exactly what Addison meant by the word: sometimes he used it in the common sense of hidden, or hidden away, as when he spoke of 'secret springs and motives',[3] 'secret shame',[4] or the distributions perfomed by the organs of our body.[5] So also did he use it to refer to the 'rest' and the 'graces' in a man that are seen only by God.[6] But it could not have meant this when Sir Roger, in asking after a tenant absent from church administered thereby a 'secret reprimand'.[7] Further, the word is frequently used quite gratuitously, or at best as padding to eke out the failing balance of a sentence: it is hardly ever necessary, sometimes it is tautological, often it is entirely meaningless. Why should Mr. Spectator be touched by a 'secret joy' at meeting Sir Roger,[8] or be pleased to observe 'the secret joy' Will Wimble 'discovered' at the sight of the good old knight? [9] Why should the prospect of immortality fill Mr. Spectator with 'secret joys',[10] and that of the Royal Exchange with 'secret satisfaction'? [11]

In short it is impossible to avoid the conclusion that for some reason there was an obsession. What is the

[1] *Spectator*, 256. [2] 3. [3] 475. [4] 23. [5] 115.
[6] 257, also 565, 399. [7] 112. [8] 269. [9] 108.
[10] 111. [11] 69.

force of the word in such phrases as 'a secret kind of instinct',[1] or a 'secret discontent' where the discontent was made apparent to every one?[2] Or in 'secret virtue of an innuendo',[3] or 'secret murmurings of heart',[4] or in the sentence where, discussing the structure of the state, we learn "I could never read a passage in Polybius, and another in Cicero, to this purpose, without a secret pleasure in applying it to the English constitution"?[5] Why all this——stealth?

It is bewildering until one notices that the adjective nearly always goes with expressions of gratification, as though the ideas were definitely associated. Again and again we come across 'secret' satisfaction, joy, pleasure, or delight; and almost always the use is surprising. We begin to see that privacy for Addison was inseparable from blissful emotions, and that the word does not mean hidden so much as especial, peculiar to himself, occult. Just as our first parents experienced a 'secret intoxication of pleasure' when they ate the forbidden fruit,[6] or Adam felt a 'secret pleasure' when, in *Paradise Lost*, he was granted a vision of universal death,[7] so Addison found a 'secret delight' in sudden sunshine as in cheerfulness,[8] a 'secret satisfaction and complacency' from the beauties of creation;[9] so from the 'secret effects' of God's mercy he derived 'secret comforts and refreshments'.[10] And if he once felt a 'secret horror' at his smallness in face of the Universe,[11] he felt a 'secret satisfaction and contentment' in his own good-nature,[12] and a 'secret pride' that his speculations had met with a very kind reception.[13]

This stress upon the recondite nature of enjoyment is curious: it is significant, it is even illuminating. The

[1] *Spectator*, 130. [2] 440. [3] 567. [4] 387. [5] 287.
[6] 351. [7] 363. [8] 381 [9] 393. [10] 571.
[11] 565. [12] 177. [13] 553; and see Appendix III.

use of the word betrays at once Addison's ambition and his timidity ; it may even account for many of his actions. By it we see how he hedged himself about ; how, for fear of hurt, of loss, of disappointment, he learned to be sufficient to himself, to guard unspotted the image of his being he could not be sure of imposing upon society. It reveals how he was his own refuge from the buffets and assaults of a crude, indelicate world. And however much we may hesitate to draw further conclusions, this partly explains why he preferred to take his ease in a circle where he could rule, and rule alone, and where, by his very superiority, he could gain a ' secret satisfaction ' nobody present could share with him, or roughly disturb.

For Addison did not care to pass his time in the houses of the great or the powerful—except to certain types of mind that is apt to be boring—but neither did he like to consort with his compeers in letters, nor seek yet more learning at the lips of still greater pundits than he. He preferred instead to linger at a coffee-house in Russell Street, Covent Garden, where he had helped to establish as proprietor an old family servant of the Warwicks' called Button. There he found relaxation and stimulus, amid a ' little senate ' of young admirers, Tickell, Philips, Budgell (who at this time shared rooms with him), and, of course, his revering contemporary Steele, although the last was rather less his confidant than formerly.

And there were others : D'Avenant, the son of the great Sir William of theatrical fame, the only member of the circle older than Addison ; Henry Carey, the baby of the group, a charming, witty youth and a lively companion, who had something of the genius of his natural father George Savile, Marquis of Halifax. There was Hughes, who aspired after dramatic fame, and who, five years younger than Addison, was already fighting a fatal consumption. For a while there was Harrison, Swift's friend, " a pretty little fellow, with a great deal of wit, good sense and good-nature ",[1] but who failed when he tried to carry on *The Tatler*: and we catch a glimpse of 'little Thomson', who was an 'excellent youth'.[2] There was also Colonel Brett, whose inclusion in the clique would seem to need some explanation, for he alone of them all had no literary pretensions. On the other hand he had " an uncommon share of social wit, and a handsome person, with a sanguine bloom in his complexion ".[3] As successful in seducing the minds of men as he was in overcoming the hearts of women, his sprightly sallies of venial flattery were such that no man left his company without feeling cleverer than he had before, for none could escape the spell of his 'amicable adulation'. And lastly, more especially as Tickell's college friend, there was Edward Young, " very pleasant in conversation ",[4] who was to expiate twenty years of gaiety by writing his *Night Thoughts* in the dull seclusion of the rectory at Welwyn.

All these names save Steele's would be obscure were it not for the happy chance that caused Dr. Johnson to give some of them an immortality their poetry could not earn for them. He wrote their lives. Perhaps, however, Carey's name lives independently, through 'Sally in Our Alley'. But it must be admitted it was a second-rate gathering to form the social *milieu* of a man like Addison, when he might have seen more of Berkeley, or cultivated the acquaintance of Newton, Bentley, or Wren. One never hears of him with Vanbrugh, and Congreve he only met at strange dinner-

[1] *Stella*, 13th Oct. 1710. [2] Addison to Philips, 25th April 1710.
[3] Cibber, xi. [4] Boswell, iv. 58.

tables. We have seen what happened with Swift, but in any case Harley's pocket philosopher could not have frequented the Whig enclave at Button's. Addison, however, seems deliberately to have avoided the society of his semblables, and to have chosen this mediocre gathering of men nearly all younger than himself, where, owing to Steele's deference, he was far removed from intellectual competition.

> " 'Tis amazing to me, I own, that with so much of the gentleman, such a general knowledge of books and men, such a skill in the learned as well as modern languages, he can take so much delight as he does in the company of such persons as I have described . . . I can think of but one reason for it . . . his vanity; which makes him desirous of being considered as the head of the people he consorts with. A man to love praise; yet be content to draw it from such contaminated springs!"

So Miss Clarissa Harlowe to her friend Miss Howe, the subject Lovelace;[1] but they are the thoughts that naturally arise when we muse upon Addison and his little senate. They must be followed out if we are to understand his character.

Addison was above all things sensitive to the opinions of his fellow men; this formed the basis of his social philosophy. The first words on the title page of this essay, though not his, typify his attitude. He could not be negligent of what any one thought of him.

> "A man's first care", he wrote, "should be to avoid the reproaches of his own heart; his next, to escape the censures of the world: If the last interferes with the former, it ought to be entirely neglected; but otherwise there cannot be a greater satisfaction to an honest mind, than to see those approbations which it gives itself

[1] Letter LXVI.

seconded by the applauses of the public: a man is more sure of his conduct, when the verdict which he passes on his own behaviour is thus warranted and confirmed by the opinion of all that know him." [1]

That is one part of the philosophy of the *qu'en dira-t-on?*; it is sound worldly common sense, but it has its obvious limitations, and its dangers. It is rarely that a keen sensitiveness to the censures of the world does not in some measure affect the dictates of the heart.

But there was more than the desire to escape the censure of the world in Addison's choice of companions; there was the intense need to ensure its applause, to experience the 'secret pride' of being approved, and, as well, the wish to lead its opinions. For there can be no doubt that Pope's famous satire is bottomed on truth. Addison loved to give laws, to see the foolish face of praise, and although these are human attributes, he carried them so far as to be content to swim a sprat among minnows. In his case the social philosophy of the Victorians overreached itself: even his contemporaries saw through it. " I love good creditable acquaintance; I love to be the worst of the company ", Swift wrote, and the allusion seems plain; " I am not of those that say, for want of company, welcome trumpery." [2]

Pope recorded the facts, but facts are always susceptible of being wrongly stressed, and maybe there was something deeper than vanity in Addison's behaviour here, something even more fundamental. It occasionally happens with men in whom the desire to dominate has from one cause or another not been gratified—as was the case with Addison from reasons partly social, partly subjective—that their ambition is transformed into a craving to be loved. And at Button's Addison found that intimacy,

[1] *Spectator*, 122. [2] *Stella*, 17th May 1711.

that immediate, prejudiced sympathy, which men usually seek in the society of one or two women, a society so impossible to him. There he was regarded as one to be treated tenderly, to be protected and compassionated as well as worshipped, to be cherished in his never-admitted weaknesses, so that all his energies might go to swell his genius. Such a view tallies with his writings; and if this attitude too is vanity, it is a form on which no one need be severe.

Apart from this it might be argued that after all Addison was free to choose the company in which he felt at ease; that he was at liberty to say with Gibbon, "I am too modest, or too proud, to rate my own value by that of my associates", and that "after the morning has been occupied by the labours of the library, I wish to unbend rather than exercise my mind". But it was not exactly to unbend that Addison frequented Button's. He went to experience that "kind of grandeur and respect, which the meanest and most insignificant part of mankind endeavour to procure in the little circle of friends and acquaintance".[1] It was just there, far from the possibility of criticism, that he liked to exercise his mind: nowhere else could he do it. Like Pythagoras, he felt wisdom was only to be spoken among the perfect.

He felt happy, safe from the dubious judgements of the world, in that coterie of charming, handsome, and on the whole intelligent young men, who paid him so much homage, and the flattery of imitation. He needed imitators. Under that influence he burgeoned, expanded, blossomed. His talk, spangled with quotations from the Latin poets, lively with gently sarcastic hits at the fair sex, rich with unexceptionable 'speculations' on the

[1] *Spectator*, 219.

soul, gushed forth under the stimulus of wine and adoration. Perhaps, as Tupper advised the Victorians, he made ' discretion guard his asking, and discretion aid his answer ', but sometimes surely he ' gave loose to every passion and every thought that was uppermost '.[1] Certainly never, it is universally agreed, was there such a splendid conversationalist, such a stylist in spoken prose. If he needed to be a king before he could be a wizard, what matter so long as the wizardry was there? And so, plied with the cup by Steele, backed by Budgell, who ' rain'd sacrificial whisperings in his ear ', encouraged by the devoted eyes of little Philips and the approving smile of Tickell, he would divagate for hours at a stretch, and the fewer and the more select the listeners, the better the talk would be. The ' stiff kind of silence ' that enveloped him when a stranger was present seemed a myth. The clock of St. Paul's Church would strike two, three, or even four, and still the calm voice would go on, invoking Plato and Aristotle to prove the immortality of the soul, Boileau and Bouhours to witness the necessity for correctness, Socrates to ensample the nobility of man. And as the company walked out into the dim light of early morning there seemed a spell of beauty cast over the meanest of life's activities, an assurance of the goodness of existence, a warmth in the heart which even the chill of dawn could not immediately dispel.

Sometimes, no doubt, they read each other their work—some scraps of prose, perhaps, destined for a *Tatler*, *Spectator*, or *Guardian* ; or some poems—Tickell's or Hughes's latest verses in praise of Addison, or Philips's latest pastoral. And when they came to read poetry the voice of the reader would change, soften, become un-

[1] *Spectator*, 68.

recognizable : and the laboured lines would be drawled with as rapturous an intonation as ever parson used to bog a collect in canorous orismology.[1]

But there was not poetry every day, and all the talk was not on the high philosophic level. There was political and literary gossip, and a good deal of tittle-tattle, when men would be criticized together with, and as freely as, their work. But Addison could never bring himself to formulate an adverse criticism, and when he heard one made would smile deprecatingly. If a poem was torn to pieces he would point out some passage that might, after all, be worse : he would seek to praise, however faintly honesty might compel him to do so. Hesitating to condemn, he would sometimes just hint a fault, and would never be too blunt, seeing how easy it is to make a mistake in literary judgement. His only error was not to be sharp enough on the Parnassian sneers of his friends, though he himself was never guilty of so invidious a gesture. Was it not his role to be

> A most incomparable man, breath'd as it were
> To an untiring and continuate goodness?

But there are times when one can be a little too careful ; and a touch more virility, a tithe more, even, of prejudice, would have saved him later some of the shattering verses of the 'Character of Atticus'.

For Pope came ; he heard, he libelled. He should never have been admitted. His gratitude for *The Spectator's* praise of the *Essay on Criticism* was no fitting passport to that *cénacle.* Although not without a certain elfin charm of feature, a beauty such as might befit a sick sprite, his 'crazy little carcass' must have shown

[1] Misson. "Quand ils passent en lisant, de la Prose aux Vers, vous diriez que ce n'est plus la même personne qui parle : leur ton de voix devient doux et langoureux : ils sont charmez, ils se pâment."

strangely in that passably foppish gathering where personal grace was not despised. Nor could he take his wine well; it upset his stomach, and fevered an imagination already prone to malignancy. For a year or so he was a fairly constant attendant, but he was not happy there. For he also was avid of praise. He knew himself to be a better poet than even the lord of Button's, and did not like to take a back seat to Tickell, nor enjoy tumbling in the ruck with Budgell. There he sat like Judas at the feast, ready not only to betray, but to usurp, visioning the time when he would be, not Cato giving his little senate laws, but King Alexander in a realm where to be his enemy was to be dubbed a dunce and 'ridiculed into immortality'.

Only two of the senate did he really like, transparent Steele, and Tickell; and, as Macaulay remarked, those two loved Addison too well to love each other. And buzzing insidiously, 'the little wasp of Twickenham' scented and encouraged jealousies. For all was not always harmony in Addison's choir. Not only was there Tickell to be played off against Steele, but Carey could be egged on to banter Philips, at whose expense he enriched the language with the term 'namby-pamby'. And the senate made the mistake of under-estimating the new member. Satisfied with themselves, they did not guess the extraordinary linguistic power, that allied with a fiery and distorted temperament as with a mind whose very limitations made it lucid, would bring the literary world to his feet, make the great writhe, and create immortal masterpieces of virulent satire.

But they had a taste of it. In the spring of 1713, when *The Guardian* had replaced *The Spectator*, a paper was thrust into the lion-headed letter-box at Button's that received contributions to the journal, while it declared in Latin that it fed only on the finest game.[1] It proved to be an essay justifying the omission of Pope's name from a previous number dealing with pastoral poetry, wherein, as in a *Spectator*,[2] Philips had been praised, and declared a true descendant, in the direct line, of Spenser, Virgil, and Theocritus. Steele read over the contribution : he shook his head dubiously, said he would ask Pope if he would mind . . . pursed his lips, but —there was a twinkle in his eye.

In due course the paper appeared,[3] and Philips, full of pleasurable anticipation, settled down to read it. But as he perused the panegyric of himself at Pope's expense, he began to feel uneasy. Was not the butter spread just a trifle too thick? Was it not carrying the pastoral theory rather far to say, when lauding the Ambrosian plainness, that the other writer in this style " in expressing the same thought, deviates into downright poetry " ? He read on. He was gratified to see quoted some lines he really did think rather good :

> O woeful day ! O day of woe, quoth he,
> And woeful I, who live the day to see,

upon which the critic commented : " The simplicity of diction, the melancholy flowing of the numbers, the solemnity of the sound, and the easy turn of the words in this dirge, to make use of our author's expression, are extremely elegant."

Even Philips could not fail to see : the paper was spoof. It was in fact a superb, exquisitely delicate, masterly piece of irony. It was devastating, catastrophic. ' Pastoral ' Philips would grow ashamed of his honourable title. He raged, he swore, he put his hand upon the hilt

[1] Servantur Magnis/Isti Cervicibus Ungues ;/Non Nisi Delectâ Pascitur/Ille Ferâ. (Ashton.)

[2] No. 523. [3] *Guardian*, 40.

of his sword, and—turned upon Steele. Dicky professed the blandest innocence. He was very sorry. He had been taken in. He had thought the paper was in praise of Philips. Why, hadn't he even asked Pope's leave to publish it? The poetaster appealed to Addison; but much as the latter loved Philips, he could not help smiling at the admirable piece of pointed writing, clearly by Pope himself. Baffled upon every side, Philips hung up a cane at Button's, and vowed that if Pope showed his face there he would give him a drubbing. The renowned fencer obviously could not use his sword on a man who was half a cripple, but he would show him the cudgel was mightier than the pen. No doubt the threat met with the contempt it deserved, for Pope was not lacking in physical bravery, and probably did not keep away on Philips's account. But if he did appear the incident could not have improved the amenities of Button's, and from that time forth the two pastoral poets lived in the Johnsonian 'perpetual reciprocation of malevolence'.

The senate, however, could unite to form a powerful dramatic claque, in this respect vying in influence with its ally the Kit-Cat. Like that formidable club it could make a play go, as it did in the case of Philips's tragedy, *The Distressed Mother*, a version of Racine's *Andromaque*, 'improved', as was the custom, to suit the English taste. Steele undertook to pack the house; the play was puffed in *The Spectator*,[1] Sir Roger was taken to see it,[2] and it was a huge success. It pleased the town, even those who were not easily pleased. "Here is a new play which has taken extremly," Lady Strafford wrote, "call'd the distrest mothere. I had not seen it tell last night for

[1] No. 290. [2] *Spectator*, 335.

I dont much love Traidys, but I think its a very good won." [1]

Moreover, its success was not a little due to the epilogue, written by Budgell, which caused great enthusiasm. It used to be encored repeatedly, and instead of being dropped after the third performance, as was usual, was continued long after, at the noisy solicitation of the audience. It seemed to give just the right tone to send people happily away after too wearing a tragedy, for Andromache, their tried favourite Mrs. Oldfield, then at the height of her figure, declaimed in her famous silvery tones :

> I hope you'll own, that with becoming Art
> I've played my game, and topp'd the Widow's Part,
> My Spouse, poor Man ! could not live out the Play,
> But dy'd commodiously on Wedding-Day . . .

and much more on the same note, thus raising the painful view of mortality crawling on the dung of earth to the level of aesthetic indifference. No wonder the audience cheered and cheered again ! No wonder they would not be denied it ! One fact, however, which caused some surprise, was that Budgell himself would sit in the pit and call loudly for the verses he had written. It was as though he thought some other writer responsible for them. Indeed, could so mediocre a tagger of lines really have written so well ? Addison was asked about it. " Ah ! " he smiled modestly, " it was very different when he first brought it to me." But perhaps he was only thinking of the final couplet, a bold *non sequitur* to the preceding lines, which exhorted the listeners to

> Take then, ye Circles of the Brave and Fair,
> The Fatherless and Widow to your Care.

Thus the whole occasion gives a pleasing picture of how

[1] Wentworth, 280 : 25th March 1712.

loyally the little senate worked for the glory of its individual members, and with what a gentle hand Addison ruled his friends. Finally, when some pedantic curmudgeon wrote to *The Spectator* protesting against the epilogue, the letter was printed[1] to be suitably pulverized in a later number.[2]

[1] *Spectator*, 338. [2] *Spectator*, 341.

Emery Walker

ALEXANDER POPE

(*National Portrait Gallery*)

2

The Spectator

"La sagesse! quel thème inépuisable!"—*Amiel.*

ADDISON's period of enforced political idleness was not given over only to such occasions, for he was chiefly engaged upon the work whereon his fame most firmly rests, journalistic essay writing.

In 1709, bettering a method initiated by Defoe, Steele launched *The Tatler*, of which the name was chosen in compliment to the Fair Sex. The sheets were sent to Dublin, whence Addison, guessing by an allusion in one of them that their author was his friend, at once began to contribute. It was the very thing for him; there, without fear of exposure, he could try his hand. It was, as Miss Aikin said, "what his diffidence required, a safe and private channel". If he failed, the papers need never be known to be his; if he succeeded, he could in course of time step forward to take the honours due. In any case, modesty apart, it was a wise precaution to be anonymous, for the expression of views might be attended by uncomfortable results: bread cast upon calm waters might return in an unpleasant form after many days, when the waters were stormy. But in such a journal as *The Tatler* Addison really could express himself—and did, with the result that nothing reveals him more clearly than the long series of essays he wrote for various periodicals.

Of course absolute concealment over a great stretch of time could not be hoped for, but there would always be a doubt as to who had written any particular paper.

And here Steele, with his lamentable recklessness, came in useful. He was the ideal collaborator; he served as whipping-boy, a happy state of affairs not unobserved by Gay. "I have thought", he wrote of Steele and Addison, "that the conjunction of those two great geniuses (who seem to stand in a class by themselves, so high above all other wits), resembles that of two famous statesmen [Somers and Halifax] in a late reign . . . the first was continually at work behind the curtain; drew up and prepared all the schemes and designs which the latter still drove on, and stood out exposed to the world, to receive its praise or censures." [1]

Indeed, left by himself, Addison had not the nerve to 'drive on' a journal, and his attempt to set up *The Whig Examiner* in 1710 proved a failure, though to be sure political polemics were not his *forte*. If Somers and Halifax had reared him for this, they made a mistake in the subject they chose for training, for in that field he was no match for Prior, whom they had foolishly allowed to secede. Addison's *Whig Examiners* have, as Macaulay said, "as little merit as anything that he wrote",[2] and in December, after eight numbers, hearing that Swift was to take over *The Examiner*, the Tory instrument, he "avoided the contest as at once doubtful, harassing and invidious".[3]

At about this time Steele abruptly ended *The Tatler*, not that it was beginning to be thought dull, except by Swift, but that one or two opinions too Whiggish for the ruling powers had made certain difficulties. It was impossible to keep Steele's pen out of the political inkpot. But the venture had been so successful, so much to Addison's taste, that the friends almost at once started another journal: but this time it was Addison

[1] *Present State of Wit.* [2] Macaulay MS. [3] Scott, 112.

who decided on the tone. This paper would be on the same lines as *The Tatler*—less the news items—but would go at once farther and more carefully, while Steele was firmly kept in check. This journal would have as author a ' man ' who was strictly impartial, observing " an exact neutrality between Whigs and Tories ",[1] in fact a mere Spectator commenting with perfect aloofness, and never risking the loss of his ears, like Defoe—for no one else under such conditions could stand ' unabashed on high '. Far from being a party organ, it would direct men's minds away from faction, thus seconding the efforts of the Royal Society, which, as everybody knew, had with its ' air-pump, barometer, quadrant ' and the like fal-de-lals, been founded for that very purpose.[2] It would deal particularly with those seemingly trivial, but in reality grave errors incident to mankind living in society, and would " endeavour to enliven morality with wit and to temper wit with morality ". " But there are none ", Mr. Spectator promised, " to whom this paper will be more useful than to the female world." [3]

To some this might seem a small conception ; but in Addison's hand its scope was well-nigh limitless. " It was said of Socrates ", he wrote, " that he brought philosophy down from heaven, to inhabit among men ; and I shall be ambitious to have it said of me, that I have brought philosophy out of closets and libraries, schools and colleges, to dwell in clubs and assemblies, at tea-tables and coffee-houses." [4]

Philosophy ! It has a fine sound ; but what sort of philosophy is it that can flourish when " punctually served up as part of the tea-equipage " ? Did George Berkeley smile a little when he read the passage, and think

[1] *Spectator*, 1 : 1st March 1711.
[2] *Spectator*, 262.
[3] *Spectator*, 10.
[4] *Spectator*, 10.

of Locke, Spinoza, and his other adversaries? But it was at once clear that Mr. Spectator had not the least design of tackling those problems which are the brute material of philosophy, of dealing with those puzzling questions of reality, or of the validity of the ego. Not for him the pleasure and the pride of categories, nor the airy stilts of abstraction. Rather was the British Virgil about to become the suave and homely Marcus Aurelius of the tea-tables; and it soon appeared that his notion of philosophy was the elegant common sense apt to mould man into the *parfait honnête homme* dear to that very French society he paradoxically so much despised. Nay, it was something even more gentle. Nothing was too little for it—not the wearing of patches, the use of rings, the frivolity of the Gallic race, the exact degree of volubility proper to educated persons. The journal became a manual of deportment; and a statue of philosophy as conceived by Mr. Spectator might represent a benign grandmother knitting by the fireside, occasionally casting a slightly severe glance over her spectacles. And the old lady's more familiar name would be Common Sense.

Common sense! It was the dawn of the century that prided itself upon its mastery of it. But the principle is a negative one, the words capable of many interpretations. Yet Addison might have appealed to Berkeley for confirmation of his doctrine that common sense was the basis of philosophy, a thesis the latter was then writing his Dialogues to prove. "You see, Hylas," Philonous perorates, "the water of yonder fountain, how it is forced upwards, in a round column, to a certain height; at which it breaks, and falls back into the basin from whence it rose: its ascent as well as descent proceeding from the same uniform law or principle of *gravitation*.

Just so, the same principles which, at first view, lead to Scepticism, pursued to a certain point, bring men back to Common Sense."

But what seems common sense to one man is often uncommon nonsense to another. " Coxcombs vanquished Berkeley with a grin ", and Sir Roger de Coverley would no doubt have refuted the Irishman's peculiar form of that commodity by stamping particularly hard upon the ground. It was Dr. Johnson's method. But there was another kind of philosophy to help Mr. Spectator, that which caused La Bruyère to say that " on ne doit écrire que pour l'instruction . . . pour le changement des mœurs et la réformation de ceux qui lisent "—a view dear to Ruskin and Trollope, but which was unintelligible to Dryden, hard as he tried to assimilate it in his last years. So Mr. Spectator banished doubts ; he pinned his faith to La Bruyère, and calling his work ' philosophy ', proceeded to inculcate into the fair sex those precepts which, if followed, would make its members the most useful and agreeable of man's domestic animals.

" An ingenious man ", so Sir Charles Grandison referred to Addison ;[1] " an ingenious man, to whose works your sex, and if *yours ours*, are more obliged than to those of any single man in the British world ". If yours, ours, there 's the crux. For woman was to be the better half of man in that she was to give infinitely less trouble. She was to be intelligent, but not too clever, good-tempered, and docile to opinion ; without opinion, in fact, for nothing was worse for a face than party zeal.[2] If married, not only was she to give no cause for jealousy, she was to feel none :[3] in short, if the home was not happy, it was to be entirely her fault, never the man's. Addison's ideal was to create the Victorian helpmeet, one

[1] *Grandison*, ii, Letter 27. [2] *Spectator*, 57. [3] *Spectator*, 171.

who could write to her husband, " my own love, I will trust you. You will succeed, and I am patient. Your little wife knows you will not lose an opportunity which may lead to success, and if you are unfortunate she is there to kiss away all disappointment, and to console you as well as she can." [1] Addison, in fact, looking back in horror upon Restoration days and that monstrous regiment of women, was fitting the female neck for the virile yoke, and Henry Esmond had no illusions as to the design. " There 's not a writer of my time of any note ", he protested, " with the exception of poor Dick Steele, that does not speak of a woman as of a slave, and scorn and use her as such. Mr. Pope, Mr. Congreve, Mr. Addison, Mr. Gay, every one of 'em, sing in this key, each according to his nature and politeness." [2]

And between them they succeeded in creating the women they wished, a long line through the Jane Bennets to the Amelia Sedleys—they and the age which was tired of the Lady Betty Modishes and the Hoyden Clumseys, who seem to have displaced the Dorothy Osbornes as well as the Barbara Palmers and Olivia Vernishes. Certainly these ' writers of note ' set the fashion for the eighteenth century. If any one cares to look up Squire Western's opinions of the charms and sphere of women, he will find them, though phrased differently, identical with Addison's—and, strangely enough, with Squire Allworthy's. Addison, it is true, would not have spoken to his daughter as Western did to Sophy, but it is probable that had occasion arisen he would have acted towards her precisely as Mr. Harlowe did to Clarissa. In this matter, as in many others, he rightly interpreted the views of his contemporaries.

[1] The first Lady Esher to her husband. *Esher Letters.*
[2] *Esmond*, I. xii.

It is unlikely, of course, that Sarah Marlborough, or Marlborough's Misses, or Mrs. de la Rivière Manley, the unscrupulous pamphleteer, paid any heed to such hortations; and one wonders what bold Lady Mary Pierpoint thought of them as she made her runaway match with Addison's grave and didactic friend Mr. Wortley Montagu. But other members of the fair sex seemed to dote on *The Spectator*. They read it eagerly. It adorned three thousand tea-tables, and so universal was their suffrage, that Tickell, writing verses 'To the Supposed Author of *The Spectator*', crooned:

> Received by thee, I prophesy my rhymes
> The praise of virgins in succeeding times;

a curious compliment to a man who in the same poem was, as usual, referred to as the British Virgil, while 'Fame, Heav'n and Hell' were his 'exalted theme'.

It is true, they were. But 'the middle way is best', and these exalted themes were treated in that spirit of the golden mediocrity that is the only really safe guide either in the conduct of daily life or the promptings of the spirit. Addison did not care for Icarian flights of speculative thought, or for those emotions, so heavily paid for, plucked in the dark forests of the soul. Was not the 'artificial wildness' of Fontainebleau more welcome than the terrifying abysses of the Alps? Thus the thoughts that he developed in his modulated phrases seemed to many exactly the things they also were thinking, and indeed, his moral precepts were bound to meet with acquiescence in a post-Collier age which blossomed into Societies for the Reformation of Manners. In effect, *The Tatler* and *The Spectator* did not lead public opinion, they expressed it; they helped it to make up its mind. If, for instance, it was beginning to be felt that lap-dogs were becoming a nuisance, Isaac Bickerstaff would deluge them with whimsical scorn; but where public opinion gave no sign that venerable gentleman was silent. Petticoats might be judged too wide, bonnets too high; but since no one suggested that hanging youths for trivial offences was abominable, not the airiest breath of ridicule was wafted upon this barbarism from the club that contained Sir Roger de Coverley, Sir Andrew Freeport, and Will Honeycomb. *Vox populi, vox Dei*; and it was through the voice of the people that Addison hearkened to the voice of God. He had stumbled upon the secret of successful journalism.

Originality, alas! was out of the question, for mankind had reached the farthest stretch of wisdom. "We have little left us, but to represent the common sense of mankind in more strong, more beautiful, or more uncommon lights."[1] Boileau had said it: Horace had proved it. This being the case, Addison could never shock, for it is the new view that most revolts mankind. "The novelty, Philonous, the novelty! There 's the danger." Thus in his 'visions' he could deal with 'exalted themes' in a way that must appeal to every one. Not a virgin but could appreciate *The Vision of Mirza*, that simple allegory of life and death and future reward. It might be objected that such a theme was perilously close to religion, that such a subject if any might conceal a trap. But there, as in politics, Addison picked his way gingerly, offending none. Was it not admitted that "there is not a more melancholy object than a man who has his head turned with religious enthusiasm"?[2] Naturally he rejected superstition, not, however, on the grounds of hated science,[3] but on the solid basis of a simple faith he had no difficulty in believing. For he was never borne upward very far in the fountain of

[1] *Spectator*, 253. [2] *Spectator*, 201. [3] See *Tatlers*, 216, 221.

Philonous, and even a constant study of Bayle's Dictionary failed to undermine the thoughts he had imbibed in the Deanery at Lichfield.

His literary criticism, too, guided the steps of his readers into paths they were willing to tread. Written not in the spirit of Dryden's prefaces or of Pope's *Essay on Criticism*, it pointed out the spiritual rather than the literary beauties of Milton, as it did the simple feeling of 'Chevy Chase'. And, though resting on authority, it is not surprising that Dr. Johnson found him a poor critic, though for the wrong reasons, and that Landor preferred the judgements of Steele, for Addison was not a critic so much as a popularizer, the forbear of a manifold line. His dissertations too were so written that it needed little thought to follow them, indeed only so much as might conveniently be spared in the coffee-houses of the busy world.

Nevertheless popularity is not gained merely by dubbing oneself 'censor of manners' and uttering comfortable commonplace, by preaching the sweet doctrine of the obvious virtues—politeness; honesty, political and commercial; continence—lest disfigurement follow; truth-telling, faith, charity; and above all, prudence, respect for opinion. The public of Queen Anne's day read *The Spectator*, not because it was pious, but because it was charmingly, and on the whole freely, written. It might sometimes become a little tedious, but that was only to be expected, since Addison chose to write over the initials C.L.I.O., and the muse of that name is, as we know, "apt to be pompous". On the other hand it was full of pleasant little tales from the classics, or from Bayle's Dictionary, and miniatures of character such as would have delighted La Bruyère. Wit enlivened morality; and the fair sex, while no doubt feeling virtuously in agreement with a man who hated fashion as much as any mid-Victorian, could hold their sides with laughter at reading that one of the honorific titles of the Shah of Persia was 'nutmeg of delight'. For though Addison "would not willingly laugh but in order to instruct",[1] he was a master in the art of gentle humour. Indeed, had not his goal been the ears of the fair sex, it might be supposed his humour was too gentle.

In any case the even flow of his prose was most seductive to the circles that would only read that which could easily be read. His English lies liquid on the palate like a really happy port—but it is a ladies' port. For in his writing there is none of the rhythmed bell-note of Browne, the rolling swell of Milton's cadence, nor the vigorous thud of Dryden's galloping hoofs. Beside Swift's rapier the edge is waxy; compared with Bolingbroke's delicate architecture Addison's is—Addison Road. But, still more to jostle metaphor, his readers could, as it were, feel themselves deliciously rocked on phrases that swing like cockle-boats in the wake of a great ship. His prose, in short, like his precepts, is, in the Johnsonian phrase, "the model of the middle style".

To the student of drum-and-trumpet history, or to those whose interest lies in disentangling clear lines of development in the chaos of human strife, *The Spectator* must seem a singular growth in the hot-bed of faction presented by the last four years of Queen Anne's reign. Statesmen, soldiers, even bishops, appeared in the smithy of double-handed intrigue, dangerous with white-hot sparks, in which, not without many slain, the British Constitution was hazardously and blindly forged. Then paper and ink were barbed weapons that might easily

[1] *Spectator*, 179.

wound the many hands that wielded them, and often did. In an atmosphere of Guiscard attempts, crowds flocking to see the body of Harley's would-be murderer suspended in a window; of bandbox plots which brought so much ridicule on courageous Dr. Swift; amid rumours of attempted landings by the Chevalier St. George, the king over the water; or gripping fears as to the Queen's health; surrounded by tempers that could pass the Tory Occasional Conformity and Schism Acts and plan the Whig procession Steele was to lead;[1] when men who had not forgotten William's usurpation or the Monmouth rebellion anxiously saw to their fire-arms, and Mohocks struck terror into astrologers, it seems incredible that men should have had time to read *The Spectator*. But however stirring revolutions may be, for the most part of the time the normal life goes on—since it is that by which we live—and men pursue their favourite callings. We may remember that in 1712 the Royal Society published its vindication of Newton against Leibnitz as the inventor of the Infinitesimal Calculus, that Collins and the Arian Clarke continued their metaphysical discussions of other-worldly matters, that Berkeley composed his dialogues, Lord Mohun killed the Duke of Hamilton in a duel, and Pope took lessons in painting.

Thus through all the geyser-spouting of pamphlets and libels engendered by the ballad-breeding—and Peer-creating—Peace of Utrecht; in the midst of fierce criticism such as that contained in *The Conduct of the Allies*; in a thundery air of suppression, vituperation, calumny, and Grub Street taxes, Addison and his little senate were able calmly to write *The Spectator*, which Swift might find boring[2]—he believed they were

[1] See *ante*, Vanbrugh, p. 136.

[2] Swift to Stella, 18th Nov. 1711: "Do you read the *Spectators*? I never do."

'prettily written'—but which circles of young ladies found diverting, and breakfast-tables an excuse for silence. Yet it was indeed a staggering performance in that there was nothing 'party' about it; that is, it could not deal with subjects which at that crisis of the nation's history were the only ones of acute public interest. Non-party, when the safety of the new, hard-won régime called loudly for the fierce trying-out of opposite views! But that was just its secret. It could please Stella in Dublin, or make good bundles for maternal devotion to send to Lord Raby in Holland: and being a comment on the things of the day that did not in the least matter, it brought profit without fear to the writers and the printer. It was so eminently safe that one could hardly refuse to subscribe. If it did not cause excitement like *The Public Spirit of the Whigs*, nor raise laughter so boisterous as the account of Prior's journey into France, it was, on the other hand, as suitable to the antechamber of Lord Halifax as to the boudoir of Lady Masham. Bolingbroke and Marlborough might not waste their time over it, but Drs. Arbuthnot and Garth might without a second thought approvingly con the same passages of dramatic criticism, or smile at the same metrical version of a psalm. It shone alike upon the just and the unjust. Like a 'whimsical Tory' it seemed at once to be against war and against Jacobitism; like an occasional conformer it could compound with conscience for the sake of doing good.

It is all the same obvious that a journal like *The Spectator*, with the work falling chiefly on one man, cannot go on for ever. Polished work is not done offhand, and although Addison could dictate almost the finished essay once he had it clear in his head, he nevertheless polished considerably. Nor is elaborate and considered description, if it is not quite criticism, such as he wrote on *Paradise Lost*, lightly thrown off. Moreover, even perfect wisdom is not really inexhaustible, nor can any man pontificate urbanely for every morning's breakfast without reaching a limit, although the subject be the sum total of the universe. Universality itself begins to appear a trifle ridiculous, it becomes too much, in Corbière's phrase, a 'mélange adultère de tout', and *The Spectator* did not elude carpers.

Indeed, there was something about the Apollonian calm of Mr. Spectator, with his curt but superior statements that he would not answer critical fools,[1] that must have acted as a goad to such writers as the author of *The British Censor*, a not unamusing, nor wholly unjust pamphlet in verse which appeared towards the end of 1712. After jibing at Mr. Spectator for praising 'Chevy Chase' *because* many parallel passages can be found in Virgil—which was not altogether fair since this criticism had been forestalled—it went on to describe the activities of the Censor :

> All Things by Thee are clearly Understood
> From *Homer* to the *Children in the Wood*.
> Maxims of Schools, and the grave Ayrs of France,
> Ethics and Modes, Divinity and Dance ;
> Pain, Bliss, Hate, Friendship, Lamentation, Song,
> To thy extended Province, all belong ;
> But Poetry is thy peculiar Care,
> And here thy Judgment is . . . beyond Compare.
> Thro' thy just Praise each arch Pretender shines
> With *Blackmore's* easie, clear, and nervous lines . . .

So far good ; the reference to Blackmore's voluminous turgidity is excellent ; but now the verses tend to become personal :

[1] *Spectator*, 355.

> But Tickell is, (thy Theame's Sublimer Scope)
> Of ev'ry Muse, and Grace the springing Hope.
> Tickell, (surprizing Object of thy Love !)
> Who do's the just reverse of *Denham* prove,
> (Deep, yet not clear, not gentle and yet dull,
> Raging, yet weak, o'erflowing, yet not full ;) [1]

Such criticism contained some things too near to truth to be ignored, and if at all common, it was evidently time for Mr. Spectator ' to go off the stage ', as he said. Thus on the 6th December 1712 a number, signed by Steele in full, announced the cessation of the journal, acknowledgements being made by name of all the contributors—except one. This gentleman, while being given the place of honour, thanked with exceeding generosity for his work on *The Spectator* and *Tatler*, and for help in *The Tender Husband*, as well as being made the subject of reverend and friendly compliment, remained modestly veiled behind the discreet pseudonym of C.L.I.O.

[1] *Censor.* The forgetful reader may like to be reminded that Denham's lines on the Thames, expressing his aim in poetry, run :

> Though deep, yet clear ; though gentle, yet not dull ;
> Strong without rage, without o'erflowing full.

3

Cato

BUSY enough in the literary world, Addison was not altogether unoccupied in the political ; there may have been duties in connexion with Birmingham's Tower, and there was Parliament. The violence and unprincipled bribery practised by the Tories in the 1710 elections had not dislodged Addison, though he had found his election expensive.[1] But he went to the House of Commons only to vote, never to speak. The latter he could not do. Once he tried, but the shouts of " Hear him ! Hear him ! " that greeted his rising completely bowled him over. " I conceive . . .", he began, stammered, repeated the words, halted, tried once again, and sat down, having, as some wit said, " conceived three times and brought forth nothing ". He never tried again.

Gibbon suffered from the same disability. " Timidity ", he said, " was fortified by pride, and even the success of my pen discouraged the trial of my voice." But Addison's case would appear to be different. Writing of stage fright in a *Spectator* that may be taken as his own apology,[2] he remarked :

" As this sudden desertion of one's self shows a diffidence, which is not displeasing, it implies at the same time the greatest respect for an audience that can be. It is a sort of mute eloquence, which pleads for their favour much better than words could do ; and we find their generosity moved to support those who are in so much perplexity to entertain them."

[1] *Memorial.* [2] *Spectator*, 231.

It is not known whether Addison won over any votes by this ingenious means ; but he was content to accept his limitation seeing that it was, after all, due to a virtue. " It is impossible ", he declared, " that a person should exert himself to advantage in an assembly . . . who lies under too great oppressions of modesty."

Yet modesty with Addison did not mean the reluctance of the strong always to impose themselves upon the weak ; it did not mean the avoiding, from altruistic motives, of a deserved and supportable limelight ; nor did it mean the self-effacement sometimes practised by the great that the fun of the smaller fry may not be spoilt ; in fact, it was not humility. He described it as " a kind of quick and delicate feeling in the soul, which makes her shrink and withdraw herself from every thing that has danger in it. It is such an exquisite sensibility as warns her to shun the first appearance of any thing that is hurtful." Falstaff might have pleaded it was just such an ' exquisite sensibility ' that sent him tumbling down the road at Gadshill.

That there was a danger in speaking in Parliament, in an environment that was largely hostile, cannot be doubted. Failure would be hurtful to the reputation Addison was building up, humiliation disastrous. An inaccurate scientific illustration might draw upon him the lucid eye of Newton, the expression of an ideal elicit a coarse chuckle from the unimaginative Walpole : this was not the Irish house. Here too the middle way was best—to be, and yet not to be, a Parliament-man. Here too there was no quality so useful as that of discretion. Gibbon's charming self-analysis seems after all applicable to Addison. Pride fortified timidity, and the success of his writings made unfavourable comparison only too easy.

Moreover, there was the vexed question of sides.

Though he sat in the Whig interest, Addison steadfastly refused to be a party man. In this he was not alone; it was the fashion among literary men to repudiate party; in fact to be called a party man in the world of letters was to be branded as infamous. Swift, who wanted authors to be a compact, profit-sharing body, above faction, ridiculed the conception on philosophic grounds,[1] but Addison feared it as dangerous. Its spirit seemed to him, not without reason, to drive on to disaster. "A furious party spirit, when it rages in its full violence, exerts itself in Civil War and bloodshed; and when it is under the greatest restraints naturally breaks out in falsehood, detraction, calumny, and a partial administration of justice."[2] The most Addison felt he could do for party was to dedicate the bound volumes of *The Spectator* to Whig notables.[3] Therefore, through all the contentions of party strife, those pale eyes looked out from under the shadow of the great wig in a slightly supercilious manner, and the mask-like face fronted faction with a calm to which the occasional nervous smile waveringly gave the lie.

But at last Addison was drawn into an adventure which came perilously near to involving him in the worst horrors of the angry scene. For against his will, or at least in spite of his fears, he was lured into a dramatic declaration of his political faith. It cost him agonies of apprehension.

At this time the name of the younger Cato was, for obvious reasons, much bandied about among men with a classical smattering. Even Etherege could use him as an illustration, and his personality was familiar to readers of *The Tatler* and *The Spectator*. Abroad, too, the theme

[1] *Dissensions in Athens and Rome.* [2] *Spectator*, 125.

[3] Somers, Halifax, Boyle, Marlborough, Wharton, Sunderland. The 7th was Steele's. The 8th, when party strife was no longer dangerous, to Will Honeycomb.

of the exiled patriot was a favourite one; not only had the Frenchman Deschamps adopted it, but, when in Italy, Addison had seen it used in opera. Perhaps the play he had submitted to Dryden dealt with that subject, but in any case, immediately after his return in 1703, Steele read to Cibber four Acts of a drama called *Cato* which Addison had written, and was now, in 1712, being on all sides implored to finish and have performed.

But Addison, with one stage failure behind him, was not eager to repeat the experience. The play was undoubtedly as ‘correct’ as art could make it; throughout its four Acts the sacred surface of the unities lay unruffled: but as Farquhar, that *enfant terrible* of the theatre, had pointed out, the rules of drama “do not lie in the compass of Aristotle and his followers, but in the Pit, Box and Galleries”. The many-headed monster of the pit is a notoriously capricious judge, it often butts masterpieces away: and a stage fiasco lends too public a target to ridicule. Yet it was tempting—for as *censor morum* Addison felt a grandfatherly interest in the hero of Utica, and he could not resist dallying with the idea. But suppose it was wrongly taken! Suppose it was used as a handle against him!

At one moment it occurred to him that the responsibility might be shared, and he asked his young ailing friend Hughes to write a concluding Act. Hughes accepted with alacrity, and in a short time came back with a formidable posse of blank verses. But in the meantime it had occurred to Addison that although it might be pleasant to have some one handy to share the blame should need arise, it might be difficult to manage the matter fairly. Besides, it might be the reverse of blame that would have to be shared! So he had himself written the fifth Act, taking from the opera he had seen in Italy the idea of staging the traditional legend of Cato reading the Socratic dialogue on the immortality of the soul, to render more palatable the wormy draught of self-inflicted death.

But still Addison could not nerve himself to the plunge, and the play was handed round among his friends for perusal, for correction, and for help. Pope's advice was asked ; but he replied he thought the author would get reputation enough by having his work printed ; that it would be unwise to act it. Addison said he was of like mind, but then, his friends were so importunate. Would Pope look over it again ? All his suggestions would be acted upon.

It was important to enlist Pope's aid. For besides the danger of a fall from literary grace, there was the horrid possibility that the play might be taken for a piece of Whig propaganda ; that a Tory London would howl down as factious speeches that were meant to enrich the virtue of the world, or that a stupid group would hiss as subversive characters intended as an ensample to mankind. Addison was determined to minimize this risk also. Tory Pope wrote the prologue—the words ' Britons arise ' being on consultation amended to ' Britons attend ', in case the former might be thought to incite to rebellion ; and to stress its non-party flavour, Whig Dr. Garth wrote the epilogue.

On the management side, Steele promised once more to pack the house ; and, much the friend of Cibber and Booth, urged the company to efforts beyond the ordinary. Addison added further incitement by foregoing his profits in favour of the actors, each according to his success, and under these circumstances Cibber felt bound to spare no expense in staging.[1] Thus Juba's waistcoat

[1] *Apology*.

was stiff with gold, and Marcia's petticoat ballooned about Mrs. Oldfield's form in those lavish folds Mr. Bickerstaff's censures had failed to modify. The theatre was safe.

But it was the political side that caused Addison the most anxiety, and he went so far as to sacrifice his pride (or, as he would have said, overcome his modesty) to enlist the aid of Swift, who, if not the most important man in England, was at least flattered into this pleasing belief by those who were. Addison accepted the invitation to dine with the first Secretary of State, and once 'civility' had been thawed by wine, took the opportunity of declaring to Bolingbroke, at that time the great theorist of his party, his abhorrence of such a thing. He went farther. Since Bolingbroke seemed so complaisant, the author of *Cato* assumed that the whole company shared his own tolerance, and proposed the health of Lord Somers, Swift's ready tact alone preventing him from following up this *gaffe* with the health of Lord Wharton ![1] But 'cankered Bolingbroke', as Addison afterwards somewhat ungenerously called him, was sound ; and it has even been suggested that the play was submitted to Harley, Lord Oxford, who would command the suffrage of the 'brothers' of the Scriblerus Club.[2] Swift at any rate was as safe as houses, but to show the actors he was so, he was taken to a rehearsal, an experience which sadly frosted for him the magic mirror of stage illusion.[3]

At last the evening of "the day, The great, th' important day, big with the fate Of Cato and of—" Addison, saw all the London that counted gathered together in Drury Lane, eager for the rise of the curtain. The house was crammed, but the mixture of Whig and

[1] *Stella*, 3rd April 1713.

[2] Elwin and Courthope, i. 327.

[3] *Stella*, 6th April.

Tory was tolerably even, and Addison, from the side-box where he sat supported by friends and flasks of burgundy and champagne,[1] gazed at it troubled. What would be the audience's reception of his carefully concocted speeches upon liberty? For opposite the genial Kit-Cat faces glowered the rude visages of notorious October-Clubbists, and a formidable array of ministerial steenkirks filled the other boxes. At last, unable to bear the suspense, he took refuge in the green-room, and sat upon a bench, sweating with anxiety.

He need not have been afraid. " Le théâtre vit des passions qu'y apporte la foule ", as Renan has remarked, and were not all parties ready to die for the very name of Liberty? No party, obviously, could publicly own an aversion to it. Faction might differ as to the proper degree of monarchic power, or even as to the wielder of it, but there could be no two opinions held, or at least expressed, as to popular rights. From the first success was assured, for each group was determined to prove itself right-thinking, and Pope was disgusted to find himself clapped into a Whig from the opening lines of the prologue. When at last Booth-Cato appeared, borne in a lacquered chair, in the full glory of a brand-new fifty-pound wig, he was hailed by a mighty roar of approval that delayed the speaking of his words. Thunders of rapturous applause greeted such lines as

> A day, an hour, of virtuous liberty
> Is worth a whole eternity of bondage;

but the culminating moment of the play was when Bolingbroke, calling to Booth, leaned out of his box, and handing him a purse of fifty guineas, congratulated him in a voice everybody might hear, on so well defending the cause of liberty against a perpetual dictator. The

[1] Berkeley's *Letters*, 16th April 1713.

play was safe; at the expense, it is true, of a hit at Marlborough, whose recent demand to be made Captain-General for life was thus aimed at. Ingenious Bolingbroke, thus to turn the tables! But Marlborough was abroad, in semi-exile, and the force of the 'home-strock', as Peter Wentworth called it, was lost in the deafening clamour of Whig striving to outclap Tory, and Tory determined to be more Whig than the Whigs in the sacred cause of liberty. Pope acrimoniously reported that Addison was distressed to find the applause coming more from the hand than from the head; but what did it matter where it came from? It came; that was enough. The play was a dazzling triumph. Running for thirty nights it created a record for popularity, until beaten, long after Addison's death, by *The Beggar's Opera*.

More than a triumph for the author, an apotheosis. In the mouths of the town Addison was not only the greatest playwright of his, or of any, age—he who had once been only as Virgil strong; but austere as the great Censor, he was now also the embodiment of the Spirit of Liberty, no mere apostle, but Cato of Utica, no less, the vindicator of justice and of truth. The printers could barely contend with the eagre of praise that swept up Grub Street from the apartments and coffee-houses of frantic poetasters, who sang such strains as,

> *Britons*, with lessen'd wonder now behold
> Your former wits, and all your bards of old;
> Johnson outvy'd in his own Way confess;
> And own that Shakespeare's self now pleases less.

It was high noon at Button's, and imagination boggles at the jubilant scenes. Even 'Thersites' Dennis was silent, while the undergraduates of Oxford neglected their studies to stand in queues for local performances; and 'tried by Roman Laws', as Tickell phrased it, the play gained the august approval of most of the University dignitaries.

It is true there was a deal of party hubbub about it, but it was comparatively insignificant struggling for claiming the honours. In his care to give no stick to factions to beat each other, Addison had gone almost too far, for *The Examiner* scoffed at the Whigs for deluding themselves with the belief that there was anything in the play on their side. The Whigs, however, persisted in their error. Cato they affirmed to be Marlborough—though indeed he was more like Coriolanus—the Numidians to be the Hanoverians, and drew upon themselves a reply in the form of a curious sixpenny pamphlet by 'A Gentleman of Oxford', entitled

Mr. Addison turn'd Tory
or
The Scene Inverted:
wherein
It is made to appear that the Whigs have misunderstood
that celebrated author in his applauded tragedy
call'd
CATO
and that the Duke of M——s character, in endeavouring to be a *General for Life*, bears a much
greater Resemblance to that of *Caesar* and *Syphax*
than the Heroe of his Play.

This was to make the most of Bolingbroke's 'home-strock'; but Addison, thanks to the giver of the stroke, could afford to ignore such pribbles and prabbles.

But just as all seemed snug, a thunder-cloud darkened the sky, and Lintot published *Remarks upon Cato, a Tragedy, by Mr. Dennis*, a bulky pamphlet. Thersites had broken silence, and at his own clapper-clawing was no mean spectacle, for he had knowledge to back his virulence. The iron of failure had entered his soul, and added to a real concern for the drama, he had a passionate desire to wound to the death the work of others. A devil of destructive criticism possessed him, drove him on relentlessly ; a clever, even a brilliant devil, which even in the midst of sound and fury contrived to signify a great deal. He preluded with two savage quotations on the title page, but opened his essay by declaring that in view of public opinion he had intended to hold his tongue. Yet, urged thereto by friends, and feeling it was far worse for the public taste that one bad play should succeed than that two or three good ones should fail, he had felt it his duty to breast the tide, and show the multitudinous applauders that they were wrong.

Under his withering pen scene after scene, passage after passage, became false, turgid, without taste, or, what was worse, ridiculous. His acrid ink corroded even the fine ideals of the play, and Cato himself became an oaf " who rashly dy'd by his own Hands, when there was no Necessity for Dying, and who deserted the Cause of Liberty and of his Country, thro' Stubbornness and thro' Ignorance, or sacrifis'd them to his stoical Pride ". There was indeed, as Dryden said of Collier's polemic, ' too much horseplay in the raillery ' ; and if, as he showed, too close an adherence to the unities may lead to the absurd, he forgot that to chain a work of imagination to the kitchen table of fact may do the same. But granting his premises, as most readers at that time were ready to do, his criticism, in spite of his violence, is convincing as well as diverting, and he tore the play to tatters. There was not a shred of reasonableness, much less of tragic beauty, left in the play of *Cato* when he had done with it ; and there cannot have been many readers not enough carried away by his onslaught to be unable to agree that " this Author has found out the Secret, to make his Tragedy highly improbable, without making it wonderful, and to make parts of it highly incredible, without being in the least entertaining ".

It threw Button's into ferment. Addison might comfort himself that he had satisfied Aristotle as well as the pit, box, and galleries, but there was an insidious suggestion at the beginning of Dennis's booklet that he cared more for success than for art. Why, the malevolent critic had asked, had the author thought it necessary to take all these elaborate precautions against failure? If you believe in your play, why pack the house? If you do not . . .? The question was unasked, but the answer was implied. The hit was all the worse that only Addison could be aware of it; his little senators were sublimely ignorant of its poignancy.

So, with the best-intentioned ineptitude, they urged Addison to reply to the *Remarks*. But controversy is invidious; one cannot parry every shrewd blow an unscrupulous antagonist cares to make; one cannot preside over the debate, and to employ others is only to expose oneself further. Besides, Addison felt the attack was most unanswerable where most it hurt him. In vain his admirers put their brains and their pens at his service: he smiled, and bade them desist. Pope offered his talents; they were gently refused: the Philips affair had intervened between *Cato* and this. Steele informed the master of a coming lampoon upon Dennis, but Addison shook his head, and wished to know nothing about it. His friends were surprised at his persistent refusal—until they realized that this was only another instance of his forbearance; and then, no doubt, they found in themselves that " secret awe and veneration for the character of one who moves about us in a regular and illustrious course of virtue, without any regard for our good or ill opinions of him ".[1]

In spite of all, however, to the entertainment of a world not averse from denigration, there appeared without warning *The Narrative of Dr. Robert Norris concerning the strange and deplorable Frenzy of Mr. John Denn——An Officer of the Custom House*, a squib, if not scurrilous, at any rate in the worst of taste. But though inelegant, it was a high-spirited piece of buffoonery, so obviously aimed at the critic's person that its pretence to be a vindication of *Cato* only heightened the tone of private malice. It is a poor performance, but not unamusing to the student of human nature. Though perhaps the best piece of wit lay in the title-page quotation, which reminded readers that Democritus excluded sane poets from Helicon, it succeeded in making Dr. Norris, with his Galen and Celsus, look as pedantic an owl as Dennis, while Lintot himself was not altogether spared. The publisher of the *Remarks* was puzzled. From internal evidence it appeared to be, if not by Pope, at least by a friend of Pope—but then Pope's friend Cromwell seemed to be aimed at in one or two passages. Moreover, it was Pope himself who had suggested to him the idea of inciting Dennis to write the *Remarks*. Who could the *Frenzy* be by? The matter was made no clearer when he received a note from Steele

"Aug. 4th. 1713.

"Mr. Addison desires me to tell you that he wholly disapproves the manner of treating Mr. Dennis in a little pamphlet by way of Dr. Norris's account. When he thinks fit to take note of Mr. Dennis's objections to his writings, he will do it in a way Mr. Dennis shall have

[1] *Spectator*, 255.

no reason to complain of. But when the papers above mentioned were offered to be communicated to him, he said he could not, either in honour or conscience, be privy to such a treatment, and was sorry to hear of it." [1]

Why, Lintot wondered, should the note come from Steele and not from Addison? But Steele was soon out of reach, for resigning his pension as gentleman waiter to the late Prince of Denmark, he was off to be elected Whig member for Stockbridge, leaving the management of *The Guardian* in Addison's hands. But there were two other questions Lintot might have asked himself. First, why Steele did not contribute to the eighth volume of *The Spectator*, which appeared in 1714; and second, why Pope ceased to frequent Button's? Pope said the potations and the late hours were too much for his feeble frame; [2] and besides, he was busy over that work Mr. Addison had so kindly encouraged him to perform, the translation into rhymed couplets of the *Iliad* of Homer.

In the last volume of *The Spectator* there was a slight reference to criticism in general, which may or may not have been intended as an answer to Dennis, but probably was not. There would be no point in drawing attention to the *Remarks*, which though violent, were often irrefragable as arguments. Moreover, to keep silent often has the force of putting the other person in the wrong.

[1] See Appendix IV. [2] Spence.

III

THE JUSTIFICATION OF WISDOM

1. *Doubts*

ADDISON had written nothing for the earlier *Guardians* ; he had been too busy over *Cato*. The field had been left to Berkeley, who, with that charming simpleness which sometimes peeps through the subleties of his philosophy, used it to confound such ' monsters ' as free-thinkers, critics, and misers in one graceful damnation. And although Addison contributed some fifty papers to the second volume, he seems to have felt they were of a rather tired quality, being indeed mainly furbished-up versions of the letters he had written home when on his travels. " There is no employment so irksome as that of transcribing out of oneself next to that of transcribing out of others " [1] he was to say later ; so in the autumn he retired to Bilton to enjoy the company of his sister, ' a sort of wit, very like Addison ', to prepare for the election now due under the Triennial Act, and to gather fresh material. He refused to be drawn into any literary venture, and replied to Hughes's solicitations by saying " I must now take some time *pour me délasser*, and lay in fuel for a future work ".[2]

Moreover, in the then stormy crisis of affairs, with ballad-mongers crying out against the makers of ' the wretched damn'd sham Peace ', and piously wishing that ' Bob ' [Harley] and ' Harry ' [St. John] might be

[1] *Freeholder*, 53. [2] 12th Oct. 1713.

hanged,[1] it would be impossible to write anything out of which party capital could not be made. Steele, with characteristic courage had thrown himself into the fray with a paper called *The Englishman.* " I am in a thousand troubles for poor Dick ", Addison continued to Hughes, " and wish that his zeal for the public may not be ruinous to himself; but he has sent me word that he is determined to go on, and that any advice I may give him in this particular, will have no weight with him." But it is doubtful if Steele had ever given much more than lip-service to Addison's advice. It always seemed sound; but somehow, when it came to actuality, was impotent to check him.

No one could expect the fervent Steele to keep out of the present exciting hurly-burly, or persuade him that it was called folly to prop a falling fabric. When in April the Queen announced the signature of the Peace of Utrecht, the turbid river of pamphlets, which already seemed swollen to the utmost, doubled and redoubled itself, flooding the country with a mass of ephemeral matter. On the Whig side the treaty gave rise to a howl of execration. The Queen's ministers were traitors, Jacobites, Papists; why else such disgracefully easy terms to Louis; why the quashing of prosecutions against Scottish Jacobites; why, finally, this influx of Popish priests? When the magistrates of Dunkirk—to Captain Shandy's dismay—petitioned the Queen against the demolition of their fortifications, the cries grew louder than ever, and it is possible that even Addison secretly published one or two leaflets. The old Whig juntists, rallying their forces, carried a Bill in the House of Lords making high treason any active measures against the Protestant succession—but they only carried it by one

[1] Ballad, *Harleian Misc.*, iii. 294.

vote![1] And while the enlistments in the Pretender's army increased, they began to correspond with Marlborough, a pastime in which they were joined by Lord Oxford. Clearly, if it was wise to write anonymously, it was wiser still to keep out of the tussle altogether.

Poor Dick would not listen to reason. He saw the state was in danger, and said so at some length, with great clarity, and no lack of vigour, in *The Crisis.* Even if he made too much of the scare, he said, it was better to be frightened by a bogey than to be lulled into false security. Addison, Hoadley, and others, privately gave it a little revision, and it appeared on the 19th January 1714, a powerful indictment of the Government. Poor Dick indeed! He watched the public weal but not his own. To publish *The Crisis* was a rash act, the pamphlet one of which the new Tory Parliament could not but take notice. It was true their party was in a large majority, which it intended to increase by bringing in petitions against a hundred odd Whig members, including Steele; but however strong you may be, you do not care to nourish a really dangerous viper in your bosom for a moment longer than necessary, and since Steele was as far down as seventeenth on the list, it was found more convenient to charge him at the Bar of the House of Commons with irreligion and sedition, than to await the outcome of the other charge. The Kit-Cat took the matter in hand, not trusting Steele's impetuous nature, and forbade him to conduct his own defence. They caused him instead to stand between Walpole and General Stanhope and read a three-hour speech by Addison, who sat near by. But the case was prejudged; the speeches of Walpole and others were of no effect whatever, and the member for Stockbridge was expelled

[1] Lecky, *England*, i.

the House. "There is no need to issue orders for his commitment", Collier, the theatre patentee and Parliament-man, is reported to have said; "once he is no longer a member of this House, his creditors will see to that for us."

Addison was not attacked—there is no danger in a member who never opens his mouth—and controlling his zeal, he kept out of the murky regions, resisting Bolingbroke's attempt to win him over. How, indeed, could he change? He had written, "Nothing that is not a real crime makes a man appear more contemptible and little in the eyes of the world as inconstancy, especially when it regards religion or party". It would not have suited him to be a renegado, for, "In either of these cases, though a man perhaps does but his duty in changing his side, he not only makes himself hated by those he left, but is seldom heartily esteemed by those he came over to".[1] He held firm; and meanwhile, as the Queen's constitution sank, the struggle waxed fiercer and more vindictive. So universal were 'treachery and tergiversation' that no one could foresee the issue, and it was only by a majority of seven that the Upper House rejected a motion that the Protestant succession was in danger.[2] Foreign observers, indeed, would have supported the motion.[3] The succession was probably always safe enough, for commerce was on the side of the Hanoverians, as well as law, the dissenters, and the moderate Church party; but at that time the excitement was intense, and civil war seemed imminent. When at the end of July Bolingbroke forced Oxford from power, the country held its breath, and few dared whistle *Lilli-Burlero*. The immediate rumour 'La reine se meurt' sent a shudder throughout the kingdom.

[1] *Spectator*, 162. [2] Hallam, iii. [3] Lecky, *England*, i.

But—Addison was busied with other things. Every week there appeared three *Spectators*,[1] those by Addison being written in his suavest manner. The journal dealt with such subjects as the benefit of needlework to ladies, the cleanliness of Mahometans, the grandeur of obscurity, and, with equal urbanity, the poetry of Cowley, the ubiquity of God, or Sir Isaac Newton's noble way of regarding infinite space.

Perhaps, however, Addison was right, for when on the 1st August the news came 'La reine est morte' it was felt as an anti-climax. The Jacobite plans were found to be in a hopeless state of muddled unreadiness, and the Regency of Peers, selected to bridge the interim of King George's absence, ruled unopposed. A scarcely disturbed calm reigned over the waters, in the midst of which Addison floated in well-merited glory as Secretary to the Chief Justices, or Regents.

It was a magnificent appointment, so magnificent as to give rise to some comment, for it was thought to herald a Secretaryship of State.[2] Halifax, indeed, believing with undue optimism that he would be made head of the Government, is said to have offered the post to Addison as they went to meet the King. The offer, it is supposed, was refused, for apart from its conditional nature, if it behoves a maiden of modesty to refuse the earliest offer of marriage, and a clergyman the first offer of a bishopric,[3] it would be most improper for a politician at once to seize the chance of one of the three highest posts in the kingdom.

The Parliament elected after the King's arrival was splendidly Whig, for no expense had been spared. Steele once more took his place in the assembly, this time

[1] Nos. 556–635, 18th June–28th Dec.

[2] Wentworth, 410. [3] *Spectator*, 89.

as member for Boroughbridge, a seat in the gift of Vanbrugh's friend, the Duke of Newcastle. Yet the winter of the Whig discontent, though transformed by the sun of Hanover, had given place to a summer which, though glorious, was all the same a little clouded. Addison's friends were heaped with honours, but they could not avoid seeing that they were cold-shouldered. It appeared that the old heroes were slightly tarnished. Somers, of course, was too old for power, but Halifax, though created an earl, and triumphantly gartered, was only made Chancellor of the Exchequer ; while Wharton, though raised to a marquisate, got no post at all. And if Marlborough was once more Captain-General, his activities were rigidly confined to his military duties. The Government, in fact, was in the hands of a new group, of which Townshend was the nominal head, and Walpole the mainspring. Thus when the Regency resigned its powers into the hands of the sovereign, Addison was dismissed with many polite expressions of esteem, congratulations upon the manner in which he had discharged, unpaid, so onerous and important a task, and—a recommendation to the King.

It was not very satisfactory for Addison. He was as much as ever a great man with the junto, but where was the junto? Even that violently ambitious old intriguer, the Earl of Sunderland, was unable to obtain a post he thought suitable. The dice had been loaded against him from the beginning, as he had realized when, with paling face, he had heard the names of the Regents read out, but waited in vain to hear his own. In October he was fobbed off with the Lord-Lieutenancy of Ireland, in which post, it was thought, he would be kept well out of the way. But Sunderland had other views. Like a predecessor in this post of honourable retirement, the Earl of Rochester, he thought he could manage the business very well from London, as well as more easily keep his finger in all the other pies; so, pleading indisposition, he refused to stir from England. However, knowing Addison to be familiar with the ropes, he sent him over as his Secretary. Yet Addison does not seem to have spent much of his time in Ireland—the absence of the Viceroy cut down the emoluments to miserable proportions compared with those of other offices "in this first happy year" of George's reign[1]—though he made the most of his opportunity of renewing his friendship with Swift, safely shanghaied as Dean of St. Patrick's, in spite of being expressly warned to avoid him. But he properly claimed the freedom, as one whose loyalty could not be doubted, of having what friends he chose, and rejoiced in the companionship of a man to whom he could be generous, and who could not now injure him by proffering service.

But Addison was no more pleased with his old post than Sunderland with his new one. It was a bitter blow to his ambition, to his self-esteem. Were all his virtues and his service to go for nothing, his talents and his rectitude to waste their sweetness on the desert air of Dublin? It was certainly not for a mere compliment he had nearly killed himself by hard work as Secretary to the Chief Justices.[2] Could it be that he had, after all, not been enough of a party man, had been, in fact, a little too circumspect? Was it possible that his complete philosophy led nowhere, or that wisdom could fail to reward her children? Or was it that his all-round view of life somewhere held a flaw? He appealed to Halifax.

"My Lord," he wrote on the 17th October 1714,[3]

"I find by your Lordship's discourse that you have your reasons for laying aside the thought of bringing

[1] *Memorial.* [2] Ibid. [3] Add. MSS. 7121, f. 11.

me into a part of Lownde's place [1] and as I hope they do not proceed from any change of good will towards me I do entirely acquiesce in them. I know that one in your Lordship's high station has several opportunities of showing favour to your dependants as your generous temper does not want to be reminded of it when any such offer. I must therefore beg your Lordship to believe that I think no more of what you were pleased to mention in relation to the Treasury, tho the kind and condescending manner in which your Lordship was pleased to communicate yourself to me on that subject shall always raise in me the most constant and unfeign'd zeal for your honour and service.

"I fancy if I had a friend to represent to his Maties that I was sent abroad by King William and taken off from all other pursuits in order to be employ'd in His service, that I had the honour to wait on your Lordship to Hanover, that the post I am now in is the gift of a particular Lord in whose service I have bin employed formerly, that it is a great fall in point of honour from being Secretary to the Regents, and that their request to His Majesty still subsists in my favour, with other intimations that might be made to my advantage, I fancy I say that His Majesty upon such a representation woud be inclined to bestow on me some mark of his favour. I protest to your Lordship I never gained the value of five thousand pound by all the businesse I have yet been in and of that very near a fourth part has bin laid out in my elections. I should not insist on this subject so long were it not taken notice of by some of the Lords Justices themselves as well as many others that his Matie has yet done nothing for me tho it was once expected he woud have done something more considerable for me than I can at present have the confidence to mention. . . . I will humbly propose it to your Lordship's thoughts whether his Matie might not be inclined if I was mentioned to him to put me in the Commission of Trade or in some honorary post about the prince or by some other

[1] Secretary to the Treasury.

method to let the world see I am not wholly disregarded by him . . ."

" To let the world see . . ." He did not attempt to disguise that it was there rather than in his opinion of himself that he was grievously hurt ; but it frightened him also that the bubble of his reputation was being pricked. For people would come to solicit his aid with Halifax, and though he could put most of them off, " there are some which I cannot resist without declaring, what would go very much against me, that I have no credit with your Lordship ". It was a painful situation ; it would look like a sad collapse.

The dream of becoming Secretary of State, or perhaps more, was dwindling to the shadow of a shade, for Halifax, it appeared, was something of a broken reed, and failed in one attempt to get Addison a post.[1] By the end of November Addison saw this only too clearly, and resigning himself to obscurity, asked only for reasonable financial reward.

" My Lord," he wrote again on the 30th of that month,[2]

" Finding that I have miscarried in my pretensions to the Board of Trade I shall not trouble your Lordship with my resentments of the unhansome treatment I have met with from some of our great men in every circumstance of that affair but must beg leave to express my gratitude to your Lordship for the great favour you have shown me on this occasion which I shall never forget. Young Cragges told me about a week ago that his Ma^ty^, tho he did not think fit to gratifie me in this particular designed to give me a Recompense for my service under the Lords Justices, in which case your Lordship will most probably be consulted. Since I find I am never to rise above the station in which I first

[1] Add. MSS. 7121, f. 14. [2] Ibid., f. 15.

Enter'd upon publick Businesse (for I now begin to look upon myself like an old sergeant or corporal) I would willingly turn my secretaryship in which I have served five different masters to the best advantage I can: and as your Lordship is the only patron I glory in and have a dependance on, I hope you will honour me with your countenance in this particular. If I am offered less than a Thousand pound I shall beg leave not to accept it since it will look more like a clerk's wages than a mark of his Majesty's favour . . ."

He went on to point out that he had never abused his position to acquire wealth, or accepted any presents, and added as a kind of postscript, on one side of the signature, "I beg your Lp will give me leave to add yt I believe I am the first man that ever drew up a P. of Wales' preamble without so much as a medal for my pains". The Hanoverians, it seemed, were slightly lacking in style.

Halifax, however, did not take all these reproaches lying down; he pointed out to Addison that his eclipse was, when all was said, partly his own fault:

"Come, prithee, Addison," he wrote at about this time, "no unreasonable modesty. I made thee Secretary to the Regency with this very view [of promotion]. Thou hast now the best right of any man in England to be Secretary of State; nay, it will be a sort of displacing of thee not to make thee so. If thou could'st but get over that silly sheepishness of thine that makes thee sit in the House and hear a fellow prate for half an hour together, who has not a tenth part of thy good sense, I should be glad to see it so."

Whatever Addison may have thought of the rather brutal terms in which his Lordship referred to his modesty —'silly sheepishness' is a poor paraphrase of 'exquisite sensibility'—the *tutoiement* must have seemed to augur well; but hope diminished when in June 1715 Halifax died. Moreover, in August Addison lost even the post that he had, for Sunderland, at last successful in his wirepulling, exchanged his Irish place for that of Lord Privy Seal with a seat in the Cabinet. And since no one seemed inclined to mention the late Secretary to the King, he took the part upon himself, and addressed a Memorial to his Majesty.

The substance is much that of the letters to Halifax, down to the medal-less preamble to the Prince of Wales's patent, with an addition explaining that when the memorialist went to Hanover to help Halifax present the now King with the Garter, his Lordship had given him nothing for his pains. And there are as well some statements that come rather curiously from the man who had so sternly set his face against faction, and so carefully avoided any expressions which might by a point have raised the political temperature. For he informed the King that he "took all occasions, both by his writings and conversation, to promote y[e] cause which, God be thank'd, has so wonderfully prevail'd, and to publish those Royal virtues which the nation sees at present in your Majesty". And again: "Nor will your Memorialist's modesty"—that 'quick and delicate feeling', we remember, that warns the soul of danger—"permit him to insist upon his endeavours, which were not thought unsuccessful in securing such a spirit among the People as dispos'd 'em to favour y[e] Interest of a Prince who is so justly esteemed a Friend to y[e] Liberties of Europe." It sounds something oddly. One is tempted to think that Addison's enemies were not altogether calumniating him when they said that the man who had so scrupulously denied wishing to make any political implications in *Cato*, afterwards took great credit to himself for having been, at that difficult and dangerous time, the one man to stand up boldly and openly in the cause of liberty.[1] Here we see once more that Addison had been a little too wary, had protested a shade too much. But in any case the Memorial seems to have had some effect, for before the end of the year Addison was made Commissioner of Trade and Plantations, at a salary of a thousand pounds, the exact minimum wage consistent with honour.

Nor had Addison during this period allowed his literary career to be utterly submerged under his political labours. In spite of his killing work as Secretary to the Regents, *The Spectator* had continued to appear until the end of December 1714; and in March 1715 his play of *The Drummer* was acted at Drury Lane, of which Sir Richard Steele was now patentee. The authorship was well concealed—even Steele had to guess at it—and the comedy was supposed to emanate, so the prologue declared, from " A raw young Thing, who dare not tell his name ", and who went on to say very frankly,

> Each Wit may praise it, for his own dear sake,
> And hint He writ it, if the thing shou'd take ;
> But, if you're rough, and use him like a Dog,
> Depend upon it—He'll remain Incog.

Since Addison proposed to act precisely in this manner himself, this was to make of the stage also a 'safe and private channel' suited to his diffidence; and as the town did, in fact, prove rough, 'incog.' he remained, until Steele let the cat out of the bag after the author's death.

The year 1715 also produced another awkward literary scuffle, again with Pope, and to understand it we must go back to the beginning of the acquaintance of this diverse pair.

Shortly after the appearance of the *Essay on Criticism*

[1] Elwin and Courthope.

a laudatory article appeared in *The Spectator*.[1] Pope wrote to thank his friend Steele, who then told him the paper had not been written by him, but by Addison, to whom, if he wished, he would introduce him. They met; but Pope was not of the Philips-Budgell breed, and was past his days of literary hero-worship. He had seen through all that with Wycherley. Addison, who was nothing if not sensitive to atmosphere, could feel at once that here was no true votary. Of what use to him a friend whom he could not guide, instruct, patronize? Yet Pope came to Button's (he could not well be excluded from a public coffee-house), for it was the leading literary coterie of the day, the Kit-Cat being closed to a Papist. And then the queerest kind of minuet took place, with bowings and scrapings and asking of advice and looking over each other's work, for all the world like setting to partners. But after the affair of *Guardian* No. 40, wherein Philips was so heavily thrown, it was evident that this elaborate frivolity could not continue, and indeed, it came to an abrupt stop with *The Narrative concerning the Strange and Deplorable Frenzy of Mr. John Denn*——. After that Pope's name was made very free with at Button's,[2] and however deprecatingly Addison might smile, the most terrible slurs were cast upon the wasp who could sting so effectively. Constant battering could not fail to have an effect even upon the unblemished good-nature of the lord of Button's—" so many mischievous insects are daily at work to make people of merit suspicious of each other ", Pope corantoed it to Addison.[3] But the latter wrote to Lady Mary Wortley Montagu to have nothing to do with Pope, " he will play you some develish trick else ", a prophetic piece of advice, for her turn was to

[1] No. 253. [2] Gay to Pope, 1715.
[3] Letter, 30th July 1713. See Appendix V.

come. Pope's friends, however, went so far as to say that Addison was jealous of the younger poet's reputation—and Lady Mary continued to write burlesque Philipian pastorals with Pope.

And although in December 1713 Pope wrote to Addison that there was no one to whom he so freely opened his heart, although he told him " I really love you so well, that I would rather you should pardon me than esteem me ",[1] the relations between them seem to have been no warmer than ' civility '. They could hardly be so when Philips was always at slandering Pope, but never to his face, " although I was almost every night in the same room with him ".[2]

Lady Mary may have been diverted at the quarrel, but some viewed it with distaste, and among them was Jervas, Pope's teacher in painting. In August he spoke about it to Addison, and wrote the result to Pope, who, he said, should have been behind the wainscot to hear all the delightful things Addison had said about him. And yet, Pope probably asked himself, were these things quite sincere? For Jervas went on to state " He is sensible that nothing can have a better air for himself, than moving in your favour, especially since insinuations were spread that he did not care you should prosper too much as a poet ".[3] Here, certainly, was the chance of a generous, a noble gesture, from Mr. Addison, Secretary to the Regents, towards Mr. Pope, the notorious Tory: but was it not to turn the implication of envy over to the other side? And Addison, in the very *Spectator* in which the *Essay on Criticism* was praised, had said some very hard things about envious poets: it is, he had pointed out, only those who have not succeeded who try " to

[1] *Letters*, 14th Dec. [2] 8th June 1714.
[3] 20th Aug. 1714.

depreciate the works of those who have ". Besides, one does not leap to accept a friendship proffered only because it would look so bad not to make advances.

Lack of acuteness was not Pope's failing, and when, a week later, he answered Jervas, he complained bitterly that Philips had set Addison against him, and expressed himself pained beyond measure that Addison could have believed anything to his discredit. Under such circumstances he could not dream of accepting any favours from Addison. " I should be ashamed to receive 'em from any man who had no better opinion of my morals than to think me a party man ; nor of my temper, than to believe me capable of maligning or envying another's reputation as a poet."

By October, however, the minuettists were once more in the full swing of graceful movement. On the 10th of that month Pope expressed a ' real respect ' for Addison, and asked him if he would be so obliging as to look over the first volume of his *Iliad*. He said further that if Addison would point out in the *Essay on Criticism* the ill-natured remarks for which he had so gently chid him in *The Spectator*, he would expunge them from his new edition. "And since we are upon proofs of sincerity", he added, he generously pointed out a passage in the same *Spectator* which showed Addison either to be ignorant of Dionysius of Halicarnassus, or to have committed a deliberate plagiarism !

When Addison, stepping to the music, next met Pope, he asked him to wait until ' those people ', Philips and Budgell, should have left the room ; and then he told him that he could not look over Pope's first book as his young friend Tickell had also done a translation of the identical piece of Homer, and that he had already intended his mind upon that. He could not in honour do the same for Pope; it would have an air of double-dealing. But if Pope would send him his second book, nothing would be allowed to stand in the way of his giving it all his attention.[1]

Pope jigged it bravely; nothing was more honourable than Mr. Addison's dealing, or more pleasant than Mr. Tickell's love of Greek. But at the same time he was thunderstruck. This competing work of Tickell's was something quite new! Although, Addison said, Tickell had had it by him a long time, no word had been breathed about it during all these last years when he had been openly preparing his own. And if it was of long standing, was it not rather odd of Tickell to want to publish it at this particular moment? He mentioned the matter to Edward Young, whom he met shortly afterwards in the street, and that poet was even more astounded than Pope. It was, he declared, inconceivable that the thing should have been in existence long, for he and Tickell showed each other every line they wrote. Pope was, to say the least of it, huffed; and it is hardly to be wondered at that when in January 1715 Gay, with the help of Pope and Swift, produced *The What d'ye Call It*, that romping 'tragi-comi-pastoral-farce', it was suggested that not only were some passages aimed at Philips, but that others were designed as a skit on *Cato*.[2]

Tickell, of course, had a perfect right to publish, if he chose, a dozen translations from Homer, but there was something queer about all this tiptoe collusion with Addison. It was with some anxiety that Pope looked forward to the publication of Tickell's volume; not that he had any financial fears, for, thanks to Swift, his book was heavily subscribed; but he dreaded a blow at his reputation. He was, he knew, a better poet than Tickell,

[1] Spence. [2] *Letters*, Pope to Congreve, 7th April 1715.

but he also knew that he was a worse scholar. It appeared on the 4th June 1715, the day before his own, and he nervously awaited the result. For a time the issue was in doubt, for though Oxford, true to its political feelings, at first gave him the palm, it after a time wavered towards Tickell.[1] In London the battle raged furiously, with some acerbity. It became almost a matter of national importance, and as much as nearly a year later the following advertisement appeared in *The Flying Post*:[2]

"To prevent any farther imposition upon the publick, there is now preparing for the press, by several hands, *Homer defended*; being a detection of many *Errors* committed by Mr. Pope in his pretended Translation of Homer; wherein it is fully proved that he neither understands the Original, nor the Author's meaning, and that in several places he has falsified it on purpose. . . . Any Gentlemen who have made Observations upon Mr. Pope's Homer, and will be pleased to send them to Mr. Curll, at the Dial and Bible against St. Dunstan's church in Fleet Street, shall have them faithfully inserted in this Work."

Pope, in the meantime, was pencilling observations in his copy of Mr. Tickell's Homer, but he had no need to use them, for his adversary 'sank before him without a blow'. Nevertheless it was a trying situation for Addison. What was he to say to the multitudes that hung upon his lips for a verdict? He was far from wishing to anger Pope, but then Tickell 'he loved as a son', and his version had appeared in some measure under his protection. He therefore took the middle way, and declared that both versions were good. Sometimes among devoted friends he would add that Tickell's was the best ever written. And then, perhaps encouraged by Bentley's

[1] Young to Tickell, 28th June 1715; Johnson's *Tickell*, foot-note, ii. 324.

[2] 10th April 1716. Nichols, i. 113.

"It's a very pretty poem, Mr. Pope, but you mustn't call it Homer", he remarked that Tickell's poem 'had more Homer in it'. He forgot Bentley was used to being disliked.

Pope obviously could not publish the furious resentment he felt when Gay carried him this saying,[1] but he showed it clearly enough to Craggs, to whom he almost immediately wrote a letter about Addison, a letter which may be taken as the first rough draft of the *Character of Atticus*, containing as it does many of the famous expressions. But the minuet with its 'languishing eye and smiling mouth' was still being danced. "After all I have said of this great Man", Pope told Craggs, "there is no rupture between us. We are each of us so civil and obliging, that neither thinks he is obliged."[2] If Pope really wanted to be Addison's friend, his behaviour here shows him to have been a poor psychologist. For there precisely was the rub. A friend who could not think he was obliged to Addison, could not by the wildest stretch of the imagination be regarded as a friend at all. Nevertheless Addison treated of Pope's Homer in the paper he next published,[3] and the poet had no reason to complain that, in the open at least, the critic had ever damned him with faint praise. And the approval was the more noticeable in that Addison's organ was professedly political.

Professedly; for though called into existence by the rebellion of '15, the Government using this means to influence the public, it really differed very little from *The Spectator*. It is true that in *The Freeholder* Addison threw off all pretence of party neutrality, but his satire was so mild that his Tory Fox-Hunter is no less lovable

[1] *Letters*, 8th July 1715. [2] *Letters*, 15th July.
[3] *Freeholder*, 17th May 1716.

than his Tory brother Sir Roger de Coverley, while the Preston rebels were handled no more severely than had been the ‘ Grinners ’ or ‘ Demurrers in love ’. Steele was frankly contemptuous; the Government, he said, had chosen a flute when they ought to have chosen a trumpet. But indeed, neither trumpet nor flute was necessary. The futile hot-headedness of the Pretender, who would not listen to Bolingbroke, preferring the advice of his little court in the Bois de Boulogne, of which Fanny Oglethorpe was the ornament and the infamous Olive Trant the ‘ grand wheel ’; the cowardice of ‘ Bobbing John ’ Mar, who could not this time change sides quite quickly enough; the ineptitude of Ormond in the face of Marlborough's dispositions, were not the reagents to disturb a peaceful trading country contentedly settling down to business, and fearful of a Stuart repudiation of the National Debt. If the Fox-Hunter amused, as he continues to please, the performance is an addition to our literary wealth rather than to our stock of political writings, while the Character of Lord Somers is a model of graveside oratory. *The Freeholder* is Addison all over; one might even say, all over again.

For, it is curious to note, throughout the course of years Addison seems to have changed his attitude on no single point. Throughout his writings we read the same religious opinions, have repeated the same comments upon the French; the very phrases anent the fair sex are reiterated, and we meet the old familiar references to Milton. He had made up his mind soon—too soon one is tempted to think. Twenty years of life amid seething excitement, twenty years of the knowledge of men, seem to have added nothing to him. “ He who is the great standard of perfection ”, he once wrote,[1] “ has in him no

[1] *Spectator*, 162.

shadow of change, but is ' the same yesterday, to-day, and for ever '." He resembled his model.

Certainly in *The Freeholder* one cannot but feel here and there that he is too much drawing on old stocks, that the humour flags, has become mechanical. Use and wont seem to have dulled the sense in Addison. Even the rich theme of French frivolity and shallowness that had appealed so strongly to the readers of *The Tatler*, *Spectator*, and *Guardian*, recoils upon the wielder of the ridicule, and smothers him in ideas his very seriousness renders superbly comic. For instance, in No. 30 he attacks Misson, whom he does not mention by name, for superficiality. It is true that that admirable observer of manners fails to support any of his descriptions by long quotations from the Latin poets, but on the other hand no student of the social life of the time of William can afford to neglect his book: yet the gravamen of Addison's charge lies in the accusation that he has failed to observe the soul of the people. Why, for one thing, did he make so much of the phrase ' to come in pudding time '? Addison loosed his shaft; it was pretty enough, but it flew like a boomerang, for a careful perusal of the whole paper makes it clear that Addison had not the faintest notion that he had achieved satire: it was all meant in deadly earnest. " One cannot have the heart ", he wrote, " to be angry at this Judicious Observer, notwithstanding he treated us like a race of *Hottentots*, because he taxes us with our inordinate love of Pudding, which it must be confessed, is not so elegant a dish as Frog and Salad. Everyone who has been at Paris, knows that *Un gros milord Anglais* is a frequent Jest upon the French Stage; as if Corpulence was a proper Subject for Satyr, or a Man of Honour could help his being Fat, who Eats suitable to his Quality."

Deadly serious too were Addison's references to the fair sex, for though the paper was ostensibly political, he could not resist devoting about one-sixth part of it to his favourite theme. And now his irritation against 'the most beautiful part of the creation', 'entirely amiable', seems to have swelled to uncontrollable proportions, to have cried for outlet. He even abandoned his old measured method, his—gentility of expression seems the right term. But if his anger made him sometimes descend to mere rough scolding, his indignation bore him up to a height of prose he had never before reached; his paragraphs really have a backbone. For example:

"It is indeed a melancholy thing to see the disorders of a household that is under the conduct of an angry stateswoman, who lays out all her thoughts upon the public, and is only attentive to find out miscarriages in the ministry. Several women of this town are so earnest in contending for hereditary right, that they wholly neglect the education of their own sons and heirs; and are so taken up with their zeal for the Church, that they cannot find time to teach their children the catechism." [1]

To meet prose of that fiery quality one has to go back half a century to Dryden and the *Epistle to the Whigs*, or forward fifty odd years to Burke, and his splendid, irresistible diatribes in *Thoughts on the Present Discontents*.

This journal continued until June, when its occasion ignominiously faded away; and Addison plunged headlong into the most irretrievable action of his life, in a channel where safety cannot by any possible method be assured.

[1] *Freeholder*, 26.

Emery Walker

The Right Honourable JOSEPH ADDISON

(*National Portrait Gallery*)

2

Victory

It must have surprised a world accustomed to regard Addison as a man who required too much perfection in the fair sex ever to love it, when, on the 3rd August 1716, he married the Countess of Warwick. It certainly does seem a little strange that a man so suspicious of the minds and the activities of women, regarding them as essentially childish, given to tiresome social errors, should have taken this leap. It smacks of indiscretion, even though Lady Warwick, mother of a grown-up son, would be unlikely to commit any superannuated folly.

Yet the strangeness does not end there; how, one cannot but ask, had Addison overcome not only his aversion, but his diffidence? "Les âmes tendres", Stendhal has told us, "ont besoin de la facilité chez une femme pour encourager la cristallisation", and it does not appear that Lady Warwick had been at all easily persuaded. It is usually supposed that she was the 'mistress'[1] he complained of having lost in 1711. Some have gone so far as to see in Sir Roger's remarks on widows Addison's own soft reproof to this feminine 'demurrer in love', and Tonson used to say that from the moment Addison entered the family he had determined upon that conquest. Nor is it easy to understand why she on her side yielded now, why now she overcame her reluctance to an 'iteration of nuptials', to use Lady Wishfort's phrase. For Addison was not growing more

[1] The word in those days had not, of course, its modern specialized meaning.

attractive as the years went by; from placidity his features were passing to woodenness, the brightness of his eye was being dimmed, an awful austerity dwelt in the folds gathered about his mouth; and, to appeal once more to Stendhal, " Je doute fort que l'air Caton ait jamais occasionné de coup de foudre ". Perhaps at first she had thought the marriage beneath her, but that the wisdom, the disappointments, of advancing years, had shown her that after all that consideration was not of the first importance. In any case Addison's prospects were incomparably brighter than they had been five years earlier.

And he, on his part, perhaps wanted a relation more constant, more day by day, than his friendships: a woman might be less independent than a man; a wife would always be at hand. After all, the fair sex had been expressly designed for man's comfort, and now that Addison was, at forty-four, past the probable meridian of life, he felt, no doubt, that it was time to experience that conjugal state *The Spectator* had so often and so warmly advocated.

For his friends were scattering, and there were no new ones, except ' young Craggs ', and he was everybody's friend, even Pope's. Budgell was in Ireland; Tickell, Addison's last under-secretary in that country, was forming new ties there; Swift at this period never stirred from Dublin. Philips, now a rather pompous J. P., was no longer a faithful shadow, and even talked of starting a paper himself. Steele, finally, was every day getting more difficult. He was often in Scotland on business, or ruining himself in madcap schemes for bringing Irish salmon alive to London: and although he was aided in this by Vanbrugh's old enemy Benson, the enterprise was no more likely to succeed than his old alchemistic tomfooleries. Nor was he quite so deferential as he had been ; he had even attacked a number of *The Freeholder* in one of his numerous journals, and though whenever the pair met they spoke with all the old ease and intimacy, since they shunned each other [1] they met but seldom. Perhaps it was just as well. Poor Dick with his zeal, his incurable carelessness of himself and his money, had always been a source of trouble to Addison. He liked, it is true, to feel responsible for his friends, but Steele provoked unworkable situations : Addison would be held responsible for him by others, yet Steele would simply fly in the face of his advice. By such behaviour he had almost finally embroiled him with Swift, who, when Steele attacked him in *The Guardian*, had written Addison a letter complaining of it, the letter of an angry man which did not contain one phrase friendship might have dictated. The patience, even of an Addison, has its limits.

Such a marriage as he contemplated would, moreover, have social advantages ; it would, for instance, be pleasant to live in Holland House. And if the Countess had any worldly qualms, these were quieted in the next year by Addison's political elevation.

In the winter of 1716–17, Sunderland, while paying a visit to the King in Germany, suggested to him that Townshend was by no means the prime minister for the royal purposes. Stanhope would be much better. It was true he had been an ignominiously unsuccessful General, but that was no reason why he should not make a first-rate Lord Treasurer. Sunderland was a not unworthy son of a father who, whatsoever king might reign, would always manage by his consummate cleverness to be at the head of affairs, and he over-persuaded the too easily

[1] *The Theatre*, xii. Quoted by Aitken, ii. 216.

managed monarch. In March Townshend was dismissed; Walpole, in spite of the King's sevenfold appeal, insisted upon resigning, and their places were exactly taken by Stanhope and Sunderland, the former being the figure-head, the latter enjoying all the real power. And whether for old sake's sake, or warned by the history of Harley and St. John that it does not do to have too brilliant and active a subordinate, he offered the post of Secretary of State to Addison, who could be trusted never to open his mouth in the House of Commons.

And, this being the second time of asking, Addison, somewhat to the general surprise, accepted. It was thought that he was hardly a fit person for so arduous a place. Lady Mary Wortley Montagu was especially troubled.

"I received the news of Mr. Addison's being declared Secretary of State", she wrote, "with the less surprise that I know the post was offered him before. At that time he declined it; and I really believe he would have done well to decline it now. Such a post as that, and such a wife as the Countess, do not seem to be in prudence eligible for a man that is asthmatic, and we may see the day when he will be glad to resign them both."

It may be that the Countess had insisted;[1] but why should Addison not have at least tried his hand in the post which must, after all, have been the goal of his ambition? So, making Tickell his under-secretary, he took a house in Albemarle Street,[2] where, no doubt, he held his official levees, Holland House being too far in the country. Here his friends must have gathered to congratulate, and solicit. Only Steele kept strangely aloof. "I ask nothing of Mr. Secretary Addison", he wrote. But Mr. Secretary Addison could not have given

[1] Spence. [2] Egerton MSS.

anything of importance to a man whose zeal would be sure to lead him into indefensible extravagances.

Lady Mary, however, had been right. Addison was glad to resign his Secretaryship before a year was out. It is easy to see that the harsh world of politics, the "systematic organization of hatreds", was no world for the gentle writer of the *Vision of Mirza*, the creator of Sir Roger de Coverley, or the arbiter of the modes and manners of the fair sex. His interest was in the eternal rather than in the immediate actualities. He might write a clear dispatch, or a mild letter of recall to an unsuitable ambassador, but would scarcely be quick enough amid the wiles of the council-table. It is no detraction from his virtues to say he was incompetent, any more than it would be to hint that he could not ride to hounds. It was 'commonly said' that he "was by no means qualified for the office of secretary, being not skilled in business, and not knowing how to speak".[1] But it is not true, as was at the time suggested, that he was turned out of office, though it is probable that he himself felt that his inadequacy made resignation the only course.

He retired to Holland House with a pension of fifteen hundred pounds a year, but it is doubtful if he was happy. Rumour had it that he "married discord with a noble wife", but that is likely to be an overstatement. It is probable, however, that in the one instance where he might have given so much, he failed to give enough. Besides, Lady Warwick may have been too exacting: she had given up position to marry him, and no doubt she found that, in spite of the four thousand pounds she had received in compensation for loss of a jointure, that her husband was too fond of slipping off to Button's to discuss

[1] Hearne, ii. 54.

that odious Boileau, or to find new parallels between the *Aeneid* and absurd English ballads. Addison was too old a dog to learn new tricks of domesticity.

He was now definitely retired from politics; he had attained the highest position possible to one of his birth, and had relinquished it. But he busied himself with many things; projecting a tragedy on the death of Socrates, anticipating Johnson in the idea of a Dictionary, and Paley in compiling *Evidences of Christianity*; with making metrical versions of the psalms. The 'parson in a tye-wig' was at last finding his true bent, returning to the dreams of his youth. Tonson vowed he had his eye on a bishopric. But he had not all his old energy; more and more did he need that stimulus to the mind without which he had never been able to think freely—burgundy. It was popularly said that he found the cup did "more than Milton can To justify God's ways to man", and the heavier wines are not good for sufferers from asthma.

Retired as he might be in a life filled with 'secret pleasures', he was not unguarded from the claims of friendship or the poisoned shafts of enmity. The former obtruded vexingly in the form of Eustace Budgell. This young man—he was still only about thirty—had been very well established in several lucrative Irish posts during Addison's last tenure of office in that island, but he was ill-advised enough to quarrel with Addison's successor, Webster. Budgell wanted a certain clerkship for his brother, Webster was determined to dispose of it elsewhere; and of course the chief secretary won, sealing his victory by obtaining the discharge of Budgell from all his posts. In high distress the unfortunate young man ran to his wise cousin for advice. The advice he got was good: to keep quiet. But Budgell could not keep quiet; it was his destiny to "charge low Grub-Street on his quill", and in spite of Addison's disapproval, he insisted on publishing an account of his quarrel with Webster. Naturally it did him no good; and it lost him besides much of the consideration of his mentor, who rightly thought that dirty linen should be washed in private.

That certainly was the method he adopted when in 1718 he once more came into collision with Pope.

At the end of 1716, the aged Wycherley, who had for twenty years lived a ghost-like existence, married a young woman to inconvenience a spiteful heir, and died. It was expected that some one would write a memoir to put on record the really magnificent qualities of the author of so great a masterpiece as *The Country Wife*. But since no author of rank offered himself, Gildon, the printer, announced that he would compose a small commemorative pamphlet. It was mentioned to Addison, who said he was very glad to hear of it, and would even contribute towards the expense of the publication in the case of its proving a failure. It was suggested that something about Pope would have to be put in, as no life of Wycherley could be complete which did not contain some account of the strange confederacy between the dazzling but decayed old dramatist, and the brilliant but deformed young poet. Addison could not but agree; perhaps he smiled deprecatingly, and hoped that nothing hard would be said about Pope. However it was, the young Earl of Warwick went off to Pope and amiably told him that his stepfather had given Gildon ten guineas to libel him in the 'thing about Wycherley'.

Whatever Addison may have thought would be said about Pope, he can have had no inkling of the outrageous things that actually were written in the booklet that appeared in May 1718. It was published by Pope's sworn enemy Curll, and was entitled :

Memoirs of the Life
of
William Wycherley, Esq.
with a
Character of his Writings
By the Right Honourable George
Lord Lansdowne,

the phrasing ingeniously suggesting that Lansdowne had written the whole scurrilous lampoon, whereas he was only responsible for the admirably dignified prose of the *Character of his Writings*. If Addison had indeed encouraged the publication, he must have been as much horror-struck as Pope was enraged, to read such passages as :

" About this time there came to Town, and to *Will's*, one *Pope*, a little diminutive Creature, who had got a sort of Knack in smooth Vercification and with it was for setting up for a Wit and a Poet."

After descanting awhile on his " Plausible, or at least Cringing Way of Insinuation ", Gildon rushed on :

" I remember I was once to wait on Mr. *Wycherley*, and found in his chamber this little *Aesopic* sort of an animal in his own cropt Hair, and Dress agreeable to the Forest he came from . . ."

and so forth ; and not content with such an attack, he concluded the paragraph with an insulting reference to the elder Mr. Pope, a respectable linendraper, who had only recently died, and of whom his son had been really fond.

Had Pope thought a moment, he must have known this was none of Addison's doing ; but very naturally inflamed with anger, he took young Lord Warwick's statement *au pied de la lettre*, and setting pen to paper dashed off at white heat the still effulgent lines now known as the *Character of Atticus*. He had long brooded over the wrongs Addison had done him, he had the headings of his satire quite clear, and the poison ran freely from his pen, distilled by a furious rage, controlled by the exigencies of a fiendish and fastidious art which made every word tell. He at once sent them to Addison.[1] He was in no mood for dancing minuets.

Addison did nothing. It was the only thing to do. It was what Pope himself did :

> Yet then did Gildon draw his venal quill ;—
> I wished the man a dinner, and sat still . . .

and it was absurd of Pope to take it as a triumph that afterwards Addison always treated him with civility, as though this were another instance of his being " Willing to wound and yet afraid to strike ". Addison was no match for Pope at this kind of literature, nor could he also be expected to hang up a cudgel in his coffee-house. In any case he knew his role better. " To forbear replying to an unjust reproach, and overlook it with a generous, or, if possible, with an entire neglect of it, is one of the most heroic acts of a great mind." [2]

And if neither friends nor foes were to leave Addison alone in his retirement, nor were politics altogether to do so.

In 1719 Sunderland set the Peerage Bill in motion. The Whigs had not forgotten that when they had allowed the Act against occasional conformity to pass it had been on the understanding that the ' whimsical ' Tories under Nottingham would support the war,[3] but that Harley had dished them by persuading the Queen to create twelve new peers to vote the peace in the House of

[1] See Appendix IV. [2] *Tatler*, 133. [3] Lecky, *England*.

Lords. The Peerage Bill, fathered by Addison's old acquaintance, the proud Duke of Somerset, was designed to prevent a repetition of such a manœuvre. It all seemed so simple, so right. The Lords, naturally, would not object to their vested interests being guarded. The King was seduced into agreeing to this limitation of his power by the pleasing idea that he was thereby injuring his son, and this very limitation made it appear on the surface an unexceptionally Whig measure. But the idea was not so pleasing to the Commoners, who saw themselves thus arbitrarily shut out of paradise, dispropertied of possible freedoms. Walpole organized an opposition, and Grub Street flew to sharpen its pens. This being the case, Sunderland called upon Addison to answer some of the critics of the Bill, the most formidable of whom was the author of an incisive pamphlet called *The Plebeian*, which appeared on the 14th March 1719.

Addison crossed swords in a sheet called *The Old Whig*, and under this pseudonym dealt some shrewd blows in return. The battle waxed bitter, all the more so that it was soon apparent that the author of *The Plebeian* was none other than Steele. Under these circumstances the most innocent remarks take upon themselves the colour of allusions. Thus the controversy was carried on on the lower level of such writings, with the usual amount of sneering and patronizing advice. On one occasion it went farther. In his first *Plebeian* Steele had drawn a parallel between a closed peerage and the Ephori of Lacedaemon; and when Addison rated him for being personal he countered the charge by adding a passage concerning the paederastic habits of the Ephori, concluding by saying "it is very plain all this was omitted to avoid the least Appearance of personal Reflection".[1]

[1] *Plebeian*, ii.

The accusation was a grave one, and difficult to refute, and Addison could only reply with, " I am informed there are two or three keen Disputants who will return a proper Answer to it when they have discover'd the author ".[1] When Steele's turn came again he wrote of the threat of violence, " The rest of this Paragraph is very mean; and this Author's Menaces in this place are as vain, as his Compassion in another part of his Pamphlet is insolent ".[2] The whole thing was sadly un-Victorian; this was an atmosphere unsuited to Addison.

Too much, however, has been made of the personal bitterness of these writings, for which biographers have laid the blame on one or the other according to the side on which they were pleading. There is nothing to choose between the controversialists in this matter. But it is unlikely that by the words ' little Dicky ' Addison meant to strike at Steele, and it is unjust to regard his references to the ' stagnant pool ' as gibes at Steele's unfortunate movable fish-ponds. For Steele himself had introduced the expression by saying that a closed House of Lords would become " as corrupt and offensive as a stagnated pool ". And probably the worst personal cut Steele dealt his sometime friend was to quote against him the speech in *Cato* beginning " Remember, O my Friends, the Laws, the Rights ", to which he referred as " that noble Exhortation of the Tragedian ". The rest are merely strokes given in the heat of conflict, and may be disregarded, except perhaps for Steele's insinuation that the Old Whig was used to masquerading, which, incomprehensible to the generality of readers, can have been meant for Addison alone. How far his suggestion that six of the most ardent supporters of the Bill in the

[1] *Old Whig*, ii. [2] *Plebeian*, iv.

Commons had patents in their pockets for the final creations to be made before the peerage was closed was meant to apply to the Old Whig, it is impossible to guess.

In truth it was an odd controversy, which Macaulay has summed up illogically, but not unfairly, by saying, " It seems to us the premises of both the controversialists were unsound, that on these premises Addison argued well and Steele ill; and that consequently Addison brought out a false conclusion while Steele blundered upon the truth "—save that there is as little to choose in the reasoning as there is in the style. Both disputants found it difficult to keep to the point, and many of the arguments are ' clean kam '. Both became lost and embrangled in the almost theological complexity of a triune state consisting of Crown, Lords, and Commons, and often strayed to irrelevant side-issues as well as to personalities. The British Constitution in its grandeur loomed up before Addison's eyes huge and august, but—foggy; and though there might be a mystery in the soul of state, it somehow seemed less important to unravel it than to know whether the aggregate income of the Commons exceeded that of the Lords, or to discuss the attributes of age as exhibited by the slowness and testiness of the Old Whig.

The Bill, thanks to Walpole rather than to Steele, was dropped, to be defeated at the next session; but the effort to save it seems to have exhausted Addison, who, attacked by dropsy in June, was forced to realize that he was near his end.

3

Justification

LOOKING back on his life of forty-seven years, Addison must surely have felt a 'secret satisfaction and complacency' at its outcome. Without bribery, intrigue, or much self-abjection, he had attained to the highest post in the state then open to a commoner without connexions—for if he ever had hopes of a peerage, these were dreams rather than expectations. He had written the most renowned tragedy of his age, and had earned, he was sure of it, immortality in his essays. He would always rank as a revered *censor morum*, as one who had leavened the most critical period in English manners; for he had set a standard of taste in behaviour and in poetry, and directed the fair sex in the way it should go. He had moved as freely as he wished in the best intellectual circles, and was hailed as an equal by the finest minds of his generation. If some of his friendships had been tarnished by the violence of faction, as in the case of poor Dick, it was not his fault that others had been unable to see that the secret of a successful life was to live undangerously, without undue enthusiasm, or the hideous distortions of zeal.

But there was more to gratify him than mere outward success; he had lived consistently with his own standards. He had always been scrupulously honest, had always striven to do his duty without fear, favour, or—affection. He had been gentle, tolerant, submissive, even to turning the other cheek: he had tried to see the best in every thing and every one, had been, in fact, as far as lay in his power and in his purview, a sincere Christian. Even ignoble ambition, such as broke out so desperately urgent in his last letters to Halifax, that rodent passion which 'raises a secret tumult in the soul, rouses a craving it cannot allay or abate',[1] even that he had crushed in himself. That, and envy, for through all his days he had shown himself a foe to detraction, giving honour where honour was due, praising where he felt effort called for praise. He had embarked on life determined to be a model, and his treadings had never slipped.

No one familiar with the *Spectator* papers on fame [2] or envy can suppose he had achieved this perfection without a struggle, that the *mens sibi conscia recti*, the mind undoubting of its virtue, had been built up without many a severe wrestling match with the old Adam of worldly desires. He had deliberately formed, meticulously polished himself, until he glowed as a beacon for all mankind. This he had done by "adhering steadfastly to one great end as the chief and ultimate aim of all his pursuits".[3] Nor had he deceived himself as to his motives; in endeavouring "to lay down some rules for the discovery of those vices that lurk in the secret corners of the soul", he had 'come at a true and impartial knowledge of himself'.[4] If he had been a hypocrite, he had been so of set purpose, for the sake of the general picture; for motives do not matter so long as the final action is good. The commendable, the commended deed, is what we should strive after. Again and again in his essays he had preached the duty of standing well with one's neighbours; of so ordering one's person and one's actions as to give no handle to calumny; of so behaving that the mud cast by an imperfect world should

[1] *Spectator*, 256. [2] *Spectator*, 255, 256, 257. [3] *Spectator*, 162.
[4] *Spectator*, 399

glance off without leaving a smirch. And he hoped, he must have believed, that in his case the result had been an almost perfect pattern. His modesty, he knew, had already become proverbial. Surely the wisdom of the *Qu'en dira-t-on?* was justified of this child of hers!

To us, in rebellion against the Victorian view, with more faith in the human being, and much less in his ideals, approaching as we do indeed a nihilism in values, a character such as Addison's must seem unsatisfactory. We cannot but regard some of his moral operations much as we look upon the crushing of the feet of Chinese girls. We care little for a virtue that is not spontaneous, for a charitable action that is the result of thought rather than of impulse. We cannot say, as did one of the greatest and most lovable of the Victorians: "I protest that if some great Power would agree to make me always think what is true and do what is right, on condition of being turned into a sort of clock and wound up every morning before I got out of bed, I should instantly close with the offer." A decade of passionate vice we feel to be infinitely superior to a cycle of such Cathay rectitude. But since we have not to conform, we need not condemn. After all, Addison had solved the problem of his life with the greatest satisfaction to himself. To use Huxley's phrase, he had found the mean between his self-assertion and his self-restraint, his ambition and his fears, best suited to his character and circumstances. After all, his assumptions worked—as they did in the case of the Victorians—'in so far forth'. We may not admire; but are we sure we do not a little, now and again, with reservations, envy the tranquillity, the certitude?

There was, however, one thing that troubled Addison in his last days; fears for his reputation in the eyes of posterity, a matter at least as important as his actual fame. It was a thing no man had a right to neglect, as he had more than once insisted. The shining example was of no use if the immediate years were to sully it. And there was one man—apart from Pope, with whom it was impossible to deal—who might do him hurt in this respect.

When, in 1717, Gay had produced a farce called *Three Hours After Marriage*, Addison and his followers had professed themselves shocked at the indelicacies it contained. Impulsive, child-like Gay had been much pained at this accusation, and had compiled a document in which passages from the works of Addison and Steele were placed side by side with those to which the little senate had most objected in his own. He threatened to publish it, and Addison, running his eye over his own volumes, saw that it would be possible to make out a most damaging case against him, for though prudent, he had never been a prude. He sent for Gay, apologized generously for the harm he had done him, and asked his forgiveness. He omitted to mention for what offence.

Gay was bewildered, but he was too much moved at the sight of the dying man to ask him what he meant, and left the room with tears in his eyes. What could Addison mean? Had he, during his tenure of office, vetoed a suggestion of giving Gay a place? That must be it. Of course he forgave him! Poor, artless Gay! Light, airy, irresponsible figure, fit only in the commerce of the world to be a lively companion of the wits, letter-writer to a Duchess, or gentleman-in-waiting to an infant Princess! How could he have had any place, even if he had not been a Tory? So his document was never published. But it was Pope who took to himself the credit for its suppression: his regard for Addison, he declared, his knowledge of Mr. Spectator's fear of ridicule, had made him prevail upon Gay to hand it over to him for safe keeping. He kept it very safely; he had had a hand in *Three Hours After Marriage*.

And now Addison could face the final moment, the test, as he thought, of a man's life. *Finis coronat opus*, Sir Andrew Freeport had quoted;[1] a man was to be judged by the figure he made at his death. Since the life of no man can be marked up as either virtuous or vicious before the conclusion of it, no change of mind or temper must be observable. "As there is not a more melancholy consideration to a good man than his being obnoxious to such a change, so there is nothing more glorious than to keep up an uniformity in his actions and preserve his beauty of character to the last."[2] His teaching would continue even beyond the grave, for "there is nothing in history which is so improving to the reader, as those accounts which we meet with of the deaths of eminent persons, and of their behaviour in that dreadful season".[3] And, indeed, Addison had studied much for his model, for the end of philosophy, Plato had taught him, was to teach a man how to die. He rejected the indifference of Petronius as smacking too much of levity[4]—but he had written of the glorious death of Cato, and had pondered much over the brave end made by Socrates. They had died well; but he would have one advantage denied them, for 'religious hope' filled his mind with 'secret comfort and refreshment'.[5] As he felt the end approach he summoned his step-son, Lord Warwick, in the hope of recovering the profligate. "I have sent for you", he said, "that you may see in what peace a Christian can die." In this manner he illustrated his saying that 'the practice of the

[1] *Spectator*, 549. [2] Ibid., 349. [3] Ibid., 289. [4] Ibid., 349.
[5] Ibid., 471.

virtue of faith administers great comfort to the mind of man in the hour of death '.[1]

His own took place on the 17th June 1719.

. . . .

When the play is played out—and who can deny that for Addison the world was a stage?—it is perhaps as well to shut up the box. But after all, human beings are not puppets. If they are rapt away from passionate life, the passions they have aroused do not necessarily die with them; new ones even may gather around their names, and they live in the memories of their friends, perhaps of their enemies. *Finis coronat opus*, yes; but the edges are blurred, and no one can say where, precisely, is the end. There are eddies, little gusts, sudden whirlpools, that make a noise almost as loud as life, and die away: but it seems as though the presence had been real.

To Tickell at least the memory of Addison was actual. That ' awful form ' visited him in his dreams, or ' roused by Fancy, met his waking eyes '. It haunted him. At business or at Court, he would be elbowed by the phantom of the ' unblemished statesman '; if he went to the theatre, the form of Cato dominated the scene. He invaded, he permeated, the placid countryside:

If pensive to the rural shades I rove,
His shape o'ertakes me in the lonely grove;
'Twas there of just and good he reason'd strong;
Clear'd some great truth, or raised some serious song:
There patient show'd us the wise course to steer,
A candid censor, and a friend severe.

It could not be otherwise for Tickell. As, day by day, he turned over the pages of his friend and mentor's

[1] *Spectator*, 441.

writings, labouring at the edition of his works which had been Addison's last charge to him, the intonations of his voice, the very gestures that he made, rare as they were, compelled his imagination. Addison was there, not only as he went through the published works, but again as he perused the dissertation upon *Medals*, or grappled with the flimsy *Evidences of the Christian Religion.* "He taught us how to live", he cried out at last, "and (Oh too high The price for knowledge) taught us how to die." Nor can his anguish have been lightened by the comfort addressed him by Young; rather must the loss have seemed more poignant when he read:

> In joy once join'd, in sorrow now, for years—
> Partner in grief, and brother of my tears,
> Tickell, accept this verse, thy mournful due . . .

and it is curious to conjecture what lay in the mind of Dr. Johnson when he sought for 'secret history' in those limpid lines.

Steele's first feeling on learning of Addison's death was one of bitterness. Regret for his friend was overwhelmed by his jealousy of Tickell—Tickell the upstart, who had done nothing for Addison but flatter him; Tickell, who had been recommended to the protection of Craggs; Tickell to whom Addison had at the last entrusted his works, ignoring his old companion. As he heard of the progress of the edition he wrote wildly to the elder Tonson, an incoherent letter that does little but reveal the sore.

"I apprehend certain Persons desire to separate the works of Mr. Addison from mine in a book called the *Tatler*. Be pleased to observe that I paid Mr. Addison for what he writ under that title, and made a Title of the whole to Nutt, and as there is a remainder according to act of Parliament in Writings to authors of which my

Family shall not be bereft, Mr. Addison is the last man who shall be patiently suffer'd in doing unreasonable things (that He has you must know) to

Sr

Your Most Humble Ser^{nt}

July 19th 1719.[1] RICHARD STEELE."

Tickell, indeed, taking a mean advantage of the trust, cast a slur upon the one quality in Steele no one else has ever thought to doubt, his lavish generosity of temper. He suggested in the preface to the collected works that Steele had never done Addison full justice, Steele who had sung his friend's praise wherever he could, in the preface to the *Tatlers*, in the last number of their joint *Spectators*, acknowledging without stint his superiority, his genius, his greatness in every respect, roundly stating that his greatest pride was in the linking together of their names. And Tickell had the effrontery to say:

"As the acknowledgement was made in general terms, without directing the Publick to the several papers: Mr. Addison, who was content with the Praise arising from his own Works, and too delicate to take any part of that which belonged to others, afterwards thought fit to distinguish his writings in the *Spectators* and *Guardians* by such marks as might remove the least possibility of Mistake in the most undiscerning readers."

But Steele had his chance to reply, for Tickell did not imagine that Addison had written *The Drummer*, and Steele was tolerably certain that he had. Therefore in December 1721 he republished the comedy, with his vindication in the form of a dedicatory letter to Congreve.

It is a queer, and to those who know the history of it, a profoundly moving document. The bountiful heart of Steele poured over it, his love for his departed some-

[1] Aitken, ii. 216.

time ally mingling with his hatred for Tickell, " in preference of whom [Addison] had incurred the warmest resentments of other Gentlemen "—so Steele laid bare the domestic secrets of the little senate. But he forgot his later differences with Addison, he forgot the matter of the debt, he forgot he had been unable to ask anything of Mr. Secretary Addison, as he did even the insults of *The Old Whig*. He remembered only that when he had too recklessly plunged into the torrent of life, Addison had stood " weeping on the brink for his safety ".[1] His generous, foolish, impulsive soul burned as he answered Tickell, who, he said, spoke of the man who had done so much for him in cold, unaffectionate terms, and who could make no revelation of his hero other than that he ' had never had a regular pulse '.

Except for the revelation Tickell, in his eagerness to defame Steele, had blundered into making about the ' marks ' to the *Spectators*. It was true that Addison had caused them to be printed, but it was because he could not bear that others should possibly ' take any part ' of that which belonged to him. After Addison had done this, without Steele's knowledge, the latter ' made it his own act, since, he wrote, " I thought it too great a sensibility in my friend, and thought it, since it was done, better to be supposed marked by me than by the author himself; the real state of which this zealot rashly and injudiciously exposes " '. He was naturally angry that Tickell had tried to disparage him by saying Addison had marked the essays as ' a caution against him ', when he had done it ' out of tenderness ' to Addison. The real state was now worse exposed than ever.

No, he could not quite forgive Addison everything; it was too much. That vanity, parading as modesty,

[1] The Theatre, 12.

should put him in this false position, him, the almost lifelong friend, the friend from boyhood, was intolerable, and his distress was ever and anon tossed up on the boiling sea of his rage against Tickell. For the greatest part of his life, he wrote, he had been Addison's " Bosom Friend, and shielded him from all the resentments which many of his own works would have brought upon him at the time in which they were written ". " What I never did declare was Mr. Addison's," he continued, " I had his direct injunctions to hide. . . . Many of the Writings now published as his I have been very patiently traduced and calumniated for."

And this was his reward. For writing *The Plebeian* he had already been hunted out of his posts by Addison's patrons, and now he was 'traduced and calumniated' by his friend. However, there was one retort that was easy, for to accuse a man of gaining glory by Addison's writings might prove a double-edged weapon. Let the 'reputed translator of Homer', he lunged back, get to work, and see, now that Addison was dead, if he could produce another book half so good! He left it at that.

He left it; but it was just at this point that Pope took it up. The phrase 'the reputed translator of Homer' fastened very insistently upon his imagination. He thought about Addison, and he too forgot a number of things, but his forgetfulness was not of the same nature as Steele's. His tortuous and vivid fancy led him back over the years of his acquaintance with Addison, and he remembered Addison had advised him badly over the 'machinery' of the *Rape of the Lock*, while he forgot that he had advised Addison badly over *Cato*. He remembered the *Spectator* that began by praising him and ended by over-praising Philips; he forgot the flattering things said about his Homer in *The Freeholder*.

He remembered Addison had given away his participation in *The Guardian* and made it known that he ' writ with Steele ' ; he remembered the ' thing about Wycherley ' ; in short he remembered and invented all sorts of incidents, and forgot he had no vestige of proof about any of them. But ' the reputed translator ' was enough for him. He was convinced that Addison himself had written the so-called Tickell *Iliad* with the sole design, hoped-for but foiled, of humiliating him, but that, as usual, he had preferred to father the work on to another until its success was assured. The notion matured darkly and slowly, until its very familiarity made it incontrovertible. Then Pope deleted from the satire on Addison the couplet which ran :

Who when two wits on rival themes contest,
Approves them both, but likes the worst the best,

as inconsistent with his new-gained knowledge.

Swift felt differently. His heart, though cracked, was great ; it was its very greatness that had cracked it. He could forgive Addison everything, would say nothing but good of him. Feeling in his own breast all the tempers of humankind, he could understand Addison's coldness to him in the years 1710–14. Such behaviour had its obvious excuses ; he could sympathize even where he could not condone. Thus when, in 1728, he and Pope issued their joint miscellany, the preface informed the world that

" In regard to two persons only, we wish our raillery, though ever so tender, or resentment, though ever so just, had not been indulged. We speak of Sir John Vanbrugh . . . ; and of Mr. Addison, whose name deserves all respect from every lover of learning."

The juxtaposition is strange. In one sentence were

bracketed together the names of two most opposite men; the one freely careless of himself and his powers; the other who never took the smallest step without infinite regard to his reputation, or uttered the most trivial word without being studious of his character. Was this apparent compliment, with its antithesis of epithet—we remember Vanbrugh was described as a man of wit and of honour—Pope's last shaft, so subtle as to be invisible even to the probing eye of Swift? We cannot but believe that Pope's agility deceived Swift's generosity, the lacerated heart conceding what the wounded vanity could not. The Dean did not realize how heartily Pope meant the words "our resentments, though ever so just", which could not possibly apply to Vanbrugh. De mortuis . . . of course; but the miscellany contained the first published version of the Satire on Addison!

After Addison's death most of his friends lapsed into obscurity, of all the little senate only Tickell establishing himself, and earning a deserved reputation, in Ireland: though young, less intimate, obtained a belated fame. Steele spent a wretched old age exiled in Wales, for the enmity of the Duke of Newcastle, who had embarked on that long career of borough-mongering which was to bring him into such glorious collaboration with the elder Pitt, proved too strong for him. Craggs, of brilliant promise, was almost at once cut off by the 'small-pox', victim of one of those curiously sudden deaths which overtook so many of the leading members of the Government that had supported the South Sea Bubble. Carey committed suicide. Brett died in 1724, leaving his daughter to become the first English mistress of George I. Philips sank into oblivion as secretary to an Irish bishop, dragged into the light only to figure as a sprat in Pope's wide-flung satiric net. Budgell declined lower and lower in the Grub Street scale, after a brief period of prosperity with the Boyle family. He finally became involved in an ugly affair over the will of the heretical Dr. Tindal, whose second volume of *Christianity as Old as the Creation* was mercifully burned by an orthodox bishop. Scorned and reviled, Eustace one day filled his pocket with stones, and taking boat at London Bridge, was never again seen alive. He left on his desk a paper with the words,

> What Cato did and Addison approved
> Cannot be wrong—

a touching, if mistaken tribute, to a friendship twenty years overpast. Addison's daughter turned out half-witted, and the two young men over whom he might have been supposed to have an influence, Lords Wharton and Warwick, earned distinction only in profligacy.

Happily Addison was unknowing of these developments and these ends, as his coffin, at midnight, amid defunctive music, was borne to the Henry VII chapel in Westminster Abbey. There he was laid, ' to sleep in peace next his lov'd Mountague ', side by side with his honoured patron. Two epitaphs, cut in the usual lapidary style, tell the idle visitor only half the truth ; yet, we may well think, they tell more than is revealed by those faceted half-truths that lie side by side, they also, in the immortal but envenomed pages of the *Prologue to the Satires*.

APPENDICES AND BIBLIOGRAPHIES

APPENDIX I

GODOLPHIN'S WARRANT TO VANBRUGH

This very important document runs as follows :

To all to whom these presents shall come, The Right Honourable Sidney Lord Godolphin, Lord High Treasurer of England sendeth greeting. Whereas his Grace, John Duke of Marlborough, hath resolved to erect a large fabric for a mansion house, at Woodstock in the county of Oxon, Know ye, That I the said Sidney Lord Godolphin, At the request and desire of the said Duke of Marlborough have constituted and appointed, and do hereby, for, and on behalf of the said Duke, constitute and appoint John Vanbrugh Esq; to be surveyor of all the works and buildings so intended to be erected or made at Woodstock aforesaid ; and do hereby authorise and empower the said John Vanbrugh, to make and sign contracts with any persons for materials, and also with any artificers or workmen to be employed about the said buildings, in such manner as he shall judge proper, for carrying out the said work in the best and most advantageous manner that may be, And likewise to employ such day labourers and carriages from time to time, as he shall find necessary for the said service, and do all other matters and things, as may be in any ways conducive to the effectual performance of what is directed by the said Duke of Marlborough in relation to the said works.

June 9th 1705.
GODOLPHIN.

From Coxe Papers, Add. MSS. 9123, f. 79.
Vanbrugh quotes it in full in his *Justification.*

APPENDIX II

MRS. YARBURGH

There are some difficulties here. In her letter, Lady Mary states Vanbrugh as possibly " endeavouring at the honourable state of matrimony ", as though the lady were unmarried.

Leigh Hunt, Palmer, Swain, and Ward all assume that the lady in question was a daughter of Mrs. Yarburgh, either the Henrietta he did actually marry in 1719, or an elder sister. But she had no elder sister.

'Mrs.' of course, has no significance as to the married state, but if Lady Mary meant Henrietta, would she refer to her as a ruin? For Henrietta was some three years *younger* than Lady Mary, having been born in 1693—and was at the date of the letter at most twenty years of age. One is not a ruin at that period of life.

'The date of the letter.' There is some doubt here. Lord Wharncliffe in his edition of Lady Mary Wortley Montagu's *Letters* gives it as 1710, and in this he is followed by Leigh Hunt, Palmer, and Swain. Other editions give November 1713, the date preferred by Ward. If it is signed M.P. it must have been 1710, for in 1713 Lady Mary was not Pierpont but Wortley; all editions do not give the initials.

The matter is not of great importance in this connexion: we have only to consider the reference to marriage. Now Mrs. Yarburgh was evidently only met by Vanbrugh on market-days; she was but a visitor, and it is not necessary to assume that Lady Mary was well informed as to her state in life. This would not in any case affect the possibility of a friendship, or more, between her and Vanbrugh.

It is unlikely that a man of Vanbrugh's age and temperament would be attracted by a slip of a girl who was perhaps only seventeen at the time the letter was written, though of course one never knows. When he did eventually marry Henrietta she was twenty-six—a great difference in those days, and had grown much older correspondingly than he had.

The case seems to me to be probably thus. In 1710 or 1713 he carried on a mild, half-humorous flirtation with the mother, to whom Lady Mary might very well refer as a 'ruin'; and when in 1718 she died, transferred his affection to her daughter, perhaps half protectively, and developed it to the stage of love. Previous biographers in wanting to make of the episode an example of touching fidelity, have been too ready to accept the ladies as the same person.

Perhaps, however, altogether too much importance is attached to the letter of a very vivacious, not to say frisky young woman, who was evidently determined to find life as amusing as she could, and make her letters as entertaining as possible.

The authority for the Yarburgh family is C. R. Robinson's *History of the Priory and Peculiar of Snaith.*

APPENDIX III

'SECRET'

Did not the word occur so frequently its use might be put down to a fashion. "I descended a little on the side of that delicious vale, surveying it with a secret kind of pleasure . . ." That is not from a 'vision', but from *Robinson Crusoe*. "The purple sky, those wild but sweet notes of birds, the fragrant bloom upon the trees and flowers, the gentle influence of the rising sun, these and a thousand nameless beauties of nature, inspire the soul with secret transports." That is not the short-faced gentleman writing from Sir Roger's country seat, but Philonous preluding to Hylas. The first passage, written probably before Addison's death, reads suspiciously like parody. Berkeley, at the time he was writing his dialogues, was an acquaintance, and probably an admirer of Addison. Steele uses the word, but much more rarely, and less gratuitously than Addison.

APPENDIX IV

THE *FRENZY*

It is impossible to arrive at any certainty with respect to any of these Pope-Addison episodes. It is generally agreed that the *Narrative* is by Pope, though were it not for internal evidence, C. W. Dilke's contention that it is by Steele would be very convincing.[1] It seems likely, however, that Steele knew about it, and perhaps took a minor hand in it. Addison's behaviour in this affair seems not only natural, but in conformity with his character. He could not *forbid* the publication, but one may doubt if his disapproval was couched in terms strong enough to dissuade Steele. Certainly, if his influence was strong enough to make Steele write that very humiliating letter to Lintot, it was strong enough for anything. One can but guess. I can only hope my version will seem to the reader familiar with the subject, to be fair to all parties concerned.

The above remarks may serve also as a note on the Homer episode, and on the 'thing about Wycherley'.

With regard to the latter, it is probable that Pope did send his satire on Addison (Atticus) to the subject of it. Such a procedure would not be contrary to his habit. The discovery of Gildon's book (see *Times Literary Supplement*, 11th May 1922, letter from Mr. George Sherburn) invalidates all previous accounts in biographies of Addison or Pope.

[1] *Papers of a Critic*, i. 253 seq.

APPENDIX V

POPE'S LETTERS

To use Pope's letters as evidence is, of course, full of dangers. The extraordinary pranks of falsification of names and dates, the extravagant antics he went through with regard to their publication, make it almost impossible to say anything certain about them. Nor, to my thinking, does the discovery of the Caryll correspondence by any means dispose of many things. Because Pope wrote something to Caryll it does not follow he did not write the same thing to somebody else. Most of us, writing at the same period to different friends, have probably been guilty of this enormity, and possibly used the very same phrases. Where the dates are wide apart it is a different matter—but even so Pope may have kept copies, and used them; for in spite of his protestations, he certainly made a literary exercise of his letters.

I need hardly remind the reader that besides the full discussion given to this subject in Elwin and Courthope's *Pope*, there is an admirable short account of Pope's epistolary adventures in Sir Leslie Stephen's *Life of Pope* in the English Men of Letters series.

BIBLIOGRAPHY

ETHEREGE

The authorities for this study of Etherege are so few, that I have not thought it necessary to note them in the text, as has been done in the case of the two succeeding essays. Most of the important material is to be found in the Letterbook.

The Etherege Letterbook. Brit. Mus. MSS.
Etherege's *Works*. Verity Ed., 1880.
Aubrey. *Brief Lives*. Clark. Oxford Univ. Press, 1898.
Buckingham. *Works*. 1704.
Burnet. *History of his Own Times*.
Encyclopaedia Britannica.
Garnett, R. *The Age of Dryden*.
Gosse, E. *Seventeenth Century Studies*.
Hamilton, A. *Mémoires de Gramont*.
Oldys. *Biographia Britannica*.
Palmer, J. *The Comedy of Manners*.
Spence. *Anecdotes*.
Times Literary Supplement:
  10th Nov. 1921.
  16th Feb. 1922.
  23rd Feb. 1922.

Authorities referred to in the Notes

VANBRUGH

Add. MSS. British Museum Additional Manuscripts.
  751. Stowe MSS.
  4253.
  7125. Harleian MSS.
  9011.
  9123. Coxe Papers. (Marlborough.)
  9125.
  19591.
  19605.
  28275. Tonson Correspondence.
  33064. Newcastle MSS.
Aitken [G. A.]. Preface to Mermaid. *Steele*. 1 vol.
—— *Life of Steele*. 2 vols. Isbister, 1889.
Ashton. *Social Life in the Reign of Queen Anne*. 2 vols.

Athenaeum. Bound Volumes British Museum.
Aubrey [John]. *Miscellanies*. Reeves, 1890. 1 vol.
Baker. *Biographia Dramatica*.
Barman [Christian]. *Sir John Vanbrugh*. Masters of Architecture Series. Benn, 1924. 1 vol.
Beltz. *Memorials of the Order of the Garter*. 1841. 1 vol.
Berguer [Rev.]. Preface to *Tatler*. *British Essayists*.
Bickley. *Life of Prior*.
Blomfield [Sir R.]. *A Short History of Renaissance Architecture, 1500–1800*. 1900. 1 vol.
Bolingbroke. Letter to Windham, 1753.
Boswell. *Life of Johnson*. Notes. 1822 Ed. 4 vols.
Broadsides and Ballads. British Museum Collections.
Burnet [Bishop]. *History of His Own Times*. 1775 Ed. 6 vols.
Cibber [Colley]. *Apology*. Everyman. 1 vol.
Cibber [Theophilus]. *Lives of the Poets*. Vol. iv. 1753.
Conduct. *An Account of the Conduct of the Dowager Duchess of Marlborough from her first coming to Court to the year 1710*. By the Duchess. 1742. 1 vol.
Courthope [W. J.]. *Addison*. English Men of Letters. 1 vol.
Coxe [Archdeacon]. *Life of Marlborough*. 3 vols.
Cunningham [Alan]. *Lives of the Most Eminent British Architects*. 1 vol.
D.N.B. *Dictionary of National Biography*.
D'Israeli [I.]. *Curiosities of Literature*. Secret History of the Building of Blenheim. 1 vol.
Downes. *Roscius Anglicanus*.
Dunciad. Pope. People's Standard Library.
Dunton. *Life and Errors*. 1705.
Escott [T. H. S.]. *Club Makers and Club Members*. 1 vol.
Faction Display'd. Shippen ? State Poems.
Gent. Mag. *Gentleman's Magazine*. Brit. Mus. bound copies.
Gosse [E.]. *Congreve*. Scott, 1888. 1 vol.
Gotch [J. A.]. *The Growth of the English House*. 1 vol.
Green [J. R.]. *A Short History of the English People*. Everyman. 2 vols.
Hazlitt [W.]. *Comic Dramatists of the Restoration*.
Hearne. *Diaries of Thomas Hearne*. Ed. Bliss, 1857. 3 vols.
Hist. Comm. Historical MSS. Commission.
Hunt : *see* Leigh Hunt.
Johnson [Samuel]. *Lives of the Poets*. Dryden, Garth, Addison, Rowe, Congreve, &c.
Justification. *Sir John Vanbrugh's Justification of What he Depos'd in the Duke of Marlborough's Late Tryall*. c. 1721. Pamphlet.
Luttrell [Narcissus]. *Relation of State Affairs*. 1857.

Leigh Hunt. Preface to Ed. of *Restoration Dramatists.* 1840.
Lovegrove. *Life, Work, and Influence of Sir John Vanbrugh.*
Macaulay. *Comic Dramatists of the Restoration.* 1841.
—— *Addison.* 1843.
—— *History.* 8th Edition, 1852. 5 vols.
Margaret Godolphin. By John Evelyn. King's Classics. 1 vol.
Marshall. *Woodstock.* 1 vol.
Molloy. *The Queen's Comrade* (S. Duchess of Marlborough). 2 vols.
Montagu [Lady Mary Wortley]. *Letters.* 3 vols.
Morley [Lord]. *Life of Walpole.* 1 vol.
Nichols. *Literary Anecdotes of the 18th Century.*
Noble. *History of the College of Arms.* 1804. 1 vol.
Palmer [John]. *The Comedy of Manners.* 1913. 1 vol.
Price [Sir W.]. *Essays on the Picturesque.* 1798.
Priv. Cor. Private Correspondence of Sarah, Duchess of Marlborough. 1 vol.
Rariora. J. E. Hodgkin. c. 1904.
Reconcilement. Rowe. *Collected Poems.* Reconcilement of the late Quarrel between Mr. Congreve and Mr. Jacob Tonson. Chalmers's *English Poets.*
Reynolds [Sir Joshua]. *Discourses to Students.*
Robinson [C. B.]. *History of the Priory and Peculiar of Snaith.* 1861. 1 vol.
Rosamond. Addison's opera of that name.
Scott [Sir W.]. *Life of Dryden.* 1834. 1 vol.
Spence. *Anecdotes.*
Statham [H. H.]. *A Short Critical History of Architecture.* 1 vol.
Stella. Swift's *Journal* to. Bohn. 1 vol.
Strachey [Lytton]. *Books and Characters.* 1922. 1 vol.
Summers [Montague]. Ed. of Aphra Behn.
Swain [A. E. H.]. Preface to Mermaid ed. of Vanbrugh.
Thomson [Mrs.]. *Memoirs of the Duchess of Marlborough.* 2 vols.
Upcott. *Diary.* c. 1720.
Vitruvius Britannicus. Colen Campbell. c. 1720. 3 vols.
Vanbrugh. *Collected Works.* Ward Ed. 1893. 2 vols.
Ward [W. C.]. Preface to ed. of Vanbrugh.
Ward [E.]. *A Compleat and Humourous Account of all the Remarkable Clubs and Societies in the Cities of London and Westminster.* 1756. Published Anonymously. 1 vol.
Wentworth Papers. Cartwright Edition. 1883. 1 vol.

ADDISON

Aikin [Lucy]. *Life of Joseph Addison.* Longmans, 1843. 2 vols.
Courthope [W. J.]. *Addison.* English Men of Letters. Macmillan, 1884. 1 vol.
Johnson [Samuel]. *Lives of the Poets.* Addison. Cunningham Ed. Murray, 1854. 3 vols.
Macaulay. Review of Aikin. 1843. *Collected Essays.*

[The above lives are so well known that facts taken from any of them—and they form the basis of this essay—have not usually been given a reference.]

Add. MSS. 22908.
" " 7121. } British Museum Additional Manuscripts.
Egerton MS.

Aitken [G. A.]. *Life of Steele.* Isbister, 1889. 2 vols.
Ashton [John]. *Social Life in the Reign of Queen Anne.* 2 vols.
Mr. Addison Turn'd Tory, by a Gentleman of Oxford. Pamphlet, 1713.
Berkeley [Bishop]. *Letters.*
Boswell. *Life of Johnson.* Longmans &c., 1822. 4 vols.
Budgell [Eustace]. *Memoirs of the Life and Character of the late Earl of Orrery and the family of the Boyles.* Mears, 1732. 1 vol.
Burnet [Bishop]. *History of His Own Times.* Donaldson, 1775. 6 vols.
Censor. The British. Verse Pamphlet. 1712. Brit. Mus.
Cibber [Colley]. *Apology.* Everyman. 1 vol.
Curiosities. D'Israeli's *Curiosities of Literature.*
D.N.B. Dictionary of National Biography.
Elwin and Courthope. *Pope's Works.* The definitive edition.
Grammont. Hamilton's *Mémoires du Comte de Gramont.*
Hearne [Thomas]. *Diaries.* Bliss Ed. Smith, 1869. 3 vols.
Hallam [H.]. *Constitutional History of England.* Everyman. 4 vols.
Luttrell [Narcissus]. *Relation of State Affairs.* Oxford Univ. Press, 1857. 6 vols.
Lecky, *England.* [W. E. H.] *Hist. of England in 18th Cent.* Longmans.
Lecky, *Ireland.* [W. E. H.] *Hist. of Ireland in 18th Cent.* 1892.
Letter to Windham. Bolingbroke's *Works.* 1753.
Letters, Hughes. John Hughes, *Correspondence.* Johnson, 1772. 2 vols.
Letters. Pope's. Curll's 1735 Ed. 2 vols.
Macaulay MS. Pencil notes in his edition of Addison. Brit. Mus.
Memorial. Addison's Memorial to the King. Printed in Aikin's *Life*, and in Johnson's in edition quoted.

Misson [Henri]. *Mémoires et Observations Faites par un Voyageur en Angleterre etc.* La Haye, 1698.
Nichols. *Literary Anecdotes of the 18th Century.*
Papers of a Critic. C. W. Dilke. Murray, 1875. 2 vols.
Preface to *Drummer.* Steele. See text. 1723 Ed.
Present State of Wit. Agreed to be by Gay. Pamphlet, 1712.
Reresby. *Memoirs of Sir John Reresby, 1634–1689.* 1 vol.
Scott [Sir W.]. *Life of Swift* in edition of his works.
Spence. *Anecdotes.*
Steele. *Memoirs of the Life and Writings of the Rt. Honble. Joseph Addison Esq.* Curll, 1724.
Stella. Swift's *Journal* to. Bohn, 1900. 1 vol.
Tickell. Preface to Edition of Addison's *Works.* 1723.
Tindall. *A Summary of Mr. Rapin de Toyras's History of England,* and Mr. Tindall's continuation. 1751.
Traill [H. D.]. *William III.* Twelve English Statesmen Series. Macmillan, 1888. 1 vol.
Tyers [T.]. *An Historical Essay on Mr. Addison.* 1783.
Victor [Benjamin]. *Original Letters, &c.* Beckett. 1774.
Walpole [Horace]. *Letters.*
Wentworth. *Wentworth Papers.* Wyman, 1883. 1 vol.

INDEX